OVERSIZED   146541

959.704q
Vie   The Vietnam experience:
         Setting the stage

v.1

Setting the Stage

The Vietnam Experience

Setting the Stage

by Edward Doyle, Samuel Lipsman
and the editors of Boston Publishing Company

Preface by Henry Cabot Lodge,
former United States Ambassador to the Republic of Vietnam

Boston Publishing Company/Boston, MA

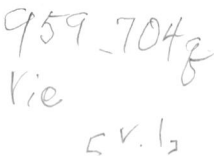

In memory of
Robert Lee Wolff
1915–1980

Boston Publishing Company

President and Publisher: Robert J. George
Vice President: Richard S. Perkins, Jr.
Editor-in-Chief: Robert Manning
Senior Editor: Robert Lee Wolff
Managing Editor: Paul Dreyfus
Assistant Editor: Karen E. English

Staff Writers:
Edward Doyle, Samuel Lipsman,
Stephen Weiss
Research Assistants:
Matthew H. Lynch, Frederick C. Ruby,
Jeffrey L. Seglin

Picture Editors:
Julene A. Fischer, Victoria Pope
Picture Researchers:
Catherine Antoine (Paris), Ann Leyhe

Historical Consultant: David P. Chandler
Picture Consultant: Ngo Vinh Long
Project Consultants:
James T. Avery III, William Bean

Production Coordinator: Douglas B. Rhodes
Production Editor: Patricia Leal Welch
Editorial Production:
Elizabeth S. Brownell, Pamela George,
Cassandra J. Malloy

Design: Designworks, Sally Bindari

Marketing Director: Linda M. Scenna
Circulation Manager: Jane Colpoys
Business Staff:
Jeanne C. Gibson, Elizabeth Schultz

About the editors and authors

Editor-in-Chief *Robert Manning,* a long-time journalist, has previously been editor-in-chief of the *Atlantic Monthly* magazine and its press. He served as assistant secretary of state for public affairs under Presidents John F. Kennedy and Lyndon B. Johnson. He has also been a fellow at the Institute for Politics at the John F. Kennedy School of Government at Harvard University.

Robert Lee Wolff, senior editor, was Coolidge Professor of History at Harvard University. He had been on the Harvard faculty since 1950. During World War II, he headed the Balkan Section Research and Analysis Branch of the Office of Strategic Services. He wrote numerous history books, including *A History of Civilization* (two volumes) and *The Balkans in our Time,* and has written several books on the Victorian fiction of England.

Staff writers: *Edward Doyle,* an historian, received his masters degree at the University of Notre Dame and his Ph.D. at Harvard University. *Samuel Lipsman,* a former Fulbright Scholar, received his M.A. and M.Phil. in history at Yale. *Stephen Weiss* has been a fellow at the Newberry Library in Chicago. An American historian, he received his M.A. and M.Phil. at Yale.

Historical Consultant *David P. Chandler* is research director of the Centre of Southeast Asian Studies at Monash University in Melbourne, Australia. He has served as a U.S. State Department foreign service officer in Colombia and Cambodia. His major publications include *In Search of Southeast Asia:*

A Modern History (coauthor) and *The Land and People of Cambodia.*

Picture Consultant *Ngo Vinh Long* is a social historian specializing in China and Vietnam. Born in Vietnam and living in the United States, he returned there most recently in 1980. He has published several books and many articles on Vietnam. His books include *Before the Revolution: The Vietnamese Peasants Under the French* and *Report From a Vietnamese Village.*

Cover photographs:
(Upper right) A young Vietminh guerrilla. The Vietminh's military branch, formed to fight the French, would become the North Vietnamese Army that the United States opposed.

(Lower right) Peasants pull weeds from a rice field near Hanoi.

(Lower left) A wounded French foreign legion officer stands ready shortly before 10,000 French troops surrendered at Dien Bien Phu on May 7, 1954.

(Upper left) A UH-1 (Huey), the workhorse of the American military in Vietnam, deposits U.S. First Cavalry troopers in Vietnam's highlands.

Library of Congress Catalog Card Number: 81-65796

ISBN: 0-939526-00-X

Contents

Preface

I welcome the publication of "Setting the Stage," the first volume of *The Vietnam Experience*. As former United States Ambassador to the Republic of Vietnam, I have long awaited a thorough and balanced account of our country's ordeal in Indochina. During my years in South Vietnam, it seemed to me that the issue of Vietnam was perhaps the most important problem facing America. Yet, even now, the dilemmas of the Vietnam era remain unresolved. Today we shoulder the task of leadership in a world of armed conflict and ideological upheaval. It is thus especially vital that we understand that very strange war in which we became so bitterly embroiled.

When I arrived in Saigon in 1963, I entered a city besieged. For nine years the United States had taken an increasingly active role in the maintenance and support of South Vietnam. Yet, I found myself in a land without a western democratic tradition, presided over by a repressive and ineffective government, vainly attempting to carry on a war amid mounting popular disaffection. How had we come to be there?

We came, it seemed to many Americans then, to defend South Vietnam from the aggression of the North. If America failed to press the conflict to a satisfactory end, communism would, we feared, engulf all Asia and raise the specter of armed confrontation between the United States, the Soviet Union, and the People's Republic of China. Our objective was to help the Republic of Vietnam achieve and then maintain its independence. But how were these aims to be accomplished?

An exclusively military solution was impossible. To preclude the intervention of Moscow or Peking, we were constrained to conduct a "limited" war. Moreover, "seek out and destroy" or a "war of attrition" through massive bombing could not be the objectives as they rightly were in World War II. This war could not be won by killing the southern Vietcong or the soldiers of North Vietnam but only by destroying the guerrilla organization in the villages and hamlets of South Vietnam. Our military might alone was in effect a net with a large mesh with which to catch whales. But the problem was to catch the small but deadly fish of guerrilla warfare. This required a fine-mesh net which we did not then possess. How could we acquire one?

We needed localized police methods. We needed the patience to wait for the right moment. We needed the capacity to strike swiftly and thus achieve surprise. But most of all we needed a revolutionary movement at the village level to rid the region of the old structures of colonialism and feudalism that beset it; a true revolution, in freedom, would be more potent than the standard Communist revolution could ever be. Top priority had to be given to the creation of local organizations capable of formulating and executing all economic and social—revolutionary— purposes. For more than twenty years we Americans, a people with our own revolutionary tradition, labored at this work. Why were we so rarely successful?

It became apparent to me that any attempt to answer one question about Vietnam simply raised many more. Was the United States mistaken in its determination to intervene? Or have subsequent events in Southeast Asia confirmed the necessity of what we set out to do? Was the United States engaged in an imperialist adventure far from our own shores? Or were we defending a small nation, pledged to democratic government, from the naked aggression of a neighbor? Did the limitations placed on our use of military force keep us from a swift and decisive victory? Or were we engaged in a war that could not be won even with the most sophisticated and lethal weapons? Were the Vietcong freedom fighters seeking to liberate their country from centuries of foreign domination? Or were they simply terrorists, willing to use any means to gain power? Did the ultimate collapse of South Vietnam signify a loss of will on the part of the American people? Or were we fighting the wrong war, in the wrong place, at the wrong time?

I appreciate how deep and sincere are the disagreements over the Vietnam question. As a nation, we may never come to full accord. In the final analysis, however, and in a democratic society, we must answer these questions for ourselves. It is the goal of *The Vietnam Experience* to present, in a more complete and systematic way than has so far been attempted, the story of the longest war Americans have had to fight. As such, it represents a singular opportunity. For it remains true that our only sure guides to a present which so often seems bewildering are the lessons—the often terrible lessons—of the past.

Henry Cabot Lodge

The Contending Parties:

The Allies
South Vietnam
United States
South Korea
Australia
New Zealand
Thailand
Philippines

The Communists
North Vietnam
National Liberation Front (Vietcong)

A Chronology:

1950–President Truman provides U.S. aid to French military in Indochina; 35 American advisers sent to Vietnam.

1954–Geneva Conference on Indochina.
President Eisenhower pledges aid to South Vietnam.

1961–President Kennedy increases number of American military advisers to South Vietnam.

1964–American and North Vietnamese forces clash in the Gulf of Tonkin.
Congress grants President Johnson authority to "take all necessary steps to repel armed attacks against the forces of the United States and to prevent further aggression." (Gulf of Tonkin Resolution)

1965–U.S. initiates bombing of North Vietnam.
First American ground combat troops arrive in Vietnam.

1968–Tet offensive.
Johnson orders bombing halt, providing basis for negotiations.

1969–Paris peace talks begin in earnest.
President Nixon calls for "Vietnamization" of the war, orders staged withdrawal of American troops.

1970–U.S. troops enter Cambodia to destroy North Vietnamese supply bases.

1971–Secret peace negotiations with North Vietnam begun by presidential adviser Henry Kissinger.

1972–Last U.S. combat troops leave South Vietnam.
Christmas bombing of Hanoi-Haiphong.

1973–Truce agreement signed in Paris, cease-fire in Vietnam.
Last U.S. military personnel leave South Vietnam. U.S. prisoners of war released.

1975–Fall of Saigon.
Evacuation of American embassy.

The American Commitment:

Americans who served:	3,300,000
Americans killed:	57,605
Americans wounded:	303,700
Americans taken prisoner:	766
• returned	651
• died in captivity	114
• still in captivity (as of 3/81)	1
Americans declared missing (1965–75):	5,011
• returned	121
• declared dead while missing	4,872
• still missing (9/80)	18
Costs:	
American aid to South Vietnam (1955–75):	$24 billion
Direct American expenditures for the war:	$165 billion

U.S. Draft Statistics:

Eligible:	26,800,000
Rejected or disqualified:	7,908,000
Examined:	8,611,000
Deferred or exempted:	10,047,000
Conscientious objectors:	171,000
Draft evaders:	570,000
Convicted of draft offenses:	8,750

At the Height of the War, 1968–69:

American troops:	543,000
South Vietnamese troops:	819,200
Allied troops:	1,593,300
Communist forces:	810,000
• in South Vietnam	250,000
American ground attacks (battalion or larger)	1,100/year
Communist ground attacks (battalion or larger)	126/year
American air attacks:	400,000/year
Bombs dropped:	1.2 million tons/year
U.S. expenditures for bombing:	$14 billion/year
Military defoliation:	1,195,000 acres/year
Military crop destruction:	220,000 acres/year
Americans killed in action:	20,000/year
Communists killed in action:	200,000/year
Refugees generated:	585,000/year
Civilian casualties:	130,000/month

The Evacuation, April 1975:

Americans evacuated:	1,373
Vietnamese evacuated:	5,595
Value of U.S. military equipment seized by the Communists:	$1 billion

The Aftermath:

Military and civilian dead (all forces):	1,313,000
Americans in captivity (3/81):	1
Americans missing (9/80):	18
Americans awarded Medal of Honor:	237
Land defoliated:	5.2 million acres
Indochinese refugees generated:	9,000,000
Indochinese refugees resettled in the U.S. (4/79):	220,000
Living U.S. veterans with Vietnam service (9/77)	2,730,000
Vietnam veterans receiving government compensation (9/77):	496,800
Disabled U.S. Vietnam veterans:	519,000

Casualties:

	killed	wounded
U.S. military	57,605	303,700
South Vietnam military	220,357	499,000
Other Allied forces	5,227	NA
North Vietnam/Vietcong	444,000	NA
Civilian	587,000	3,000,000

All figures estimated
NA—not available
Note: Because of the nature of the Vietnam War and its aftermath, definitive statistics on all aspects of the war are difficult to obtain. The figures cited above, many of them approximate, have been reviewed with appropriate U.S. government agencies.

Vietnam: The End

On April 27, 1975, the confused, leaderless city of Saigon awaited the inevitable. It was two years since the United States had quit the war, leaving the South Vietnamese to continue the struggle against the advancing North Vietnamese Army. Now fourteen North Vietnamese Army divisions with one hundred and fifty to two hundred thousand combat-ready troops stood poised for attack, their artillery trained upon the city. The tense stillness of the early morning was shattered by North Vietnamese rockets exploding in downtown Saigon—the first attack since the cease-fire dictated by the Paris agreements in 1973. The explosions killed at least ten people and ignited an enormous fire which destroyed five hundred houses and left five thousand people homeless. John Pilger, a British reporter, recalled the suffering caused by a rocket that completely razed a half acre of tightly packed houses:

There are people standing motionless, as if in a tableau, looking at the corrugated iron which is all that remains of their homes and under which there is still fire, and people. A French photographer blunders across the smoldering iron, sobbing; he pulls at my arm and leads me to a pyre that was a kitchen. Beside it is a little girl, about five, who is still alive. . . . The skin on her chest has opened like a page. . . .

During their advance to the South, the North Vietnamese had captured entire South Vietnamese Army divisions, enormous stores of arms and equipment, and valuable technical equipment and aircraft, readily turned against their retreating owners. Against only occasional resistance, the North Vietnamese in a matter of a few months had swallowed up most of South Vietnam. By the end of April, they were in a position to demand unconditional surrender.

As the tide of battle went overwhelmingly in their favor, the mood of the North Vietnamese became curiously restrained. People who barely escaped reported that North Vietnamese soldiers, just teenagers, were anything but brutal as they jubilantly marched south. A thirty-seven-year-old school teacher said: "They were so confident when they caught us they just let us go. They laughed at us for running. They said, 'Wherever you run, we will be there soon anyway.'"

Fearful of the fighting, an uncountable number of refugees, fleeing the Communists advancing from the North, crowded into the city. Many of them had been convinced that the South Vietnamese capital was invincible and safe. But this, like so many other hopes during the past two months of the North Vietnamese offensive, proved illusory. For the first time, the people of Saigon started looking for a place to hide.

"No surrender of territory to the enemy"-

Nguyen Van Thieu, president of South Vietnam

Since January, when North Vietnamese forces had launched their offensive by taking Song Be, the capital of Phuoc Long Province, the pace of the war had accelerated. Shortly before Christmas the North Vietnamese Army cut South Vietnamese ground communications to Song Be. The South Vietnamese Air

Preceding page. Fear and panic: No room is left on the last aircraft out of Nha Trang, April 1, 1975.

Force tried to restore air communications to Song Be, but the massive Khe Sanh airlift of 1968 was not to be repeated. The South Vietnamese were short of aircraft to drop vital supplies to the garrisons there, and in early January the North Vietnamese overran the city.

Song Be was not an arsenal or a major population center, but its capture had ominous overtones: It meant the loss of all of Phuoc Long Province, only fifty miles from Saigon. This was the first time the North Vietnamese had taken an entire South Vietnamese province. By controlling Phuoc Long, the gateway to the central highlands, the North Vietnamese had easy access to Pleiku and other major towns to the north.

Having so easily captured a province in the heart of South Vietnam, North Vietnamese leaders substantially altered their original strategy of a "mini-offensive" intended to "test the reactions" of South Vietnam's forces. They decided the time was ripe to launch their long-awaited, full-scale offensive against the South. After a high-level strategy session in Hanoi, Le Duan, North Vietnam's Communist party chief, optimistically announced: "This year the attack on the central highlands will begin."

On March 11, South Vietnamese President Nguyen Van Thieu made a disastrous decision: He withdrew government forces from the central highlands in order to protect Saigon. From then on, the South Vietnamese were on the run, soldiers and civilians alike. Thieu had called for a tactical retreat, but the general in charge of the withdrawal packed up his staff and left the highlands, turning over the operation to an officer with little command experience. A disorderly retreat ensued, then came general panic. South Vietnamese soldiers, many with their families in tow, began an exodus toward southern coastal cities. Frightened civilians joined the withdrawal column. Route 7B, a little-used highway badly in need of repair, became choked with more than fifteen hundred cars and trucks.

The convoy of tears

The trek to the coast was one of the most tragic episodes of the war. Perhaps 30,000–40,000 lives were lost before the fifteen-day "convoy of tears" was over. The North Vietnamese Army harried the retreat column, a confused mass of soldiers and civilians, all the way to the coast. As one Vietnamese described it:

The evacuees jammed on trucks along the blooded way included soldiers, children, very old people. They were spilled all over by the impacting Communist shells. Refugees moving on foot were hit by Communist machine guns, falling down on the road. The blood flowed on the road like a tiny stream. The sound of roaring artillery and small arms, the screams of seriously wounded people at death's door, and children, created a voice out of hell.

Units of the South Vietnamese Air Force, finding themselves alone and unable to defend the highland air base at Pleiku, sought escape on all operable aircraft. Thousands of civilians also jammed the airfield, vainly trying to get aboard. South Vietnamese soldiers fired shots, and people fell to the ground, wounded or dead.

A Vietnamese colonel, who was attempting to evacuate people and equipment from Pleiku by C-130 transport planes to Saigon, recalled the disorder:

An anguished father and his family flee along South Vietnam's coastal Highway One after government forces abandoned the central highlands in March 1975. Some 1.5 million people joined this "convoy of tears" from the central highlands to the coastal cities—and an uncertain fate there.

The airfield at Pleiku was in a state of panic. Sometimes the planes could land, but they couldn't do the job. I had to go there and use my pistol to restore order. Of course, I didn't shoot anybody, just shot in the air. And when the people saw me there was order. But soon I had to go back to headquarters. And the enemy kept shelling the headquarters at Pleiku and the airfield.

The debacle in the central highlands was repeated many times during South Vietnam's hasty and disorganized retreat to the South. The hysteria only intensified when the ragged remnants of South Viet-

Vietnamese soldiers and peasants and Americans press to get their babies and briefcases alike onto one of the last planes out of Nha Trang, on the coast of South Vietnam. In a scene repeated throughout the evacuation, 500 people compete for the 100 places aboard the plane.

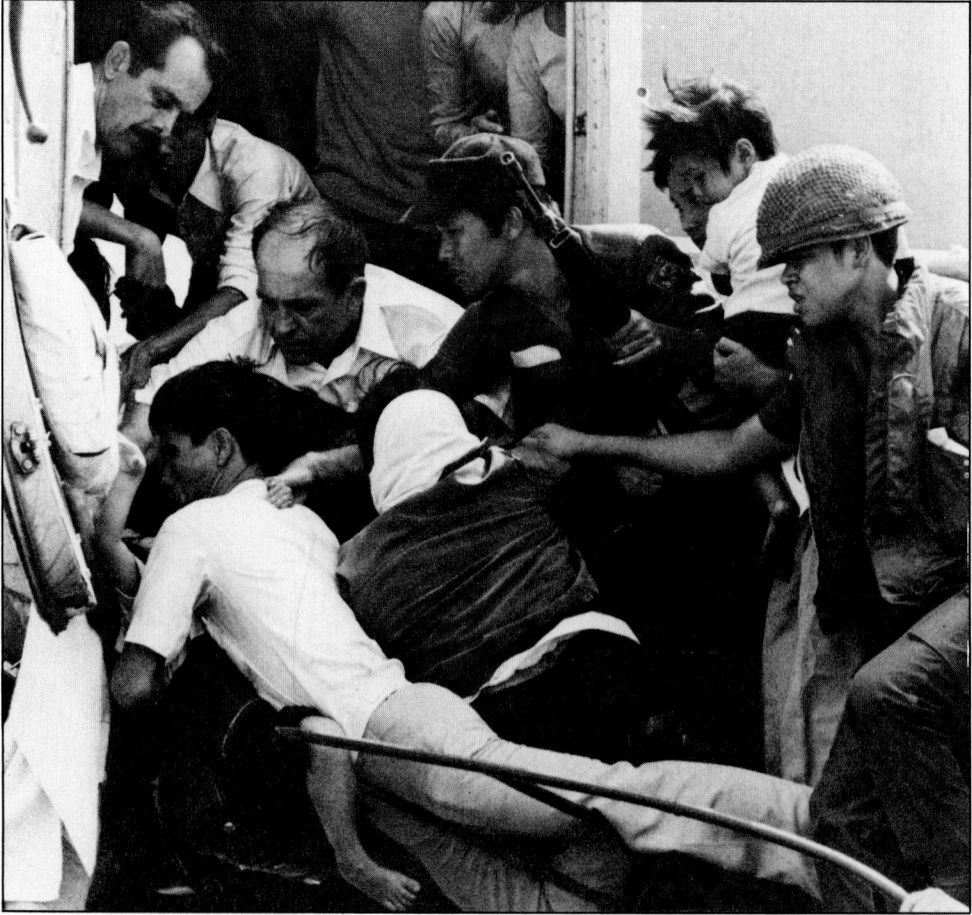

As the plane reaches capacity, frustrated refugees cling to the doors and wings. Some planes took off with refugees still holding on to the wings and wheels.

NHA TRANG: Desperate Crush to Escape

The sea lift from Nha Trang is no less frantic and desperate than the air evacuation. Refugees crowd the dock at Nha Trang, anxious to board a boat and escape advancing Communist troops.

Shielding himself from the sun, a father searches Nha Trang dock for his daughter among the bodies of children killed in the crush to flee to Saigon (left).

His grim search over, the father bears away his daughter's body in a jute sack (above).

nam's finest highland troops straggled to the coast alongside terrified civilian refugees. Instead of rest and security, the convoy's survivors found the coastal roads already clogged with another swarm of refugees from the North. The events at Pleiku had precipitated a psychological collapse that affected many South Vietnamese and led to inconceivable strategic mistakes. The shifting of troops from the Quang Tri area near the North Vietnamese border back to Da Nang caused fearful civilians to flee southward.

As the undisciplined soldiers and civilians passed through Hue, the stream became a torrent of panic-stricken people, all seeking haven at the once-impregnable air base at Da Nang to the south. The military and refugee situation at Hue deteriorated to such a degree that General Truong, the South Vietnamese commander, ordered the evacuation of the city on March 25.

Hue, the old imperial capital, had always held much patriotic and emotional significance for the South Vietnamese. Its evacuation greatly disheartened the army and lowered the morale of the people. A Vietnamese officer related how one commander at Hue announced the evacuation to his staff:

He came to the meeting room with a sad and uneasy voice, saying, "We've been betrayed! We have to abandon Hue, the loveliest part of South Vietnam. . . . The purpose of the Hue abandonment is: save our forces. It now is 'sauve qui peut' ['every man for himself']."

In an uninterrupted caravan, trucks and buses carry frightened Hue evacuees and their possessions toward Da Nang, a city already engulfed by refugees and destined to capture by the North Vietnamese.

Da Nang's giant air and naval base had once been the symbol of American military power in Vietnam. It was the base of the first American combat troops in Vietnam. But now it teemed with thousands of people determined to make their way farther south, at any cost. Within the city many thousands of South Vietnamese soldiers milled about, armed and desperate. Although the Saigon government did its best to organize a refugee program and to reunite separated family members, its efforts to control the pandemonium were futile. With Communist troops threatening to envelop the city, South Vietnamese soldiers, who had arrived in Da Nang with no supplies, no equipment, and no commanders, turned to violence to obtain food and shelter. Some soldiers went on rampages of looting and killing. Amid the anarchy, Communist rockets and artillery pounded the city and its defenseless inhabitants.

America watches

Americans followed events in Vietnam with mixed emotions. For some the growing likelihood of a North Vietnamese victory was a welcome end to an unjust war waged by a corrupt South Vietnamese regime. Others observed the rapid demise of South Vietnam with shock and dismay: A trusted ally against Communist aggression in Southeast Asia was quickly succumbing to a tragic death.

For most Americans, however, the impending defeat of South Vietnam presented a bitter irony. The U.S. had pulled its troops out of Vietnam in 1973, and the American prisoners of war had come home. Following that, millions of Americans had made peace with a conflict in which the country had sacrificed thousands of lives but had still not won. Yet the conflict had gone on, and American involvement had not really ended. Although the U.S. had withdrawn its soldiers, it was supporting South Vietnam's continuing struggle with billions of dollars worth of economic aid and military equipment.

To Americans watching the fall of South Vietnam on television, it seemed as if they were losing the war a second time. As one Vietnam veteran said, "One of the best people I ever knew died in Vietnam. He had so much to offer the world. I can't imagine the feelings of parents who had sons who died in [South Vietnam] as they watch the region fall. ...."

The sudden collapse of South Vietnam's defensive capability against the North Vietnamese had apparently surprised the U.S. Defense Department as well.

On March 13 Secretary of Defense James Schlesinger acknowledged that a major Communist offensive was underway, but he said that South Vietnam intended to hold coastal cities. He also said that Saigon would not be attacked until the following year. Within three weeks, as South Vietnamese forces fled south from the central highlands, Schlesinger revised his forecast. Instead, he predicted an attack on Saigon "in the next month or two."

As pressure mounted during March for an American response to the Vietnamese crisis, the debate over military aid to Vietnam raged in the halls of Congress. In early March President Thieu sent a delegation to Washington to request a substantial increase in military and economic assistance to his war-torn country. U.S. Ambassador Graham Martin, who thought the aid increase was crucial to the survival of South Vietnam, made the trip to Washington

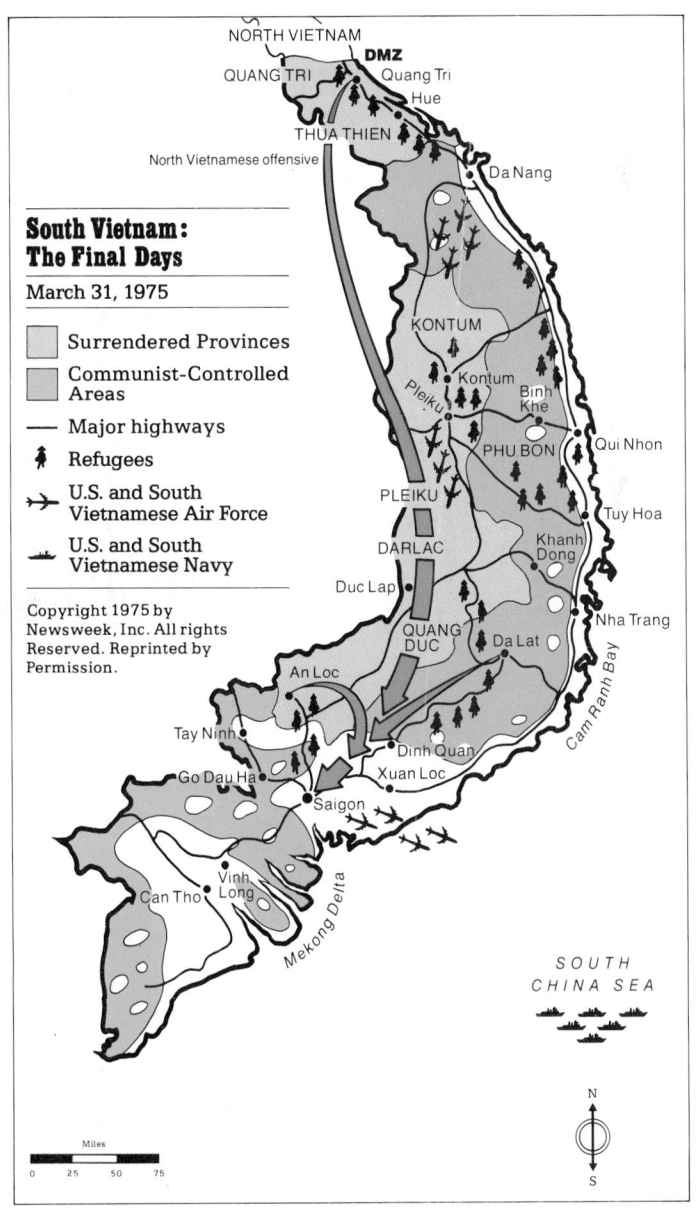

South Vietnam: The Final Days

March 31, 1975

- [ ] Surrendered Provinces
- [ ] Communist-Controlled Areas
- — Major highways
- 🯄 Refugees
- ✈ U.S. and South Vietnamese Air Force
- ⛴ U.S. and South Vietnamese Navy

NORTH VIETNAM · DMZ · QUANG TRI · Quang Tri · Hue · THUA THIEN · North Vietnamese offensive · Da Nang · KONTUM · Kontum · Pleiku · Binh Khe · PHU BON · Qui Nhon · PLEIKU · DARLAC · Khanh Dong · Tuy Hoa · Duc Lap · QUANG DUC · Da Lat · Nha Trang · Cam Ranh Bay · An Loc · Tay Ninh · Dinh Quan · Go Dau Ha · Xuan Loc · Saigon · Vinh Long · Can Tho · Mekong Delta · SOUTH CHINA SEA

Miles
0 25 50 75

N
S

In a beach scene reminiscent of Dunkirk, South Vietnamese soldiers lucky enough to get aboard the last American evacuation ship depart the once-invincible port at Da Nang (top).

The legs of dead South Vietnamese soldiers hang from the last American aircraft out of Da Nang after its landing at Saigon's Tan Son Nhut Airport. The soldiers, unable to force their way aboard the plane, had crept into the wheel wells and were crushed on takeoff.

When the Saigon government decided not to make a military stand in Da Nang, the troops that had massed there took any way out they could find. Here South Vietnamese Marines, after a heavily shelled passage to the ship, crowd an evacuation LST (landing ship tank) in Da Nang (right).

himself to present Thieu's case to the president and Congress.

The plea for more aid to South Vietnam received a favorable hearing from President Gerald Ford. Congress, however, was wary of pouring money into what looked like a losing cause. Besides, Washington was already preoccupied with the deepening recession of 1975. Congressional leaders were unwilling to divert money from economic recovery programs to a then distant problem. Still, some favored more military assistance as a pledge of continuing loyalty to a faltering ally. President Ford's angry comments echoed the opinion of those who deplored Congress' refusal to expand U.S. aid commitments to South Vietnam:

For just a relatively small additional commitment in economic and military aid, relatively small compared to the $150 billion that we spent, [it is sad] that at the last minute of the last quarter we don't make that special effort and now we are faced with this human tragedy. It just makes me sick every day I hear about it, read about it, and see it.

All roads lead to Saigon

In Saigon, President Thieu greeted America's unwillingness to increase aid to his struggling country with a combination of anger and despair. Angry at what he would call the "shameful inadequacy" of American assistance, Thieu later said:

The Americans promised us—we trusted them. But they have not given us the aid they promised. To fight we have to have ammunition and the wherewithal. ... We lost tanks, we lost artillery. The United States, when this happened, should have reacted. ... You [Americans] signed the Paris agreement, which said you would do this.

As Thieu anxiously awaited news from Washington, creeping paralysis overtook him. He had counted on the military and economic support of the U.S. for so long—even to the point of believing that the U.S. might resume bombing the North with B-52s—that he never anticipated that South Vietnam might have to stand and fight on its own. The ultimate realization that his blind faith in the U.S. would be of no avail, and his underlying pessimism about South Vietnam's military capability, engendered a despair in Thieu that eventually crippled the country's entire leadership structure.

Thieu's ability to lead was impaired further by the fact that he trusted nobody and few trusted him. He was so fearful of a coup that much of his thinking was aimed solely at staying in power. To solidify his position, he generally appointed to high-level government and military posts only those who would not or could not act independently of him. As a result, when indecision immobilized Thieu, the entire government nearly ceased to function.

A high-ranking South Vietnamese minister described the paralysis affecting military and political officials who looked to Saigon for guidance:

While the country was plunged in unprecedented turmoil and on the verge of collapse, the government adopted a strange attitude, a silence that was hard to understand except for a few appearances on TV and radio by President Thieu. People asked themselves questions and they tried to answer them themselves. Rumors circulated in place of government announcements. The Ministry of Information was mute, because the minister himself didn't know much about the situation and didn't know what the president's intention was. Furthermore, he didn't dare to take the initiative and talk about the things the president might not like or agree with.

While the people of South Vietnam awaited leadership from Saigon, the refugees at Da Nang, trapped by Communist forces, pleaded for help. But Thieu's government seemed powerless to rescue even a few of the million refugees crammed into Da Nang. As it had been so many times during the Vietnam conflict, the initiative was left to the U.S. The plight of Da Nang's refugees, which included some of the seven thousand Americans still thought to be in South Vietnam, spurred the U.S. to action.

An ill-fated rescue

The U.S. hastily chartered three Boeing 727s and sought a 747 jumbo jet. It was hoped that together the four planes could carry thousands of refugees per day in an emergency airlift to Saigon. On March 26 the American military consul for northern South Vietnam ordered the evacuation of his American personnel by way of Da Nang. The evacuation began smoothly enough, but soon panic and confusion took over. After a World Airways Boeing 727 landed at Da Nang to bring out more passengers, an unruly crowd surrounded the airplane. Everyone tried to scramble on board, endangering the safety of the aircraft. It eventually succeeded in taking off.

The following day several Air America and World Airways pilots flew into Da Nang. In their return to

Saigon, they complained that their planes had been nearly swamped by mobs completely out of control. It appeared that the airlift was doomed. But Ed Daly, president of World Airways, decided to make one more attempt to fly one of his 727s into Da Nang's now tumultuous airport on March 29. The refugees, sensing that Daly's might be the last plane out, erupted into a riot. The plane barely got off the ground, since it had to take off on a taxi-way obstructed by hostile refugees and South Vietnamese soldiers.

Reporter Paul Vogle, who had spent eighteen years in Vietnam, found his trip on board the last plane out of Da Nang to be the most terrifying experience of his life.

Mobs of people are pushing and shoving, trying to get aboard. The plane is taxiing away from the mob. The crew is scared. The mob is panic-stricken. There's a man with an M16 pointed at us, trying to get us to stop. We're loading [refugees]. . . . People are storming aboard, shouting . . . pushing . . . soldiers, civilians. People climbing up on wings, falling down off wings. Soldiers are firing in the air to frighten other people away . . . no control at all.

. . . women and children lying on the ground. Some people trying to lie in front of the wheels. . . . The pilot gooses the plane. They'll die when the plane takes off. People are still on the landing ramps as the aircraft picks up speed . . . fall off on the ground as it goes, pulled out by suction.

Although the plane reached Saigon safely with about two hundred and ninety refugees aboard, no one dared suggest a return trip. It turned out that most of its passengers had not been civilian refugees but South Vietnamese soldiers who had forced their way onto the plane. This alarmed U.S. authorities who had counted on the South Vietnamese army to maintain order during the evacuation. Some of these soldiers had shot family members who stood in the way of their escape. At least seven refugees had clung to the plane's wheel wells and were saved only because the body of a soldier entangled during takeoff had jammed the gear retraction mechanism.

An attempted sea lift from Da Nang was more successful. The *Pioneer Commander*, one of the three vessels promised by the White House and the U.S. Embassy, dropped anchor off Da Nang on March 28. It took on ten thousand people, among them nonessential staff of the U.S. Consulate. Arriving right behind the *Pioneer Commander* were the *Pioneer Con-*

South Vietnamese President Nguyen Van Thieu faces his nation on television on April 5, 1975, to announce the resignation of his cabinet and vow continued resistance against the advancing North Vietnamese. Two weeks later Thieu resigned and fled the country.

tender and a U.S. Navy ship, the *Miller*. Together the three ships carried over twenty-eight thousand refugees south to the former American naval base at Cam Ranh Bay. Returning the next day for more, the crews found that the Communists were overrunning Da Nang. The evacuation ships were besieged by a crush of refugees as well as by South Vietnamese Marines bitter at being abandoned by their government.

The tragic scene on the beaches resembled that at Dunkirk thirty-five years before, but few of those involved expected that they would ever return to Da Nang in victory, as the French and British had to Dunkirk:

By chance the [South Vietnamese Marines] wound up on two ships . . . two thousand or so made it to the *Pioneer Commander* . . . some came out in sampans and lifeboats, motorboats, and fishing boats. On nets and stairs, they scrambled aboard the big American ship. Perhaps fifty persons died when they made the mistake of trying to clamber on the ship in front of armed marines. [South Vietnamese] Marines opened up with their M16s and fought with their hands to kill. The toll of those who drowned or were crushed between the *Commander* and smaller boats is unknown.

Refugees who made it aboard the evacuation ships endured overcrowding and atrocious sanitary conditions. The decks were often covered with excrement and strewn with dead bodies. Many of the dead were

Commandeering a helicopter (background), Nguyen Cao Ky, former vice president and prime minister of South Vietnam, prepares to flee Saigon. He flew the helicopter safely to the deck of the USS Midway on April 29, 1975, shortly after exhorting a crowd of Catholic supporters in Saigon to stay and fight.

simply pushed overboard. Armed soldiers fought over what little food there was while defenseless refugees huddled together, fearful for their lives and few belongings.

Hope springs eternal

Four weeks after the fall of Da Nang, the first rockets fell on Saigon. By then Communist forces controlled most of the country. Now Saigon was a last, tiny island of sanctuary. First Hue, then Da Nang, then Cam Ranh Bay had been lost. Although many of the government air bases, military outposts, and fortified areas had simply been abandoned, the South Vietnamese army had also made a few courageous stands against the enemy.

At Xuan Loc, a provincial capital thirty-eight miles northeast of Saigon, South Vietnamese units held out for more than two weeks against superior North Vietnamese forces and a continuous barrage of mortar and artillery. South Vietnamese defenders at Xuan Loc seemed determined to demonstrate that they could fight despite the poor performance of their comrades at Hue and Da Nang. But their last-ditch resistance was not enough. By April 21 Xuan Loc lay in ruins and had to be evacuated. A South Vietnamese military officer described the North Vietnamese assault:

There was nothing we could do. The Communists shelled us with thousands of rounds—thousands. Then they attacked this morning with two regiments of infantry. Our casualties were not light, so we ran through the jungle to escape.

In the aftermath of Xuan Loc, South Vietnam appeared irretrievably lost to the North Vietnamese. President Thieu's once heralded defense policy—no negotiating with the enemy, no Communist activity in the country, no coalition government, and no surrender of territory—was all but forgotten. Thieu himself resigned on April 21 under heavy political pressure. It was hoped that Thieu's successor might reverse his uncompromising policy and negotiate a cease-fire with the Communists in exchange for a coalition government.

While announcing his resignation, Thieu vowed to stay on and fight, no matter what the consequences:

I resign but I do not desert. From this minute I will put myself at the disposal of the president and people. I will continue to stay close to you all in the coming task of national defense.

Thieu did stay in Saigon, briefly; five days after his speech he packed fifteen tons of "baggage" into a U.S. Air Force C-118 transport plane and flew to Taipei. It was reported that three and one-half tons of South Vietnamese gold accompanied him.

Air Marshall Nguyen Cao Ky, former South Vietnamese premier and vice president, was not far behind. Ky had told a rally of Catholics in Saigon to "let the cowards run away with the Americans" and promised to lead a defense of the capital. But soon after, he commandeered a helicopter and piloted it to the deck of the USS *Midway* standing by off the coast. Like so many promises made during the Vietnam War, Thieu's and Ky's went unfulfilled.

A few surprises

The collapse of South Vietnam astounded many American officials in Saigon, in particular, U.S. Ambassador Graham Martin. The U.S. had long tried as hard to believe in the South Vietnamese as the South Vietnamese actually believed in the Americans. Even as South Vietnam crumbled, some U.S. Embassy officials clung to the hope that all was not lost. Ambassador Martin surprised a congressional delegation in Saigon by running a "business as usual" operation at the U.S. Embassy. Delegation members had also been astonished by Martin's seemingly unshakable confidence in Thieu's regime and the ability of South Vietnam to defend itself against the Communist offensive. A State Department official said that, despite the hopelessness of the situation, Martin was still planning for future economic and social programs in South Vietnam.

The swiftness of South Vietnam's downfall startled North Vietnamese leaders, too. They were as puzzled as the Americans by the erratic behavior of the South Vietnamese. General Van Tien Dung, the North Vietnamese army chief of staff, was shocked by the swift success of an offensive he had expected to last two years or more:

A Russian-made tank manned by Communist soldiers advances on Da Nang during the spring 1975 offensive. Memories of Communist acts of terror, such as the alleged killing of some three thousand civilians in Hue during the Tet offensive of 1968, caused South Vietnamese to flee the North Vietnamese advance.

Why, he [Dung] wondered, had Thieu decided to abandon the highlands. It was, he noted in his diary, probably a "fatal mistake." In previous offensives, he might have spent weeks or months pondering, discussing, waiting for orders. But this was the difference in 1975. . . . He was able to issue the orders to take advantage of the Saigon retreat and move his troops in fast pursuit.

The blood bath predicted for so long by U.S. and South Vietnamese leaders did not take place. Roland-Pierre Paringaux, the only non-Communist journalist allowed in Da Nang shortly after its capture, described what had once been South Vietnam's second largest city as a "picture of calm":

The city's streets are full of life, the military presence is inconspicuous, and soldiers on patrol are indulgent, even after the 9 P.M. curfew, which is ignored by a few strollers and street merchants. . . . Foreigners who stayed in Da Nang were issued papers giving them freedom to move through the city. Among them were 120 French citizens; some 50 Indians, Chinese, and Canadian and American Roman Catholic priests.

Saigon: a city under siege

As the North Vietnamese tightened their strangle hold on Saigon in the last week of April, the city appeared resigned to its fate. President Thieu was gone. The new president, Duong Van "Big" Minh—nicknamed "Big" by Americans because of his height and to distinguish him from another Vietnamese official named Minh—was frantically trying to arrange a cease-fire or some other way to prevent the destruction of the city. But most Saigonese and their uninvited refugee guests knew that the end was approaching.

For some the finality of it all induced a strange sense of exhilaration or at least promised a welcome release, one way or the other, from the tension that gripped the city. Others sought escape in movie houses, which remained packed even as the Communists entered Saigon on April 30. There were also those who looked for a miracle that would lift the siege and save the city. Rumors abounded that the U.S. had succeeded in winning an eleventh-hour cease-fire agreement from Hanoi; that General Giap, North Vietnam's military mastermind, had been killed in a coup, and all Communist forces were being recalled to the North; and that the mighty American B-52s would appear in the sky once again to preserve the nation.

The severity of the crisis also brought formerly hostile factions together for one last prayer for the peace and solidarity that had eluded South Vietnam for so many years. Catholic priests and Buddhist monks gathered at Saigon's cathedral for the city's first joint religious service. In the words of one Buddhist monk, prayers were offered to Buddha "To seek harmony and protect and help the Vietnamese people. It would be very good to help us sufferers."

But there were many in Saigon who, like Thieu and Ky, did not wait for the final act of a drama whose climax they fully anticipated. Throughout March and April, all who could afford or scrape together the means to get out of Vietnam did so. The last commercial flights from Saigon were filled with South Vietnamese officials and their families, wealthy businessmen, and others with the necessary funds and papers.

Saigon, which had been transformed into a booming metropolis by the steady flow of American dollars, unraveled. People sold houses, cars, and expensive appliances at drastic losses to buy gold, U.S. dollars, preserved food for traveling, and ocean-going junks. Though there were many bargains, there were few buyers. In two weeks a palatial Saigon villa dropped in price from $125,000 to $31,000—and still wasn't sold.

Saigon's prostitutes, who had prospered when there were five hundred thousand American GIs in South Vietnam, also felt the sting of war. Dinh My Linh, the uncontested queen of Saigon's bar girls, did not know where to turn. She said:

Every night when I go home I drink three or four bottles of beer to try to make myself sleep, but how can I? I think about my mother and father, that I will never see them again. When the VC come, probably they will kill me.

Other prostitutes, who had supported large families by their profession, washed their faces clean of make-up, donned peasant attire, and returned to their villages to prepare for the inevitable.

Private U.S. companies began withdrawing their American employees and their dependents in late March. The American banks in Saigon quietly removed their American managers and employees and most U.S. currency on Friday, April 4 on specially arranged flights. Their departure was not discovered until the next Monday morning when the banks, staffed only by Vietnamese, refused to handle any more foreign currency transactions. This left hundreds of people stranded with worthless travelers' checks.

The last good-bye

For some time before the North Vietnamese had launched their final offensive, U.S. authorities in Vietnam had been developing contingency evacuation

Some of the thousands of desperate people who, beginning in March 1975, line up daily outside the U.S. Embassy to seek emigration papers.

plans if the "worst" were to occur. Their Talon Vise Plan, or Operation Frequent Wind as it was later called, was extremely complex. Top priority was the evacuation from Vietnam of all of the estimated seven thousand American troops and civilians. Talon Vise as originally proposed gave the American ambassador four options—evacuation by:

1. Commercial airlift from Tan Son Nhut, the airport outside Saigon, or any other available airports.
2. Military airlift from Tan Son Nhut.
3. Sea lift from the port serving Saigon.
4. Helicopter lift to U.S. Navy ships nearby.

Not even the most careful planners could have foreseen the military catastrophe that befell South Vietnam in spring 1975. All four evacuation options had assumed the cooperation and protection of the South Vietnamese armed forces. But the unreliability of South Vietnamese troops would pose a dangerous threat to Talon Vise.

A further complication was the vaguely conceived plan to evacuate up to two hundred thousand endangered South Vietnamese. The endangered category applied to all South Vietnamese who had worked closely with U.S. military or government agencies and were supposedly on a North Vietnamese execution list. The list included political figures, military officers, and government employees. Also on the list were those employed in the Central Intelligence

Agency's Phoenix program, who had killed thousands of Vietcong sympathizers and supporters.

U.S. Ambassador Martin drew fire for refusing to trigger Operation Talon Vise until the final stages of the North Vietnamese offensive. To the end Martin remained an outspoken supporter of the Thieu regime and, according to his critics, "dragged his feet" on implementing the evacuation plans. Martin's critics also charged that the U.S. Embassy's evacuation procedures even in mid–April were disorganized. In the confusion, a secret embassy signal code for starting the evacuation was accidentally disclosed when a marine guard at the embassy gate mistakenly handed out copies of it to anyone going inside. The coded message was to be broadcast over the American–run radio station in Saigon followed by the playing of "White Christmas."

As part of Talon Vise, the U.S. Defense Attaché Office (DAO) had set up a command center at Tan Son Nhut to coordinate the processing and evacuation of refugees. Under its direction, the evacuation of Americans and Vietnamese proceeded quietly during the first two weeks of April. DAO officials had wanted to speed up the evacuation but had been stymied by Ambassador Martin. He feared that a full–scale evacuation might cause widespread panic. Depart-

ment of Defense officials fumed at the delays: "We were sending planes and they were coming back half and two–thirds empty."

In the third week of April, word came from Washington ordering the U.S. Embassy to evacuate all but essential American personnel as quickly as possible. When embassy officials went into action, however, they realized that they had miscalculated the number of Americans in South Vietnam. They had originally expected seven thousand Americans. But unaccounted for Americans and even military deserters soon began showing up, many with Vietnamese wives, children, and in–laws. Embassy officials now had to contend with an evacuation figure that topped thirty-five thousand Americans, including their dependents.

By April 20 the evacuation airlift from Tan Son Nhut had accelerated considerably. Instead of a few hundred per day as before, DAO supervisors were processing and evacuating three to five thousand people every twenty-four hours. At the evacuation

Children march into the belly of a huge C-130 transport plane at Tan Son Nhut Airport, April 22, 1975. An earlier flight carrying more than two hundred orphans crashed, killing most aboard.

compound they worked around the clock against seemingly insurmountable odds to fly as many people out as possible. Time was the crucial factor. The airlift could continue only so long as Tan Son Nhut remained free of enemy fire, and the North Vietnamese were expected to attack almost any time.

A human assembly line

The evacuation process at Tan Son Nhut resembled a long assembly line. Tired and frustrated refugees, both Americans and Vietnamese, moved through an endless series of checkpoints for passports, identification, baggage checking, flight assignment, and boarding. Tempers were short, and one American caught in the slow-moving line of refugees shouted, "Find out where we get our shots and let's get out of here!"

For most Americans, a free ride to safety required only the proper identification papers and a passport. Those with Vietnamese dependents, however, encountered more difficulties. U.S. and South Vietnamese government red tape demanded proof that all Vietnamese claims for dependent status were legitimate. Many Americans sought evacuation not only for immediate Vietnamese family members, as permitted by regulations, but also for distant cousins and in-laws. Some Americans even sought passage for their Vietnamese maids and servants.

For every South Vietnamese fortunate enough to have that most coveted status—an "American connection"—there were hundreds of thousands of refugees just as afraid of being killed but unable to find a way out. According to a U.S. intelligence report, the odds against a Vietnamese escaping were fifty to one if he or she did not have an American relative or friend willing to guarantee financial assistance in the U.S. Many South Vietnamese were ready to sacrifice themselves to evacuate their loved ones with an American sponsor. A forlorn widow vainly pleaded with an American, "For God's sake, take my little boy out of Vietnam and raise him. If he stays, the Communists will take him from me to raise him their way, so he is lost to me anyway. Give him this chance, please."

There were South Vietnamese military personnel at Tan Son Nhut who had no legal means of evacuating but used whatever leverage they could to flee. Members of the South Vietnamese Air Force flew themselves and their families to U.S. air bases in Thailand or seized helicopters to reach U.S. aircraft

Knowing there is no landing space aboard the USS Blue Ridge, a Vietnamese pilot jumps from his helicopter, looking to swim to the ship.

carriers off the coast. The scene at Tan Son Nhut was ugly as soldiers and refugees fought to board South Vietnamese aircraft. Many fell or were pushed off the loading ramps as the planes taxied out.

DAO officials tried to discourage these unauthorized flights, but desperate South Vietnamese pilots ignored the orders. A few crazed South Vietnamese flight crews even threatened to shoot down U.S. evacuation planes unless granted landing clearance in Thailand. Meanwhile, like a tattered flock of birds

This South Vietnamese Air Force HU-1 (Huey) helicopter flown to the deck of the USS Blue Ridge is pushed into the South China Sea to make room for more helicopters to land and unload Vietnamese military men and their families.

fleeing a storm, South Vietnamese helicopters headed for U.S. carriers. One by one they landed and, once unloaded, one by one the helicopters were dumped into the sea to make room for more.

Everybody out!

As DAO personnel carried out the herculean task of processing thousands of evacuees, the pilots of evacuation planes, delayed on the ground, grew increasingly anxious. Uncertain military conditions around Saigon made every flight in and out of Tan Son Nhut an extremely hazardous operation.

In the early morning hours of April 29, Captain Arthur Mallano, an American C-130 transport pilot, waited nervously on the ground at Tan Son Nhut for his load of refugees. For two or three days, intelligence sources had warned officials at Tan Son Nhut of North Vietnamese rocket attacks. The pilots,

Scaling the walls of the U.S. Embassy, guarded by U.S. Marines, Vietnamese make final futile efforts to find places on the evacuation flights.

in their few spare moments, maintained a close watch on the horizon. When the attack came, Mallano had a ringside seat for the fireworks.

I'll never forget that time . . . we thought at first it was lightning in the background. You know the whole sky kind of lit up and I said to the copilot, "Gee, that thunderstorm is getting a little closer. It's moving toward the field." The next thing I know, not only was it white, it was red, blue, green—it had different colored rockets and mortars and it was hitting the field. . . . They were not just firing to scare us. When I saw the intensity of the rocket attack and the accuracy with which it was hitting the field, I immediately told the loadmaster, "Let's get the last passengers on." We did!

As Mallano took off, a continuous barrage of rockets was devastating the airport. From the Continental Palace Hotel in downtown Saigon, western corre-

spondents listened to the radio chatter from Tan Son Nhut over the UHF frequency used by U.S. officials. "The ICCS [International Commission for Control and Supervision] compound is burning. . . . The back end of the gymnasium's been hit. . . . My God, control, we've got two marine KIAs [killed in action]."

A terse question followed: "Do you know where the bodies are?"

The first voice replied: "Yeah, but that area's been chewed up real bad. They're gonna be in bad shape."

The two KIAs were nineteen-year-old Marine Lance Corporal Darwin Judge and twenty-one-year-old Marine Corporal Charles McMahon, the last Americans to die in battle on Vietnamese soil.

The battle of Saigon was underway. The rocket attacks on Tan Son Nhut prompted a series of emergency meetings in Washington between President Ford and his top advisers. Within hours, they ordered

On April 29, 1975, the day before South Vietnam surrendered, Americans clamber up a last-minute escape route to helicopter pads atop the U.S. Embassy.

Ambassador Martin to evacuate all remaining Americans in Saigon. After personally checking the damage at Tan Son Nhut, the ever-cautious Martin agreed with Major General Homer Smith, military commander in Saigon, that Option Four of Talon Vise, the evacuation of the airport and embassy by helicopters, should begin. But despite the fires at the airport and the open rebellion of South Vietnamese army units there, Martin was still reluctant to make a move. Smith's appraisal of the situation, however, finally convinced him: "Either we go with Option Four or we're going to look pretty stupid or pretty dead."

As Talon Vise went into motion on April 29, a fleet of 81 helicopters embarked from U.S. ships near the coast. During the last few weeks of the evacuation the U.S. had stationed 44 naval vessels, 120 air force combat and tanker planes, 150 navy planes, and 6,000 marines in the area. Since Tan Son Nhut was now closed to airplanes, helicopters had to pick up remaining American evacuees under fire.

The airport was also beset by snipers and rioting South Vietnamese soldiers. To provide security, U.S. helicopters landed two at a time on a tennis court near the DAO compound and unloaded 840 marines. Lt. Colonel John Hilgenberg recalled the joyous reaction of the evacuees when the helicopters arrived with the rescue force. "To me the sight was almost too good to be true. ... The crowd broke into a huge cheer with hand clapping and the first smiles I had seen in days."

By 7:30 P.M. the helicopters, flying in ninety-minute cycles between the ships and Tan Son Nhut, had successfully evacuated almost all of the last few thousand refugees. The marines had intimidated reckless South Vietnamese soldiers who had sniped at U.S. aircraft, disrupting the final stages of the evacuation.

The chopper pilots and their frightened passengers

ness, was shrouded by rain and masses of clouds reducing visibility to less than a mile. To find landing zones, some helicopters had to rely on flares fired by marines inside the embassy compound. Others followed flashlight signals.

The original Talon Vise plan was intended to evacuate only one hundred to one hundred and fifty people from the embassy. When it became clear after the rocket attack that Tan Son Nhut had totally shut down, hundreds more Americans and Vietnamese had crowded into the embassy compound. All during the afternoon choppers landed, loaded, and took off from the former parking lot, now a helicopter landing zone.

Outside the embassy, South Vietnamese authorities had placed Saigon under twenty-four hour curfew. But with police and military security forces disintegrating, there was little hope of enforcing it. Tens of thousands of desperate people roamed the streets,

A weary Ambassador Graham Martin, flanked by his press spokesman John Hogan (right) and Admiral Donald Whitmire, steps on board the USS Blue Ridge from one of the last helicopters to leave Saigon.

The North Vietnamese Army commanded a reputation for fierceness in battle. But on a Saigon street after South Vietnam succumbed in April 1975, the faces of these troops seem uncertain and tense.

could scarcely relax. The North Vietnamese had already rocked the field with artillery. Everyone expected that heat-seeking missiles would come next. Each takeoff was a nightmare. "As we gained altitude, we held our breaths," a newspaper correspondent noted. "We knew the Communists had been using heat-seeking missiles, and we were prepared to be shot out of the sky. ... Forty minutes later we were aboard the U.S.S. *Denver* ... and safe."

The embassy waits

Although the rescue mission at Tan Son Nhut had been completed, the U.S. Embassy in downtown Saigon still awaited evacuation. The city, then in darkness, was shrouded

frantic for a way to escape. Some soldiers simply dropped their rifles, discarded their helmets and backpacks, and dissolved into the crowds. Others, angry and frustrated, shot their rifles aimlessly into the air.

An atmosphere of doom lay upon the people, even those hiding quietly in their homes. Many Catholics, for whom suicide was a mortal sin, contemplated taking their own lives. A Catholic mother of nine children, who had moved south when the Communists took control of the North in 1954, explained: "We cannot live with them. Since there is no longer any place to run, the only option is death."

Saigon's hostile mobs were beginning to pose a serious threat to the remaining Americans. During most of the evacuation, the Vietnamese had continued treating Americans with their customary polite-

ness. But as things fell apart many Vietnamese vented their wrath against Americans. In some areas it became dangerous for an American to be seen on the streets. Members of the French diplomatic corps started wearing small French flags to avoid being mistaken for Americans.

The French were not leaving. Even after their fall at Dien Bien Phu in 1954, the French had never ceased trying to maintain their influence in Vietnam and continued diplomatic relations with Hanoi. It was a strange twist of history: The French, who had been driven out of Vietnam after a century of colonial rule and a bloody war, now enjoyed the most secure presence in the country of all the western powers. The bizarre switch of French and American roles in Vietnam prompted one U.S. Embassy official to say: "It's so ironic. The French lost to the Communists at Dien Bien Phu, and we took their place here. Now, twenty-one years later, we're the ones being forced out, and they're coming back as the most important western political force in Indochina."

During the evening of April 29, the mob of Vietnamese surrounding the embassy began to grow. The embassy was enclosed by a ten-foot wall with barbed wire strung across the top, but hundreds hoping to reach the helicopters tried to scale it. A U.S. radio operator issued a frantic call for assistance: "Marines to the gate as soon as possible!" Minutes later, the operator called again: "There are some two thousand people in front of the gate. It's getting hostile." As the night wore on, exhausted marines struggled to keep order. They had to use tear gas and rifle butts to

After crashing through the gates of South Vietnam's presidential palace on May 1, 1975, Communist soldiers on a Russian-made T-54 tank wave their flag of victory. President Minh had surrendered to the Communists the day before.

hold off the surging people screaming and begging to be taken along.

Around 9:30 P.M. an urgent message arrived from Washington instructing Ambassador Martin to "wrap it up and get his ass out of there." The head of embassy security gathered together all the remaining Americans. When the Vietnamese evacuees saw what was happening, they made a rush for the landing zone. The radio operator shouted: "The gates are open. We've lost control of the crowd."

The marines fell back toward the main embassy building to cover the last American evacuees scrambling up the stairs inside to the helicopter on the roof. After all the Americans were safely on top, the marines followed. Behind the marines came looters, smashing and ransacking offices. When they reached the roof, the marines lobbed tear gas grenades into the elevator shaft.

By 7:52 A.M. on April 30, the last marines had left the embassy. The evacuation was complete. Three hours earlier, Ambassador Martin, still unwilling to leave, had bid final farewell to Saigon, his helicopter broadcasting the coded message, "Lady Ace Zero Nine, Code Two [Martin] is aboard."

The morning after

Just two and a half hours after the last U.S. chopper

had lifted off the roof of the American Embassy, President "Big" Minh announced in a short radio address that he was offering an unconditional surrender to the Communists. "I believe in reconciliation among Vietnamese to avoid unnecessary shedding of blood," he said. "For this reason I ask the soldiers of the Republic of Vietnam to cease hostilities in calm and to stay where they are." Later, Minh confided to a French journalist, "Yes, it [the surrender] had to be done. Human lives had to be saved."

High above Saigon, the pilot of a U.S. Air Force fighter plane escorting the last helicopters evacuating Vietnam, looked down on the scene of surrender and later recalled:

I looked back one last time, just a bit overwhelmed at having witnessed history in the making. After twenty-plus years of war, a city was falling, a government toppling, a country changing. Twenty years of bloody fighting with hundreds of thousands killed. . . . I remember a bit of the briny collecting in the corner of my eye, and my flushed reaction to this unwarriorlike emotionalism. In retrospect, though, when you say a last good-bye to a battleground that took [so many of your] countrymen, I guess it deserves one final tear.

In America, too, the impulse was to conclude that a sad and regrettable interlude was over. President Ford issued a statement about America's twenty-one years in Vietnam.

This action closes a chapter in the American experience. I ask all Americans to close ranks, to avoid recriminations about the past, to look ahead to the many goals we share, and to work together on the great tasks that remain to be accomplished.

Only a chapter was closed, however. The experience was not. The Americans were at last out of Vietnam. The long, cruel war was finished. But for Americans, as for the Vietnamese, the experience had reached beyond the soldiers, politicians, protesters, intriguers, innocent bystanders, and innocent victims, into the deeper recesses of society. Its repercussions—the plight of refugees, the problems of veterans, a plague of political disillusionment and national self-doubt—persisted in the United States.

Once the war was over, the temptation to consign Vietnam to the past was strong among Americans, but that was not possible because too many questions remained to be answered. How and why did the United States become so deeply embroiled in a small,

President Ford takes a pensive, long-distance view of the fall of South Vietnam. "Close ranks . . . avoid recriminations about the past" advised Ford on April 25, 1975, as the last episode of U.S. involvement in Vietnam was closing.

seemingly inconsequential country halfway around the world and to what effect? Why did the war end as it did? Who were the people, a divided nation, on whom America expended so many lives, so much blood, and treasure? What does the Vietnam experience tell about the application of power, of purpose, and of patriotism? What went wrong? Was it, indeed, a misbegotten adventure, a noble effort gone awry, or will it gain a profounder meaning in chronicles yet to be written?

Some of the answers are for the future to compose. Others are to be found by peering back into the character and the history of the land and the people of Vietnam.

On the day after the fall of the Saigon government, a South Vietnamese helicopter lies abandoned in a rice field outside Saigon, a solitary reminder of the bounty of American-made aircraft, vehicles, weapons, and munitions left to the conquering North Vietnamese.

The Final Day

By H.D.S. Greenway

The sound of artillery shells bursting in the city came through the open window of the Continental Hotel in the early hours before dawn. Up from a shallow sleep came the realization that this sound was different from the occasional incoming rocket that had awakened the capital on other nights. The rapid explosions could only mean that the North Vietnamese divisions that had encircled the city were now within artillery range. It was the twenty-ninth of April 1975. The fall of Saigon was upon us.

The final collapse of thirty years of American and French effort in Vietnam had come with a startling suddenness and great confusion and panic. Cities had been abandoned by their defenders before the North Vietnamese had arrived. Whole armies had deserted amid looting and killing. Hundreds had tried to claw their way aboard the last departing aircraft—some even hanging onto the wheels—as the debacle spread south.

Now there was nowhere else to go. All the roads leading in and out of Saigon were cut and, by the sound of the artillery, the air evacuation at Tan Son Nhut Airport would now have to be abandoned. The only chance for those remaining was flight by helicopter to the American fleet in the South China Sea.

City of fear

Saigon in those last weeks of the war had become a city of infectious fear and despair, of exhaustion beyond fatigue, of quick tears and tortured dreams. Vietnamese friends I had known for years would come with drawn faces to plead for help. It was hard to look into their eyes and not see a mirror of betrayal.

Strangers would clutch at foreigners in the streets, begging to be rescued. Long lines of Vietnamese could be seen waiting at the gates of foreign embassies while inside diplomats hastily burned classified documents. Ashes from the burning papers floated over the embassy walls. Beggars, transvestites, cripples, and prostitutes gathered in the shadows trying for one last pitch as the hour of the evening curfew approached. The corrupt, venal Saigon that had long ago become dependent on foreigners was dying.

Suicides spread like a virus carried by fear. A Saigon police colonel walked up to the South Vietnamese war memorial in Lam Son Square and saluted. Two newsmen watched as he then pulled out a pistol and shot himself. He died moments later in the arms of one of the reporters. A few days before, a man had stabbed himself in front of the National Assembly. A friend bought poison and said he planned to kill himself and his family when the time came. As the tension mounted such behavior no longer appeared irrational in the eyes of many Vietnamese caught up in the panic.

On that last day before the dawn I had trouble placing where I was. Dreams of being trapped in a burning city merged too easily with wakeful reality in those final days. The high, open French windows of the elegant old Continental Hotel let in the humid air, and at first I could not comprehend the sound of the guns. Nine years earlier, when I had first slept in that hotel, the sound of artillery had been outgoing rounds of desultory fire by Saigon's defenders against the occasional guerrilla in the forest outside of town. Now an invading army with heavy artillery, tanks, even planes was about to take Saigon itself.

I lay for awhile watching the ceiling fan stir the curtains and thought of the many battles that had been fought in this small country. Had I invested the same amount of my life in the days of World War II, I might have seen the sweep of armies across continents and navies across the vast oceans. Here it had been all churning up death on the same small killing ground. Youth had passed into middle age. Hundreds and thousands had died and two powerful western countries had expended their blood and treasure here for thirty years. All for nothing?

An overwhelming desire to stay in bed gave way to fear. Already my colleagues were gathering in the corridors outside their rooms. One had a radio that could pick up traffic between the American Embassy and the airport. "Tan Son Nhut being heavily shelled," said a voice. "Four rounds in five seconds on the flight line." Two American Marines had been killed and a choking voice asked where their bodies were. They, the last Americans killed in Vietnam, would be left behind in the mad scramble of Americans to evacuate the city. Their bodies would be sent home long afterwards.

Although it seemed clear that "Option Four"—evacuation from the U.S. Embassy by helicopter—was the only choice left, there seemed to be some lingering doubt in the mind of U.S. Ambassador Graham Martin. He went out to inspect the runway personally but was greeted by both small arms and artillery fire that continued intermittently all day.

A grandstand seat

As morning broke some of us went up to the roof of the Caravelle Hotel across the street from the Continental. It was one of Saigon's tallest buildings and offered a grandstand seat. We could see fires burning out of control at the airport, three miles away, and many South Vietnamese aircraft circling in the sky. With sinking stomachs we watched the lazy arc of a heat seeking missile rise from behind the airport and inexorably find its way to an airplane that immediately disintegrated over the city. None of us wanted to look at each other because we knew that very few would leave the city alive if the North Vietnamese decided to oppose the evacuation.

Years later the North Vietnamese commander, General Van Tien Dung, wrote that he had received instructions from Hanoi to press on with the attack but not to interfere with an American evacuation—an order that he protested but obeyed.

All Americans had been issued little maps with instructions telling them where to report "should it be felt necessary for U.S. personnel to report to their designated assembly areas. ..." Even to the last, the American command resorted to the same euphemistic style that had called every ambush a "meeting engagement" throughout the war. The word "evacuation" was never mentioned in the instructions. We were told to listen to the radio for the weather report "105 degrees and rising," which would be followed by thirty seconds of Bing Crosby singing "White Christmas." This would be the signal to assemble at various staging areas around the city and await the helicopters.

At the American Embassy, for so long the symbol of American power in Vietnam, marine guards could be seen furiously chopping down a tree behind the chancery in order to make room for a helicopter landing area. The tree had become something of a symbol; Ambassador Martin had refused to let his staff cut it down before this moment. To some his business-as-usual attitude was the ultimate head-in-the-sand refusal to see that disaster was coming like an onrushing train. To others his waiting to cut down the tree was part of a supreme effort to forestall panic among the Vietnamese in order that he might evacuate as many as possible before Option Four became necessary. Now tired and sick with pneumonia, the old cold war warrior was keeping up appearances till the end, even walking back to his residence to fetch his dog in time for the evacuation.

Other Americans could be seen carrying out charts with red and blue arrows showing the irrepressible advance of the North Vietnamese Army on Saigon. Still others were busy destroying thousands of dollars of U.S. currency.

At first the city seemed not to realize what was happening. But as afternoon came word spread and the city began to seeth with the rolling-eyed fear of animals caught in a burning barn. Great mobs appeared outside the gates of the American Embassy wailing and beseeching the Americans to let them inside. A few were admitted. I watched one of the most notoriously corrupt generals being squeezed in the main gate with a suitcase while others were forced back. Some would try to pass notes into the embassy courtyard: "I am working for the Americans. Please tell Mr. Jacobson [an embassy official] I am here," one read.

Men like animals

Keyes Beech, an American reporter caught outside, would later write: "Once we moved into that seething mass we ceased to be correspondents. We were only men fighting for our lives, scratching, clawing, pushing ever closer to the wall. We were like animals. Now I know what it is like to be a Vietnamese. I am one of them. But if I could get over that wall I would be an American again."

There were similar scenes all over town. A bus trying to take Americans to an assembly point was mobbed by frantic Vietnamese. The bus could not stop and some were run over in the street. A Vietnamese policeman in a rage of frustration and fear pulled out his gun and fired blindly into the crowd. Looting broke out at American installations and maddened Vietnamese tore at each other for a share of the loot.

In the afternoon the helicopters began to arrive—first the Cobra gunships sweeping low over the city and then the big transport helicopters. In the embassy compound, shredded classified material burst from its bags and rose over the compound like leaves in a storm as the hurricane force of the helicopters' down-draft hit them. Marines in full battle dress rushed off the helicopters to hold back the crowds threatening to break through the gates. Later, these marines would take a rear guard fighting action as the Vietnamese, in the end, broke into the compound. The marines threw tear gas as they backed up the stairs to the roof.

The mood inside the embassy was now one of despondency. Not only was the war being lost before their eyes, the Vietnamese were beginning to realize that hundreds of them who had served the U.S.—people whose work would guarantee them concentration camp status—

were being abandoned all over town. Pathetic telephone messages kept coming in: "There are thirty of us here. Please give us instructions. Please come and get us."

The main fear was that maddened South Vietnamese soldiers, some of whom were already shedding their uniforms, would turn and fire on the departing Americans. Sniper fire could be heard from time to time, and several helicopter pilots reported taking ground fire on their way in and out of the city. Yet no helicopters were shot down during the evacuation.

"Where are they?"

As darkness came with a sudden squall my turn came to leave. I was pushed into a helicopter beside a nervous gunner who kept asking me, "Where are they? Where are they?" I told him that the North Vietnamese had not yet entered the city, although later that evening their trucks, with headlights ablaze, could be seen moving down the main highways toward the city.

As the helicopter rose over the city I saw the rain-washed streets and, down by the waterfront, masses of panicked people trying to force their way aboard crowded boats headed down the Saigon River. Away to the northeast I could see great ammunition dumps blowing up and raging fires in the distance.

We crossed the coast in the gathering dark; an American fleet lay waiting below us. South Vietnamese helicopters, like butterflies borne on an off-shore wind, landed briefly on American ships before being tossed overboard. Some crashed at sea before reaching safety. All about us lay the flotillas of helplessly overcrowded boats drifting like the flotsam left after a shipwreck. These were the first of the boat people who in the years to come would account for a great hemorrhaging of Vietnam's population. A war was ended, but peace had not come to Indochina.

H.D.S. Greenway is National-Foreign Editor of the Boston Globe. *He covered Vietnam for* Time *magazine and the* Washington Post *from early 1967 until the American evacuation of Saigon in 1975.*

Inside Vietnam and Beyond:
A Chronology

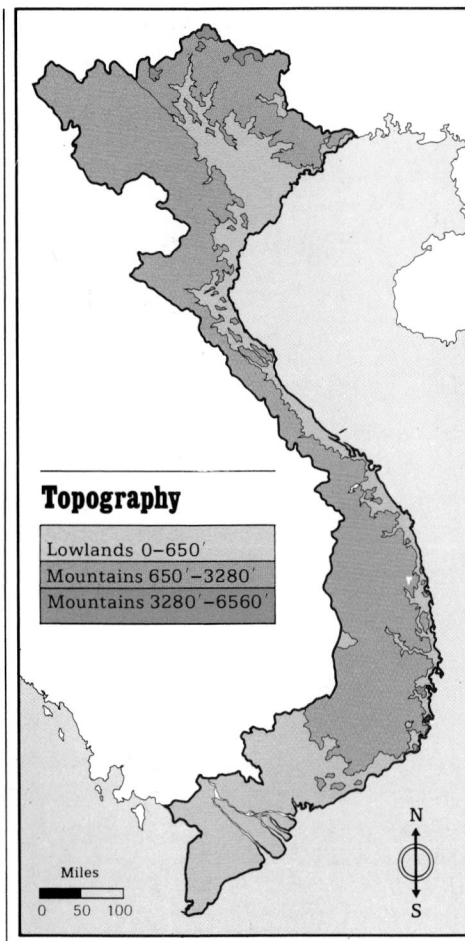

Topography

| Lowlands 0–650' |
| Mountains 650'–3280' |
| Mountains 3280'–6560' |

Miles
0 50 100

N
S

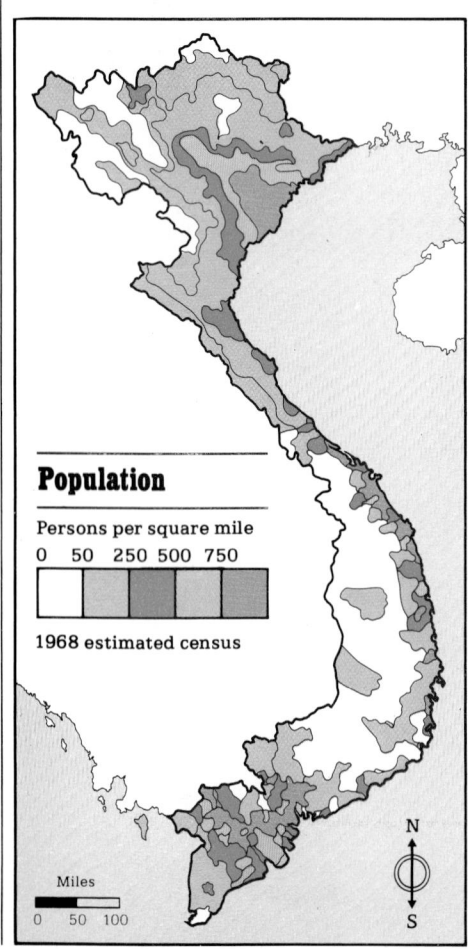

Population

Persons per square mile
0 50 250 500 750

1968 estimated census

Miles
0 50 100

N
S

Inside Vietnam

B.C.
- c. 3000–Legendary kingdom of Van Lang
- c. 450–Migration of Viets to North Vietnam
- 258–Kingdom of Au Lac
- 208–Trieu Da brings Au Lac into Nam Viet
- 111–Chinese begin 1,000-year rule of Vietnam

A.D.
- 10–Confucianism spreads into Vietnam
- 39–43–Trung sisters rebellion
- c. 100–Champa emerges between Mekong and Hue
- c. 170–Romans first visit Vietnam
- 189–Chinese bonzes bring Buddhism to Vietnam
- 248–Trieu Au rebellion
- 543–7–Ly Bon rebellion
- 938–Vietnam gains independence from China

- 969–Bo Linh proclaims kingdom of Dai Co Viet
- 1010–1225–Ly dynasty
- 1061–Champa attacked: area around Hue annexed
- 1225–1400–Tran dynasty
- 1284–Tran Hung Dao defeats Mongol army
- 1407–China retakes Vietnam
- 1418–Le Loi embarks on liberation of Vietnam
- 1428–Vietnam defeats China

- 1428–1786–Le dynasty
- 1471–Emperor Le Thanh Tong defeats Champa
- c. 1500–Portuguese land on Vietnamese coast
- 1527–Mac Dang Dung seizes power from Le emperor
- 1593–Trinh Kiem restores Le dynasty to throne
- 1620–Civil war erupts between Trinh and Nguyen
- 1637–Portuguese open trade center at Faifo
- 1640–Alexandre de Rhodes arrives in Vietnam
- 1673–Trinh and Nguyen agree to truce
- 1744–Nguyen expansion reaches Mekong Delta
- 1773–Tay Son rebellion begins
- 1786–Hanoi falls to the Tay Son
- 1802–Nguyen Anh takes Hanoi, becomes emperor
- 1820–41–Reign of Minh Mang
- 1841–7–Reign of Thieu Tri
- 1847–French ships sink Vietnam navy at Da Nang
- 1847–83–Reign of Tu Duc
- 1857–French recommend Vietnam protectorate
- 1858–Admiral de Genouilly enters Da Nang Bay
- 1859–Saigon falls to French troops
- 1866–7–Mekong expedition led by Garnier
- 1873–Garnier captures Hanoi citadel
- 1874–Colony of Cochin China ratified
- 1883–French capture Hanoi
- 1884–Treaty gives French all of Vietnam
- 1885–97–Scholars' Revolt

- 1906–8–Phan Boi Chau leads peasant rebellion
- 1913–Railroad links Saigon to Hanoi
- 1918–Nguyen Ai Quoc at Versailles Conference
- 1925–Ai Quoc founds Revolutionary Youth League
- 1926–Cao Dai religious sect founded
- 1927–Vietnamese Nationalist party organized
- 1930–French crush Nationalist uprising
  Indochinese Communist party founded
- 1930–1–Revolt of Red Soviets of Nghe-Tinh
- 1935–Communists and Trotskyists win majority on Saigon municipal council
- 1939–Communist party outlawed
  Hoa Hao Buddhist sect founded
- 1940–Communist revolt in Cochin China suppressed

- 1940–Japan attacks Tonkin
  Chinese form Vietnam Liberation League
- 1941–Japanese solidify control over Vietnam
  French initiate "policy of regard"
  Vietminh founded
- 1942–China represses Vietminh, backs Nationalists
- 1943–Nguyen Ai Quoc changes name to Ho Chi Minh
  De Gaulle rules out independence for Vietnam
- 1944–Vietnam Liberation Army created under Giap
- 1945–Japanese overthrow French March 9
  Vietminh seize power from Japan August 19
  Ho Chi Minh proclaims Vietnam free September 2

Beyond

B.C.
- 3000–Egypt unified; beginning of Old Kingdom
- c. 500–Confucius in China; Buddhism begins in India
- 399–Socrates put to death in Athens
- c. 102–Birth of Julius Caesar

A.D.
- c. 33–Jesus of Nazareth crucified in Jerusalem
- c. 60–Buddhism becomes official religion of China

- c. 220–Fall of the Han dynasty
- 410–Sack of Rome
- 618–907–T'ang dynasty in China
- 800–Charlemagne crowned Holy Roman Emperor

- c. 1000–Viking invasions of Europe
- 1066–Norman Conquest
- 1100–Khmer empire in Cambodia at its peak
- 1213–Mongols under Genghis Khan invade China
- 1271–95–Marco Polo visits China
- 1334–50–Plague kills half of Europe's population
- 1368–Ming dynasty created in China
- 1400–Aztec empire emerges in Mexico

- 1429–Joan of Arc leads French victory at Orléans
- 1453–Turks take Constantinople
- 1492–Columbus discovers the New World
- 1600–Shakespeare's *Hamlet* performed in London
- 1607–First English colony in New World
- 1637–Japan cuts foreign trade and cultural ties
- 1643–Louis XIV becomes king of France
- 1763–Treaty leaves England master of India
- 1776–American Declaration of Independence
- 1789–99–French Revolution
- 1804–Napoleon becomes emperor of France
- 1815–French forces defeated at Waterloo
- 1824–Beethoven composes *Ninth Symphony*
- 1830–July Revolution in France
- 1837–Queen Victoria crowned in England
- 1839–42–Opium War between England and China
- 1848–Revolutions across Europe
- 1852–Napoleon III restores Second French Empire
- 1859–Darwin publishes *On the Origin of Species*
- 1861–5–American Civil War
- 1864–Karl Marx presides at First Communist International
- 1870–1–Franco–Prussian War
  Establishment of the Third French Republic
- 1898–Spanish–American War
- 1899–1902–Boer War
- 1898–1900–"Boxer" Rebellion in China

- 1904–5–Russo–Japanese War
- 1905–Einstein publishes theory of relativity
- 1914–18–World War I
- 1917–Russian Revolution
- 1919–Gandhi begins civil disobedience against British in India
- 1922–Mussolini establishes Fascist rule in Italy
- 1928–Nationalist government in China proclaimed
- 1929–Wall Street crash starts Great Depression
- 1931–Civil war in China
- 1933–Adolf Hitler becomes chancellor of Germany
  U.S. President Roosevelt takes office
- 1937–Japanese attack China
- 1939–German invasion of Poland begins World War II

- 1940–Fall of France
  Battle of Britain
- 1941–Japanese attack Pearl Harbor
  Germany invades Russia
- 1942–American victories over Japanese navy
  Allied landing in Africa
- 1943–Germans retreat from Russia

- 1944–Allied invasion of Normandy
- 1945–Battle of Berlin, May 1
  UN Charter signed June 16
  Potsdam Conference, July 17
  Atomic bomb dropped on Hiroshima August 6

The Crossroads of Southeast Asia

The Beginning

The Indochinese peninsula extends like an open hand from the Asian continent into the South China Sea. It forms the southeastern extremity of Asia, reaching out from the huge arc of the Himalayas and the mountains of China. Laos, Cambodia, Thailand, Burma, and Malaysia share the peninsula with Vietnam. Southern Thailand and Malaysia, whose mountains form its backbone, jut out from Indochina's western coast to form another slender peninsula curving south toward Indonesia.

As its name suggests, Indochina lies between the two great civilizations of the East, India and China. Beginning approximately two thousand years ago, Indian and Chinese traders, missionaries, and colonists converged on Indochina by land and sea, carrying with them the vital seeds of writing, religion, art, and technology. Laos and Cambodia, like neighboring Thailand and Burma, fell at this time within the cultural sphere of India.

American Marines in combat found the jungle near Da Nang hot and inhospitable. One hundred feet above them, the humidity might vary from 95 percent at night to 60 percent during the day, but on the ground, humidity persists at a stifling 90 percent, exhausting the soldiers and literally rotting their clothing and boots.

Preceding page. Enriched with fertile silt carried by the Mekong River for twenty-five hundred miles, the delta near the Cambodian border fans out in a green expanse of flood plains.

While an Indian-inspired civilization once extended into what is now central Vietnam, the people have been influenced more by China. Running from the northwest to the southeast, Vietnam's mountain chains and major rivers formed natural barriers against the spread of Indian culture. At the same time, these natural features created a corridor for peoples from the north. Thus, the Vietnamese have always felt the intense pressure of China's civilization and, on occasion, its military might.

Vietnam: the land

Vietnam forms the eastern side of the Indochinese peninsula. The country extends some twelve hundred miles south from the China frontier to the Gulf of Thailand and covers an area somewhat larger than California. Vietnam's shape has often been compared to two rice baskets hanging at the ends of a bamboo pole, like those borne on the shoulders of so many Vietnamese peasants. The country's two major deltas, formed by the Red River in the North and the Mekong in the South, are the baskets. The Annamese mountain chain, the backbone of central Vietnam, is the pole supporting them.

Vietnam, then, divides into three distinct geographic sections: Tonkin in the North, Annam in the center, and Cochin China in the South. Each of these regions represents an important phase of Vietnam's growth as a nation. Like our colonial ancestors in the United States, the Vietnamese were migrants with a destiny. From their ancient homeland in China's southern provinces, they slowly moved into what is now Vietnam. First they took Tonkin, then Annam. Only in the nineteenth century, after centuries of warfare, settlement, and colonization, did the Vietnamese at last fulfill their destiny by wresting Cochin China from the Cambodians.

When the Vietnamese expanded from the Red River Delta, they moved through a vast network of valleys and rivers, which support an agrarian culture based on rice cultivation. Avoiding the mountainous inland sections, they settled in the coastal plains and river deltas so well suited to rice farming.

The Vietnamese were able to form and retain a national identity while settling in a diverse land. In this beautiful country, mountains and plains contrast with deep valleys, lush green fields, and flat, treeless grasslands. There are small pockets of desert in Vietnam, but about half of the country is jungle, and nearly four-fifths of the land is covered by trees and tropical vegetation.

Although beautiful, Vietnam's diverse terrain had its menacing aspect for American soldiers fighting a counterinsurgency war in the countryside. Soldiers had to adapt quickly to varied environments—jungles, rice fields, swamps—all harboring Communist guerrillas expert in using the treacherous terrain to their advantage. As early as 1962 the U.S. military implemented a defoliation program to clear extensive areas of jungle and prevent their use as enemy hide-outs and bases. Today, the more than 5 million defoliated acres remain a scar on the land and a striking reminder of twenty-one years of fierce battle.

Tonkin

Vietnam's northern rice basket is a large fertile plain of about seventy-five hundred square miles. Here the Vietnamese founded their first settlements. Its soil is enriched by many waterways, especially the Red River, sometimes called the "mother river." Flowing southward from its source in China's Yunnan Province and swelled by the Clear, Black, and Thai Binh rivers, the Red River deposits fertile loam throughout its delta. A tributary of the Thai Binh connects Haiphong, the principal port of the North, to the Gulf of Tonkin.

During the Vietnam War, Haiphong served as North Vietnam's key port for receiving Russian and Chinese aid. The U.S. military repeatedly urged the destruction of Haiphong's harbor facilities. But it was not until May 1972 that President Richard Nixon ordered the mining and bombing of Haiphong, virtually halting the flow of goods through its harbor.

Hanoi is centrally located on the Red River at the confluence of a number of streams. These serve as avenues of transportation to delta cities. After the French evacuated Hanoi, in accord with the Geneva Agreement of 1954, it became the capital of North Vietnam. Hanoi is not only a transportation hub but also a manufacturing center and an important market for agricultural and industrial products. Despite heavy U.S. bombings between 1965 and 1968 and again in 1972, the city has remained surprisingly intact. Since 1970, its population has tripled to 1,400,000, roughly equivalent to that of Cincinnati, Ohio.

The delta has always served as the region's agricultural heartland. Every year its rich soil can produce two harvests of rice, which has always been Vietnam's leading crop. So fertile is the Red River Delta that it has become one of the world's most densely populated agricultural regions.

A significant portion of Vietnam's 40 million inhabitants is crowded into this gigantic rice field. The area's population density averages sixteen hundred to two thousand people per square mile, a density almost twice that of Rhode Island, the most densely populated state in the United States. Compared to an agricultural region like Kansas, it has about one hundred times as many people per square mile. When swollen by rains, the Red River rises to dangerous

These volunteers work on a Sunday afternoon in a continual effort to shore up the land around Hanoi against the impetuous Red River. Without the dikes and canals that crisscross the Red River Delta, many of them centuries old, the river's floods would make life in the area almost impossible.

levels above the lowland plain through which it flows. Its flood waters may rise as much as thirty feet above the level of Hanoi's streets, and floods may occur several times a year without warning.

In a continual effort to protect themselves against the extremes of drought and flood, the Vietnamese have substantially altered the shape of the land. Over many years they have constructed an immense system of dams, canals, and dikes that rivals that of Holland. The dikes protecting Hanoi are so vital that, during the 1960s and 1970s, the North Vietnamese enrolled peasants in emergency labor battalions, a practice dating back to early times, to maintain and strengthen them against potential U.S. air strikes.

A network of canals also links the delta's maze of rivers. The canals lessen the floods and provide water for irrigation. Peasants transfer water from one field to another, either by simple hydraulic devices or in baskets on long ropes, transforming fields already plowed and planted with rice sprouts into endless pools of paddies. The dikes and canals have also served to reclaim land from the sea and render it fit for cultivation.

Inland from the delta, hills and then mountains rise toward China and Laos. Because of their isolation, the prevalence of malaria, and few developed agricultural resources, these highlands are still only sparsely settled. Thirty-three mountain tribes, whom the French called "montagnards," or "mountain people," are scattered throughout the high country. These tribes are for the most part culturally distinct from the lowland Vietnamese. Until recently, many of the tribes practiced only a rudimentary subsistence agriculture. In recent years, the Vietnamese have begun extensive mining of the northern highlands' considerable iron, zinc, tin, and coal deposits.

Annam

South of the Red River Delta is Annam, a strip of land which in some places is only thirty miles wide. Traditionally, the montagnards who inhabit the Annamese highlands, like those in Tonkin, have labored at subsistence farming.

Although sparsely populated, the highlands were strategically important in the Vietnamese war. In the

The Mountain People

Special Forces Montagnard troops patrol a hilltop near Dak To in the central highlands in 1969. Although these montagnards are trying to knock out North Vietnamese rocket caches, other tribesmen joined the Communists in the battle for South Vietnam's highlands.

The primitive tribes of Vietnam's central highlands, known to the French as the "montagnards," or "mountain people," came to play an important role in the guerrilla warfare that raged in Vietnam's mountain jungles between 1946 and 1975.

Prior to World War II, the montagnards had been largely isolated from the civilization of the lowlands. Vietnamese emperors had been content to leave the mountain tribes alone as long as they paid the government tribute and taxes. French colonial rulers had largely continued this policy of neglect.

The outbreak of hostilities between French and Ho Chi Minh's Vietminh in 1946, however, brought an abrupt end to the montagnards' isolation. "To seize and control the highlands," concluded Ho's brilliant tactician, General Vo Nguyen Giap, "is to solve the whole problem of South Vietnam." Soon both opposing armies were wooing the mountain tribesmen, whose knowledge of the rugged terrain made them invaluable allies in the savage guerrilla fighting.

One French sergeant told journalist Lucien Bodard: "I have the Sedangs as allies. They are great big good-looking fellows with nothing on except paint and tattooing and magic charms. They're red, like copper. ... They fight against the next-door tribe, the Katai, who are on the side of the Viets. And just as I do with the Sedangs, the Viet officers take on the Katai and train them."

After the 1954 Geneva accords, Ho Chi Minh continued to solicit the support of the montagnards. He brought as many as ten thousand tribesmen north to Hanoi, where they were trained as teachers, medical technicians, and political agents. Ho established autonomous, self-governing zones for the mountain population of the North and gave the tribes substantial representation in the National Assembly in Hanoi.

The South Vietnamese had much less success in enlisting montagnard support. While the Vietminh responded to their independent traditions, the South Vietnamese attempted to assimilate the tribesmen with force. The montagnards in turn bristled at the haughtiness of some Saigon officials, who referred to them in the traditional manner as "moi," or "savages." The relocation of Catholic refugees into lands traditionally held by the tribes further alienated the montagnards.

When American advisers appeared on the scene in the early 1960s, they attempted to rebuild alliances with certain strategically located tribes. CIA and army intelligence agents had some success in enlisting the support of the Rhade tribe, south of Pleiku. Later, General William Westmoreland would praise the "inspiring" courage of the Hre tribe, which held off an entire enemy regiment at Camp Kannach, a U.S. Special Forces outpost in Binh Dinh Province. In February 1966 U.S. military leaders convinced South Vietnamese President Ky to appoint a montagnard as special commissioner for montagnard affairs.

Despite these efforts, however, long-festering racial animosity between the South Vietnamese and the montagnards prevented effective cooperation. In 1966 American anthropologist Gerald Hickey painstakingly negotiated a treaty in which the South Vietnamese government agreed to respect montagnard tribal and property rights. But South Vietnamese military officers promptly violated the agreement. By 1975 the montagnards, who had suffered the ravages of war, the effects of defoliant chemicals, and the destruction of their traditional societies, were left on their own to face the North Vietnamese and an uncertain future.

early 1960s, the first U.S. Special Forces entered the disease-ridden region to keep the montagnards from falling under Communist control. From their highland base at Pleiku, U.S. forces also carried out defensive operations against Communist troops and supply columns moving south via the Ho Chi Minh Trail in Laos and Cambodia.

Farther north in these same highlands, the virtually unpopulated plateau of Khe Sanh was the site of one of the most important battles of the war. For seventy-seven days, U.S. forces valiantly resisted an all-out North Vietnamese attack. The North Vietnamese siege at Khe Sanh brought to mind the Communist encirclement and decisive defeat of the French at Dien Bien Phu in 1954. Combined U.S. and South Vietnamese air and ground forces finally broke the siege and routed the enemy, shattering two of North Vietnam's best divisions and frustrating its dream of a second Dien Bien Phu.

Annam's long, broken coastline and its many rivers provide both food and transportation. Most of its people live close to the sea, which supplies salt and fish, along with rice, the main ingredients of their diet. The many sheltered natural bays that dot the Annamese coast compensate for the obstacles to overland transportation presented by the mountains. Among the bays are the Bay of Tourane, later called Da Nang, and Cam Ranh Bay, once the sites of two of the United States' largest naval-air bases.

Maritime pursuits have always been important to Vietnam's coastal dwellers. The Vietnamese neglected the high seas, as they did the mountains, in their single-minded effort to pacify their frontiers and to sow freshly cleared lands with rice. They were, however, skilled coastal sailors, and internal trade was brisk in nearby waters.

Farmers in the northern Vietnam mountains cultivate every available inch of land using many techniques adopted by their forebears centuries ago.

None surpass the captains of Vietnamese junks as they navigate Vietnam's endlessly winding course of rivers and canals.

Cochin China

The mighty Mekong River, winding twenty-five hundred miles from the Tibetan highlands to the South China Sea, dominates Vietnam's larger rice basket, Cochin China. The Mekong's broad, fertile delta marks the southernmost frontier of Vietnam's national expansion. Until the nineteenth century, much of the delta was virgin territory and richer than the intensively cultivated northern regions. Under French rule, this region—including the Cambodian hinterland—exported more than a million tons of rice a year.

More benevolent than the Red River, the Mekong rises slowly in the rainy season, reaching its height in October. Farmers nearby can plan their labors without fear of sudden floods, and since the Mekong floods less often than the Red, the inhabitants have never been forced to replicate the dikes of the North.

Much of Cochin China is furrowed by streams and canals which furnish an excellent network for navigation and irrigation. Barges maintain communications among villages and carry surplus rice to Saigon, Vietnam's biggest port, which is located some forty miles from the coast. Ships pass in and out of Saigon through the tidal Dong Nai River.

Under French rule, Saigon grew from a small village to a large city. It became the capital of South Vietnam in 1954 and later expanded to a booming metropolis as a result of billions of dollars in U.S. aid. Although Saigon, unlike Hanoi, was never the target of enemy air strikes, it suffered considerable damage from Communist mortar and artillery during the Tet offensive of 1968. Until 1975, when the Communists began relocating its population to the country, Saigon, with nearly 2 million people, was also Vietnam's most populous city.

Forest lands stretch east toward the Annamese highlands. In this region, extensive areas of swamp and jungle still await clearing and development. Malaria-carrying mosquitoes and other insects have done much to make these areas unattractive except as enclaves for bandits, hermits, and toughened Vietnamese guerrillas.

Farther west are the lowland plains of Cambodia, an extension of the vast Mekong Delta. They also became a theater of operation in the Vietnam War.

Many American soldiers vividly remember border areas like the Parrot's Beak in Cambodia, where U.S. and South Vietnamese forces invaded a large stronghold of North Vietnamese guerrilla forces in 1970. In all, over two thousand Communist troops were killed at the Parrot's Beak and eight thousand bunkers destroyed.

Life in a monsoon climate

Vietnam is situated in the tropical zone. Its most northern point lies on the latitude that passes between Miami and Havana. In the far south it occupies the same latitude as Panama. No other natural condition affects the rhythm of life for the Vietnamese more than the cycle of monsoons. In many areas, these determine almost every aspect of daily life: planting and harvesting, health, housing, and dress. For six months of the year, from November to April, the winter monsoon blows from the northeast off cold and

Two Vietnamese guide their junk down the Mekong River through the early morning mist.

dry central Asia. In these months, little rain falls throughout most of Vietnam, and the country receives a welcome respite from humidity.

Between May and October, the summer monsoon blows from the southwest off the Indian Ocean. This monsoon brings tremendous heat and typhoons along with heavy rains. Vietnam's average yearly rainfall is about fifty-nine inches, slightly more than that of Miami, Florida. An average seventy-two inches of rain—fourteen in August alone—fall on Hanoi. Saigon receives about fifty inches during its rainy season.

Vietnam's diverse landscape varies the impact of the monsoons throughout the country. In Tonkin the dry and rainy seasons are not very sharply delineated, and residents of the Red River Delta enjoy a moderate winter. Averaging sixty degrees in the winter months, Tonkin's temperature sometimes tops one

Rolling clouds are about to drench the Mekong Delta during the rainy season. Huts elevated on poles are an adaptation to thwart a mighty river that regularly overflows its banks.

hundred degrees on a June day. Light rain often falls between February and April, but from June to December violent typhoons are not uncommon.

In the narrow plains of Annam, rainfall is heaviest near the highlands. The rainy season arrives later than in Cochin China and reaches its height near the

A land of extremes, Vietnam is drenched by the summer monsoon's southwest winds and scorched by dry northeast breezes during the winter monsoon. This village near Tuy Hoa is dusty after several dry months.

start of the winter monsoon. The southernmost areas are the hottest, and the extreme humidity combined with temperatures in the nineties can be oppressive.

The people of the Mekong River Delta experience the most extreme seasonal shifts although they suffer high heat most of the year. The dry months of November to April pass with barely a drop of rain while the latter months of the winter monsoon bring searing temperatures perpetually in the eighties and nineties. Clouds block the sun during the summer monsoon, but the humidity increases, and periodic storms between May and October offer little relief from the heat.

The regional weather and climate variations have, according to some people, produced differing traits among the Vietnamese. People in the North, where the winters are cool and the summers relatively moderate, tend to be particularly active and energetic. Their collective struggle for survival is intense, and peasants have a reputation as hard workers and, when necessary, valiant warriors.

In the southern delta survival is easier since land is more plentiful, and the people are freed from the mammoth dike and canal projects which dominate the lives of their northern countrymen. Furthermore, the sizzling temperatures and blazing sun make strenuous physical activity more taxing for the southern Vietnamese. For all the differences in climate and environment it is difficult to determine if these regional factors had any significant impact on the outcome of the Vietnamese conflict.

The regularity of the monsoon cycle touched every epoch of Vietnamese history and every class of its society. Before the development of engine-powered ships, Vietnamese merchant sailors adapted their schedules to the prevailing direction of the winds. But the Vietnamese peasant is most directly affected by the monsoon cycle. Although a tropical climate is normally associated with an abundance of fertile land, much of Vietnam is not easily cultivated. Only with irrigation can a Vietnamese grow enough rice for his diet. This method depends primarily upon the waters of the Red and Mekong rivers, which are yearly replenished by the monsoon rains. A late rainy season can inflict serious drought and famine upon the people.

Cristoforo Borri, a seventeenth-century Christian missionary, said that, upon the arrival of the monsoon rains, "all the people are so pleased and joyful, that they express it by visiting, feasting, and presenting one another with gifts . . . and this is done by persons

Monsoon War

When American fighting forces entered the Vietnam conflict in the mid-1960s, U.S. military commanders were keenly aware of the immense difficulties posed by Vietnam's May-to-October monsoon season.

The French, U.S. commanders knew, had been defeated as much by Vietnam's incessant rains and typhoon winds as by the fighting strength of the Vietminh. At Dien Bien Phu, the French were pounded by torrents of rain that mired their infantry soldiers in three feet of mud. The rain collapsed the French army's hastily erected bunkers, hampered their supply effort, and flooded their already miserable trenches. "The situation of the wounded is particularly tragic," General de Castries reported. "They are piled on top of each other in holes that are completely filled with mud and devoid of any hygiene. Their martyrdom increases day by day."

Ten years later Vietnam's monsoon rains became a way of life for American infantrymen. The rain and dampness seeped into their skin, rotted their clothes, and turned their boots a sickly orange color, which the "grunts," as the men called themselves, displayed with a kind of perverse pride. Some troopers shed their underwear, which fell apart from the constant dampness and caused infections.

But the monsoon season posed the greatest challenge to American airmen who, according to the hardened ground soldiers, often flew in conditions so bad that they "had no business being there." At the battle of Khe Sanh in April 1968, where U.S. Marines turned back a furious enemy attack, American fliers defined "good weather" as any condition where the cloud cover was above 500 feet and slant visibility was more than a mile and a half.

One week after Khe Sanh, in a campaign against the Communist-held A Shau Valley, American fliers underwent an even greater trial. The U.S. attack had scarcely begun when the weather became "almost unbelievably bad." Gray storm clouds, fog, and pounding rain made the operation a nightmare. Helicopter pilots were forced to climb through the low cloud cover using their navigational instruments, then regroup above the clouds to search for openings through which they could make their descents. "What should have been a simple twenty-five minute flight was usually an hour and twenty minutes of stark terror," recounted Lieutenant General John T. Tolson.

Conditions were even worse for the pilots of C-130 transport planes, who could not peer through the cloud cover for possible openings but had to rely entirely on radio-controlled instruments to make their descents. "No matter how reliable your gauges," one officer remembered, "it took a lot of guts to poke your airplane nose into clouds that are full of solid rock!"

The U.S. military command had acted on the basis of detailed weather reports, dating back to the years of French involvement, which indicated that the annual monsoon rains would not arrive until later in the spring. But in A Shau, as in many other American offensives, unpredictable weather bedeviled the most carefully laid plans. "As it turned out," one officer later reported with a hint of resignation, "May would have been a far better month—but you don't win them all."

of all degrees, even to the king himself." The king's participation in the monsoon festivities was no accident. For a Vietnamese king, as for rulers everywhere in Southeast Asia, the level of rainfall often served as a key indicator of the success and divine sanction of his reign. Too little or too much rain was an evil omen for him. It signified his loss of heaven's favor, an essential royal attribute, and cast doubt on his right to continue on the throne.

In the war against Communist insurgency, the military hardware of the U.S. and Vietnamese forces fared poorly during the summer monsoon. The rains mired artillery in a sea of mud, rendering sophisticated equipment inoperable. Clouds often grounded

aircraft. Highly mobile guerrilla forces roamed freely in the countryside and exploited the immobility of government troops.

The people: from legend to history

Vietnam's early history is shrouded in legends that Vietnamese historians have interpreted as preserving a kernel of genuine information about the origins of their people and nation. Mythical tales, passed from generation to generation before the Vietnamese could write, tell of the kingdoms of Van Lang and Au Lac. Van Lang, the first, supposedly existed as far back as 3000 B.C., but it is difficult to separate fact from fiction in accounts of kingdoms and eras so remote in time.

According to legend, the history of the Vietnamese people begins with King De Minh who descended from Chen Nong, a divine Chinese ruler revered as the father of Chinese agriculture. One day, De Minh embarked on an inspection tour of the southern part of his kingdom. On his way, he met an immortal woman from the mountains. Enticed by her charms,

One of the most ancient Vietnamese holidays, the Tet festival marking the lunar New Year—usually falling in February—is the time for every Vietnamese to return to the village of his birth. There he visits the tombs of his family, participates in celebrations and feasts, and reestablishes the bonds of kinship. This old man has purchased the traditional peach blossom branch which he will place before the door of his home to celebrate the rebirth of nature and the promise of a new beginning.

De Minh married her, and she bore him a son named Loc Duc who grew up to be king of Xich-Quy, land of the Red Devils.

Loc Duc also married an immortal from the kingdom of the sea. They had a son who eventually succeeded his father under the name Lac Long Quan, or Dragon Lord. His reign initiated a golden age for the people, and even today Vietnamese still refer to themselves in poetry as the "grandchildren of Lac."

To forge an alliance with the Chinese, Lac Long Quan married Au Co, the Chinese emperor's immortal daughter. Miraculously, she laid 100 eggs, which hatched 100 sons. One day the king, deciding they were incompatible, said to his wife: "I am a dragon, you are a fairy. We cannot remain together." So king and queen divided their sons. Fifty went with their father to rule the lowlands, fifty followed their mother into the mountains. Lac Long Quan's eldest son inherited his throne and was the founder of the first Vietnamese dynasty—the Hong Bang. His kingdom was called Van Lang, "land of the tattooed men," and legend puts its beginning as far back as 2879 B.C.

Why has such a strange legend worked its way into Vietnamese history? Vietnam has always had close political and cultural ties with China. Vietnam's long-time admiration for China's culture may explain the tradition linking De Minh, the father of the Vietnamese, with Chen Nong, one of China's legendary founders. Vietnamese patriotism may also have contributed to the myth. Despite Vietnam's esteem for things Chinese, its people have always considered themselves as a separate nation and are fiercely competitive with their northern neighbor. Van Lang's status as an autonomous kingdom justified Vietnam's proud belief in its independent heritage and its resistance to foreign aggression. The Vietnamese also probably cherish the idea of their history being as ancient as that of China.

The neighboring kingdom of Thuc overthrew the Hong Bang dynasty in 258 B.C. The Thuc leader

Tet is a time for visiting temples with a contrite heart. It is an opportunity for debts to be paid, errors to be acknowledged, and prayers offered up for good health and fortune in the coming year.

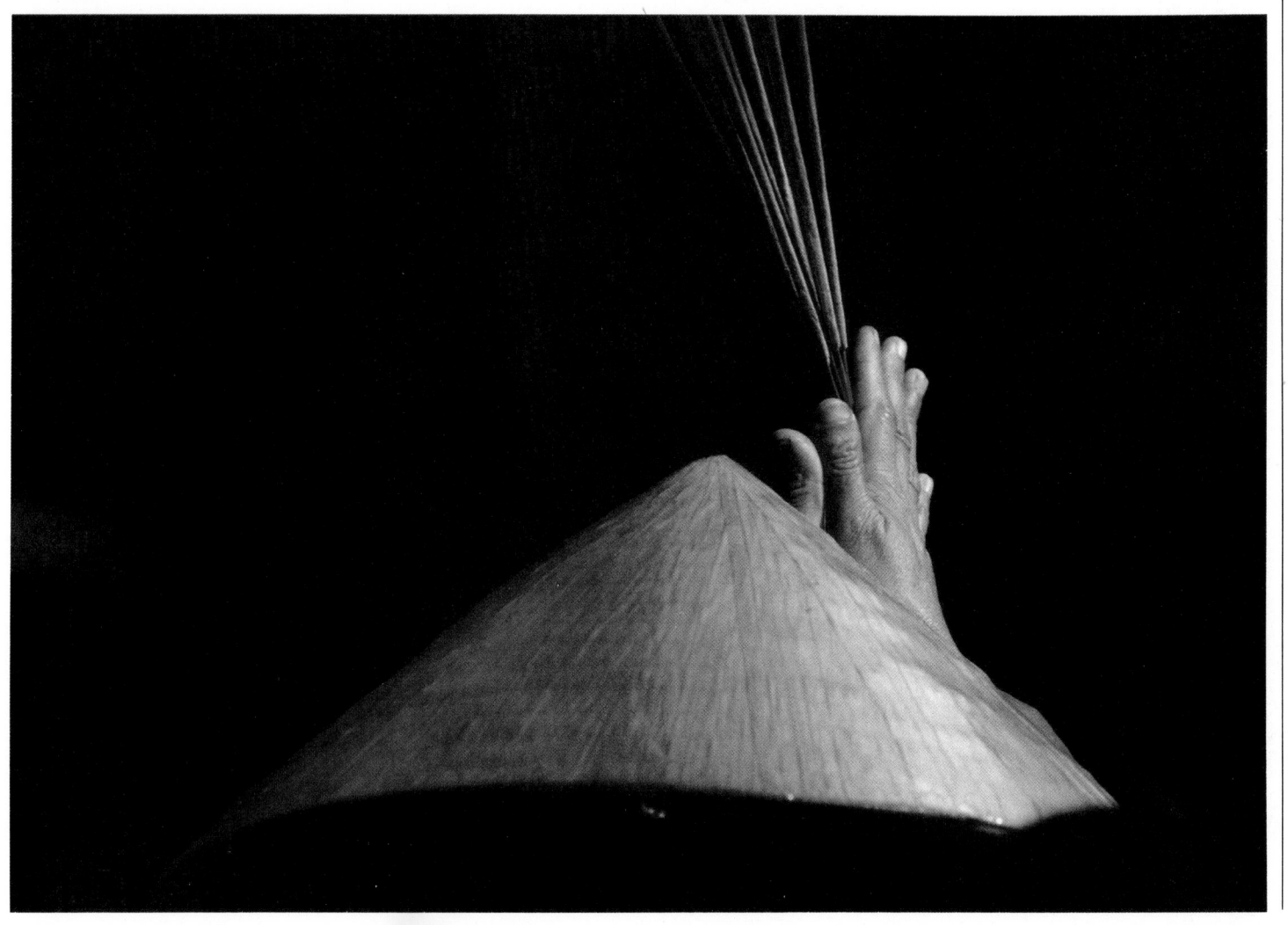

Kernels of Life: The Rice Farming Cycle

Rice farming, for centuries a central part of life in Vietnam and all of southeastern Asia, was first mentioned in historical annals in 2800 B.C., when a Chinese emperor proclaimed a ceremony honoring the planting of rice. Here, modern Vietnamese peasants plant seedlings in soil submerged by about three inches of water, which discourages weeds and nourishes the plants.

The twelfth moon for potato growing,
the first for beans, the second for egg-
   plant.
In the third, we break the land
to plant rice in the fourth while the rains
   are strong.
The man plows, the woman plants,
and in the fifth: the harvest, and the gods
   are good—
an acre yields five full baskets this year.
I grind and pound the paddy, strew husks
   to cover the manure,
and feed the hogs with bran.
Next year, if the land is extravagant,
I shall pay the taxes for you.
In plenty or in want, there will still be you
   and me,
always the two of us.
Isn't that better than always prospering,
   alone?

     —*A Farmer's Calendar*
     Traditional Vietnamese Poem

Already thirty to fifty days old when planted, the seedlings soon take hold and become bushier (right). Flowers containing the rice kernels grow from between the leaves as the plants mature.

Rice fields cover more than 12 million acres of Vietnam's land during an average year, making the country one of the world's largest rice producers. Even as war raged in 1972, North Vietnam and South Vietnam were, respectively, the ninth and eleventh largest rice-producing nations and would have been fifth largest had they been united.

Peasants pull weeds from a paddy near Hanoi. When the rice flowers bend under the mature kernels' weight, the paddy is allowed to dry, making the harvest an easier task. The kernels provide food, while the rest of the plant is used in a variety of ways, from making beer, wine, and flour to providing fuel, straw mats, garments, and fertilizer.

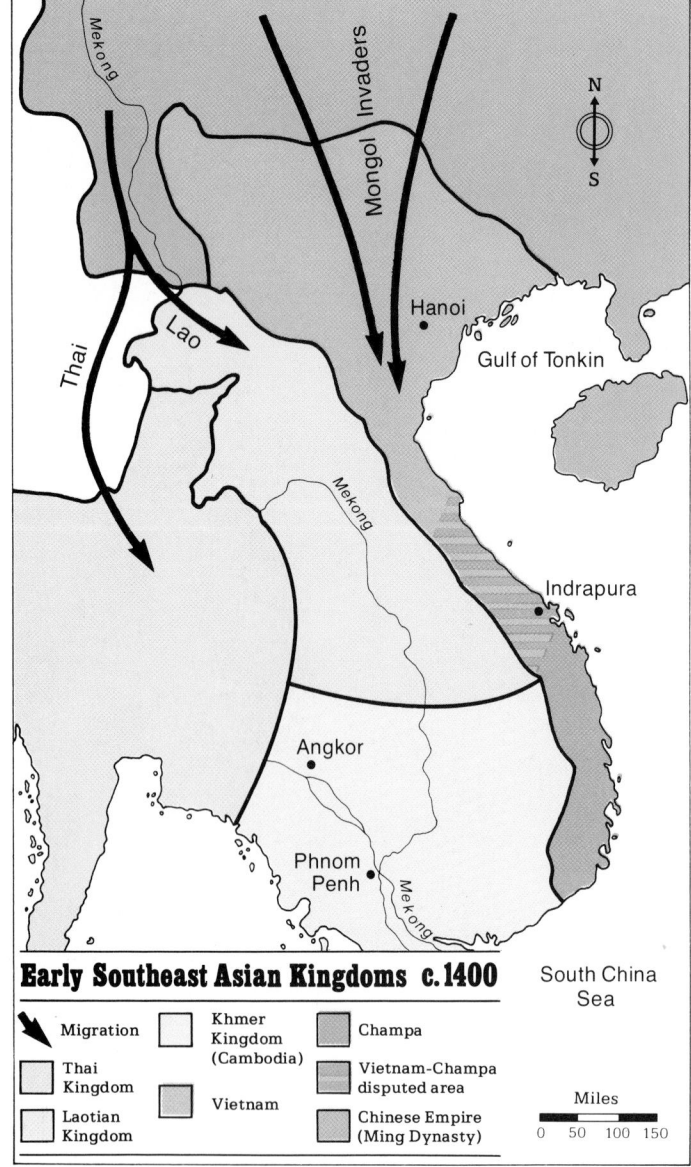

Early Southeast Asian Kingdoms c.1400

Migration

Thai Kingdom

Laotian Kingdom

Khmer Kingdom (Cambodia)

Vietnam

Champa

Vietnam-Champa disputed area

Chinese Empire (Ming Dynasty)

Miles
0 50 100 150

a Chinese province, but he had killed all the Chinese emperor's local representatives and proclaimed himself ruler of an independent kingdom. After incorporating Au Lac, Nam Viet included the Red River Delta as well as the country as far south as Da Nang.

The principal inhabitants of Nam Viet were the Viets, a non-Chinese people of Mongolian descent. These people had begun migrating toward Indochina between 500 and 300 B.C. They penetrated large areas south of the Yangtze River and were described by the Chinese as "the Hundred Viets."

Despite their name, however, the Viets do not qualify as the only racial ancestors of the Vietnamese. As they filtered south, they mingled with primitive peoples racially akin to Indonesians and Filipinos. The marriage between the Viets and these local people created the racial type that now dominates Vietnam.

Vietnam's language, which fuses Cambodian, Thai, and Chinese elements, reflects the mixed background of its people. Speaking Vietnamese has always been an exasperating exercise for foreigners, including American GIs, largely because it is a tonal language. A given syllable can be pronounced with any of six vocal inflections, each of which results in a different meaning. A classic example is the word "ma." These are the six forms of "ma" with their corresponding tones and meanings:

$$\longrightarrow \quad \nearrow \quad \searrow \quad \smile \quad \sim\!\!\nearrow$$
$$\text{ma} \quad \text{ma} \quad \text{ma} \quad \text{ma} \quad \text{ma}$$
"ghost" "cheek" "but" "grave" "horse"
$$\sim\!\!\longrightarrow$$
$$\text{ma}$$
"rice seedling."

The difficulty of learning Vietnamese not only hampered communications between U.S. and South Vietnamese forces but also posed serious problems for American soldiers in the field. To identify friend from foe in the rice fields or villages was often impossible for Americans unable to speak Vietnamese. As a result, the language barrier heightened tensions during U.S. combat operations in populated areas.

united Van Lang with his own country and called the new kingdom Au Lac. Au Lac has much of the mythical character of Van Lang, but its existence is believed to have had some basis in fact. Some think it was a small state located in the area north and east of North Vietnam's mountains. Au Lac's capital, Co Loa, has recently been excavated and is considered the most important historical vestige of ancient Vietnam.

The kingdom of the Viets

In 208 B.C. Trieu Da, a former Chinese general, attacked Au Lac and incorporated it into his kingdom of Nam Viet. Nam Viet at the time covered much of southern China. According to Chinese historical annals, Trieu Da ruled it from his capital near the present site of Canton. Trieu Da's domain had once been

Life in the Red River Delta

What was life like for the first Vietnamese in the Red River Delta? Solid historical evidence is lacking, but life in Nam Viet was undoubtedly centered around agriculture. The Vietnamese family has always organized itself around the rice-growing cycle, relying primarily on its own manual labor to farm the land.

Except when the field lay fallow, each family member performed a specific round of daily chores. Families traditionally measured their wealth according to the size and productivity of their rice fields and often paid their taxes in rice. This is still the nature of Vietnamese agriculture, despite the recent attempts of Vietnamese governments to modernize rice production and diversify the economy.

It can be said of Trieu Da's long reign (207–137 B.C.) that "the conqueror became conquered": Nam Viet's Chinese king adopted Vietnamese traditions. Independence from China, however, survived him by only twenty-five years. After a century of military friction between the Chinese Empire and Trieu Da and his heirs, China's armies finally vanquished Nam Viet in 111 B.C. China's rule over Vietnam would last a thousand years. During that time the people of Nam Viet would undergo profound changes. But they would never forget their independent heritage.

Vietnam and China

China's conquest of Vietnam proved to be one of the most momentous events in Vietnamese history. During their long occupation the Chinese imposed their language, religions, institutions, and technology on the Vietnamese. Vietnam's recorded history begins with the coming of the Chinese, who introduced writing.

The effects of such prolonged exposure to China's advanced civilization were lasting and generally beneficial to the Vietnamese. They assimilated many Chinese ways and gradually mastered the social, political, and technical skills of their colonial rulers. Ironically, China's influence set in motion a cultural process that would one day produce not a Chinese but a distinctly Vietnamese people capable of winning and maintaining their independence from China. For while the Vietnamese learned much from their Chinese masters, they also developed an unyielding determination to free themselves and resist future foreign aggression at all costs.

As a result of the long period of Chinese domination of Vietnam, Vietnamese history has since been closely affected by political and cultural events in China. Vietnam's contact with China could not have come at a more propitious time. At the time of Nam Viet's subjugation, China was at its height, both culturally and politically. From 206 B.C. to A.D. 221, China was ruled by the Han dynasty. So glorious was the Han era that the Chinese still call themselves Han

A young woman of the Rhade tribe, which inhabits areas around Da Nang, Quang Nghai, and Pleiku, enjoys a pipeful of tobacco. Bronze bracelets adorn her arms and ankles. Her earrings stretch the ear lobes and are replaced by increasingly larger pieces of ivory. Her smile would reveal upper teeth filed to the gum, another tribal cosmetic practice.

people. Arts and sciences reached unprecedented heights, and the Chinese Empire also attained its greatest size.

The Han emperors organized their strong central government around the principles of Confucius, a philosopher who lived in the sixth century B.C. No single individual has influenced Chinese and, in turn, Vietnamese thought and institutions more than Confucius. After his death, generations of disciples refined his teachings into a moral and political philosophy. Until the nineteenth century, Confucianism permeated the ideology of China and Vietnam. When the French invaded Vietnam in the 1880s, they encountered a society whose major social, political, and religious institutions were deeply rooted in Chinese Confucian thought.

Confucius taught that the state is an extension of the family and should be governed accordingly. A father, the head of the family, must provide his children

a good example to follow, as well as love and protection. He must adhere to morality and instill in his children the behavior appropriate to their social status. His children, in return, are obligated to love and obey him.

Applying these same values to the governing of the state, Confucius said that the emperor must act as a father. By dutifully protecting and caring for the people and upholding moral values in all his actions, the emperor is entitled to the complete obedience and reverence of his subjects. The example of the ruler becomes a positive force capable of making his people better. Confucius expressed the response of the people toward their king's example in a short sentence: "As the wind blows, so bows the grass."

Despite the emperor's authoritarian role, he could be removed from power. According to Confucianism, the emperor, through moral perfection, must maintain a proper relationship between himself and heaven.

Confucians regard heaven as the divine force governing the universe and the final judge of right and wrong. When the emperor violated morality, heaven revealed its judgment through natural calamities, such as flood, drought, and famine. Signs of heaven's displeasure were evil omens for an emperor. They could justify violent action by the people to replace him with another able to regain heaven's favor and restore harmony.

In Han China, the need for public virtue was not confined to the emperor. His officials were also called "the parents of the people." Imperial officials, known in the West as mandarins, won entrance to the bureaucracy through examinations that tested knowledge of Confucius' moral teachings, as well as poetry, philosophy, and history. By their culture, breeding, and education, mandarins had to prove themselves worthy of guiding the moral welfare of the people.

Chinese colonial rule

After securing its hold on the countryside, China began to exploit the economic resources of Nam Viet. Much as western merchants seventeen-hundred years later saw Vietnam as a convenient way station in trade with China and Europe, the Han hoped to use its new territory as a stopover for ships sailing the lucrative East-West trade with the Spice Islands, India, and the Near East. So they set up ports in several of Vietnam's natural harbors where vessels from other lands could deposit their goods.

When the Chinese first occupied Vietnam, they made few sweeping changes. Vietnam was administered as several territorial districts under the juris-

This detail from a Han dynasty tomb rubbing shows a chariot and cavalry procession. The Han dynasty, glorious in culture as well as warfare, conquered Vietnam in 111 B.C.

diction of military governors. No attempt was made to absorb Vietnam as simply a part of China or to place it under imperial administration. Instead, the Chinese left it as a leniently governed protectorate and did not interfere with the Vietnamese feudal aristocracy.

Many of Nam Viet's nobles collaborated with the Chinese. To retain their hereditary positions, these nobles helped collect taxes saving China the trouble of installing a colonial administration. This also helped the Chinese govern Vietnam, since the Viet lords continued to keep order among the people. China's early colonial practices made no change in the peasants' lives. They merely continued to pay the taxes they had always paid to their traditional Vietnamese masters.

At first, only a few Chinese moved to Vietnam. For military security, China sent small colonies of peasant-soldiers to establish settlements around the countryside. These colonists first built forts. Under the protection of the walls, they cultivated nearby fields. When violence threatened, soldiers would exchange their plows for swords and restore order. These colonies performed a dual function: They served as permanent outposts as well as self-sufficient agricultural communities. As a result, Chinese occupation forces were not faced with a continual supply problem.

The Vietnamese, no doubt, resented the Chinese colonists. China's peasant-soldiers were a disturbing sign that the Chinese intended to stay for good. In the long run, however, these settlements turned out to be of immense value to Vietnamese peasants. The Chinese introduced their elaborate system of dike building, which harnessed the power of the unpredictable Red River. They also taught the Vietnamese techniques to reclaim new land from the sea.

The Chinese also introduced draft animals, such as the water buffalo. Metal plows replaced the Vietnamese stone hoe. The water buffalo came to serve the Vietnamese much as horses helped American settlers. They used it as an all-purpose vehicle for plowing, hauling, and transport. In war the water buffalo carried weapons and supplies. Even during the Vietnam War, the Vietcong used buffaloes to transport rockets and artillery. The mud created by monsoon rains never hindered the water buffalo as it did trucks and jeeps.

The Vietnamese absorb Chinese ways

It was not unusual for an imperial power like the Chinese to feel a responsibility to impart their "superior" ways to "inferior"—or even "barbarian"—colonial subjects. Despite China's initial policy of leaving the Vietnamese to themselves, some military governors tried on their own to bring Chinese culture to the people. The Chinese governor of the Vietnamese provinces between A.D. 1 and 25, for example, opened schools to teach Chinese language, history, and literature to the Viets.

The Vietnamese as a whole were receptive to Chinese teachings, the consequences of which were enormous. Until the arrival of the French in the nineteenth century, written Chinese was the language for administration, education, and literary creation. Although many other Chinese innovations were integrated easily enough into the local culture, the Chinese were never able to reconcile the Vietnamese to China's political control. All Vietnamese still clung to their native tongue.

One of the first undertakings of the Chinese in Vietnam was the construction of roads, canals, and harbor facilities. Their purpose was to establish reliable communications with China and to assist the movements of soldiers and goods throughout the province. Until the coming of the Chinese, Vietnam had lacked the technical and organizational skills required for such improvements. The benefits derived from these advances, however, carried a heavy price tag for the local nobles and their peasants. The Chinese demanded labor from the peasants and compelled them to serve in the provincial militia. As could be expected, the tax burden on peasant villages increased with each new Chinese civil or military expenditure. Although the Chinese methods resulted in overall economic prosperity, the peasants saw little improvement in their lives. The agricultural wealth produced by the peasants' sweat was siphoned off by the Chinese.

First introduced by the Chinese, the water buffalo, along with the peasant, has borne the labor of rice agriculture for centuries. Water buffaloes can reach a height of six feet at the shoulder and often weigh two thousand pounds or more. The animal's strength and mobility often made it more valuable than an army jeep in moving war supplies through muddy terrain.

Vietnamese resistance

The Vietnamese aristocracy, meanwhile, witnessed a steady erosion of its power by an expanding Chinese administrative and military bureaucracy. Vietnamese nobles saw Chinese administrators gaining power over their peasants and taking over wide expanses of land. They also chafed as taxes that had once lined their pockets were funneled to the Chinese as tribute. The feudal regime resented its growing isolation from power. Resentment led to opposition and opposition to repression by Chinese authorities. Faced with eventual extinction, Vietnam's feudal chiefs chose to stand and fight.

The first Vietnamese rebellion occurred in A.D. 39. A new Chinese governor who shared none of his predecessors' benevolent attitudes provided the occasion that sparked the revolt. In order to frighten restless Vietnamese aristocrats into submission, the governor brutally executed one of their leaders. The murdered man's wife, Trung Trac, was outraged. With her sister, Trung Nhi, she mustered an army of

sympathetic vassals and their armies to avenge her husband's death.

The heroic Trung sisters fought at the head of Vietnam's warriors, but they were not the only women in the forefront of combat. One of their comrades was a woman named Phung Thi Chinh. A fanatical supporter of the Trungs, she led Vietnamese troops against the Chinese in one battle even though she was pregnant. Surrounded by Chinese attackers, she delivered her baby. She then strapped the newborn to her back, grabbed a sword in each hand, and opened a bloody escape route through the ranks of the enemy.

The Trungs founded a kingdom reaching south to Hue and north into southern China. Their kingdom, however, was destined to last but three years. Chinese armies sent to reconquer the province were more than a match for the Trungs' spirited but small band of aristocratic rebels. One of China's best generals, Ma Yuan, defeated Trung forces several times. After these setbacks, rather than accept the shame of surrender, the Trungs threw themselves into a river and drowned.

Popular tradition has venerated the Trung uprising

This covered stone bridge, built in the ninth or tenth century during the Chinese occupation, spans a riverbed in Sontay Province in the North. Few such relics have survived the many centuries of rebellions and wars.

The Trung sisters were not the only women to take up arms against the Chinese. In A.D. 248, a young woman named Trieu Au started a small but powerful revolt. Trieu Au, an orphan, lived with her brother and sister-in-law until she was twenty. But finding her sister-in-law cruel and cantankerous, Trieu Au killed her and sought refuge in the mountains.

A high-spirited and passionate young woman, Trieu Au could not bear the rule of the "cruel and cantankerous" Chinese either. In her mountain retreat she raised one thousand troops in the hope of liberating the country. Trieu Au's brother tried to discourage her, but she defiantly replied: "I want to rail against wind and tide, kill the whales in the ocean, sweep the whole country to save people from slavery, and I have no desire to take abuse."

After a short but furious struggle against the Chinese, during which she rode in golden armor on her elephant, this Vietnamese Joan of Arc was defeated. Resisting to the end, she committed suicide rather than submit to the shame of surrender. Later, Vietnamese patriots built a pagoda in her honor.

The Woman in Golden Armor

Acclaimed for her "extraordinary strength" and a mind "fertile with stratagems," Trieu Au led her army against the Chinese. The "young virgin warrior," as Trieu Au was called by her followers, is depicted in a Vietnamese print.

as striking the first blow for national independence. Some historians have even described it as a mass movement against oppression. Patriotic fervor aside, there is little evidence that the insurrection attracted the support of the peasant majority. The Trungs commanded an army consisting mostly of aristocrats and their vassals. These feudal lords struggled not for all Vietnamese—aristocrats and peasants alike—but rather to retain their hereditary powers. The real issue of the war was which ruling class, Chinese or Vietnamese, would govern Vietnam.

Sculpture, like this tenth century sandstone Buddha, keeps alive centuries-old Buddhist traditions. From the ruin of a ninth century pagoda near Hanoi, only a stone Buddha survived. In 1075 a new pagoda was built in honor of the surviving stone Buddha. Today what remains of the second pagoda is, again, its outstanding Buddhist sculpture.

The Trung episode highlights the importance of women in Vietnamese folklore and society. The Vietnamese family was strongly patriarchal, but Vietnam's women generally enjoyed a greater range of rights than did their counterparts in most Asian and European countries. Traditional Vietnamese law, for example, provided that daughters as well as sons could inherit the land of deceased parents. If there were no sons to serve as trustees of ancestral cults, daughters could take their place. The legal code also stressed the communal property rights of a wife. Children could not lawfully claim inheritance of family property until both parents died. Husbands who deserted their wives for a certain period were denied all conjugal rights.

Chinese reprisals

China responded harshly to Vietnam's bid for freedom under the Trungs. Chinese authorities abandoned their arm's-length policy, choosing instead to eradicate the Vietnamese aristocracy. Those feudal chiefs not killed or exiled were stripped of their hereditary titles. Colonial officials confiscated their property, which insured the swift demise of the remaining feudal class.

The Chinese also reversed their policy of noninterference in local affairs. China grew increasingly apprehensive about future Vietnamese resistance. To bridge the gulf between Chinese settlers and the Vietnamese, authorities launched a comprehensive program to integrate the Vietnamese people thoroughly into Chinese society. Suppressing local customs, the Chinese made a special effort to disseminate their own ideas. Vietnamese families were pressured to conform to Chinese marriage customs, to follow the cult of Confucius, and to practice other Chinese ways.

All this altered traditional Vietnamese village life. Chinese officials divided the village into several large family groupings. The head of each of these became the principal intermediary between villagers and central authorities. These family groups also received a section of land which they privately farmed. The state, however, reserved for itself a portion of village land, which villagers were required to cultivate.

While the Chinese were busy spreading their culture throughout Vietnam, something unexpected happened: Over the centuries China's colonial officials in Vietnam eventually evolved into a new provincial aristocracy. What's more, members of this elite soon took on some of the old Vietnamese aristocratic characteristics that Chinese authorities had so deliberately suppressed. The new Chinese landed gentry settled amid the Vietnamese villagers and came into closer contact with the natives. They married local women and learned the Vietnamese language. As their interaction with the Vietnamese increased, Chinese officials grew accustomed to native habits of dress and began to participate in local religious traditions and cults. As had happened to Trieu Da centuries earlier, the conquerors became conquered.

Like the leaders of the American Revolution, these Sino-Vietnamese nobles believed themselves quite capable of governing their country without outside interference. In A.D. 543 they began to flex their muscles. A Chinese aristocrat and scholar named Ly Bon launched a formidable campaign for independence. Raising an army, he led a revolt against Chinese rule. A master strategist, Ly Bon led several battles against the Chinese and for a brief time drove them out of Vietnam. He proclaimed himself emperor in 544. His kingdom covered the whole of what is now northern and central Vietnam.

The Chinese returned in 545 to reclaim the province, their military strength far outnumbering the troops and supplies available to Ly Bon. But they met Vietnam's two perennial defenses: guerrilla warfare and the tropical climate. Ly Bon, shrewd strategist that he was, recognized his inferior position and slowly withdrew southward after several inconclusive engagements with the Chinese. Stationing his men in strategically located grottoes, he sent them out at night against the Chinese, whose numbers were thinned by the heat and jungle diseases.

In 546, Ly Bon marched out with twenty thousand men and met the Chinese in battle. His troops suffered a resounding defeat, however, and Ly Bon fled to Laos. There, a Laotian tribe in league with China captured him, cut off his head, and sent it back to the victorious Chinese general. After Ly Bon's death, the Vietnamese provinces once again fell under China's yoke. But his guerrilla strategy showed the Vietnamese that it could be possible to defeat a superior force by using tactics designed to wear down an enemy through attrition and hit-and-run attacks. That the North Vietnamese never forgot Ly Bon's example is well shown by the eventual success of the Communist guerrilla tactics in the Vietnam War.

A supplicant worships "the Buddha of a Thousand Arms and a Thousand Eyes" in the Ninh Phuc temple near Hanoi. Between 1200 and 1600, Chinese and Vietnamese cooperated to build this temple, which reflects the synthesis of Sino-Viet religion and architecture.

Part of the reason Ly Bon's revolt ended in failure was that it did not involve the mass participation of peasants. Ly Bon's army, like that of the Trungs, drew its main support from an aristocratic faction. It has become an important theme in Vietnamese history that no liberation movement can succeed without widespread peasant support. Early Vietnamese nationalist leaders against the French, many of whom were from the upper classes, eventually recognized this political reality and strove to enlist peasants to their cause. The man who most successfully attracted peasants to the Vietnamese nationalist struggle came on the scene centuries later. His name was Ho Chi Minh.

Buddhism and Vietnamese unity

Buddhism was China's second major religion. It had a much more pervasive impact upon peasant life than did its counterpart, Confucianism. Buddhism was founded by Gautama Buddha, an Indian prince, in the sixth century B.C. Indian missionaries and traders carried his spiritual teachings over the Silk Road to China. The Indian faith reached Vietnam as early as A.D. 189, when Chinese Buddhist monks, called bonzes, sought refuge there from political dissension at home. Vietnam also became the way station for thousands of Buddhist pilgrims and missionaries traveling by sea between India and China.

Like many other religions, Buddhism generated a number of different schools of thought. The dominant Buddhist sect that took root in Vietnam was called Mahayana, or the "Greater Vehicle," a progressive school adaptable to any conditions of land and time. Mahayana Buddhists considered Gautama Buddha to be God's earthly incarnation. They believed that anyone, through a life of spiritual and moral perfection, could become a Buddha. The morally perfect person saved others before himself through acts of love and charity. By eliminating selfish desires, one could avoid continuous rebirth or reincarnation and attain Nirvana, a state of perpetual blessedness and peace.

Buddhist missionaries achieved tremendous success among the peasants. Confucianism, with its more intellectual philosophy, had limited relevance to them. Buddhism on the other hand stressed the more universal facets of religion: the existence of heaven and hell, the promise of relief from suffering in an afterlife, and belief in the universal presence of spirits. In time, the Vietnamese assimilated Buddhism into their local religious practices. Buddhist monks began to take a prominent place in village religious affairs. The image of Buddha stood beside other idols.

"We Have Always Had Heroes"

A Chinese historian once wrote, "The people of Vietnam do not like the past." Certainly Vietnam's history, filled with the ravages of war and the affliction of colonial occupations, holds few pleasant memories for the Vietnamese. But that country's history also presents numerous examples of Vietnam's fierce resistance to foreign aggression and successful efforts by the people to fight for their independence no matter what the sacrifice in lives and hardship. The lessons of Vietnam's "revolutionary" tradition, even going as far back as the Trung sisters, have not been forgotten.

During the Vietnam War, the Communists in the North used the popularity of the Trung sisters as propaganda to support their military actions against the South and U.S. "imperialism." The North Vietnamese government sponsored annual ceremonies to honor the Trungs at the numerous temples dedicated to them throughout the country. These events had a twofold purpose: to identify the struggle against the South with the nationalist rebellion of the Trungs and to enlist the active participation of women.

The leaders of the South also attempted to use the popular memory of the Trung sisters' rebellion to their advantage. In the early 1960s, President Ngo Dinh Diem and his sister-in-law, Madame Ngo Dinh Nhu, tried to transform the anniversary of the Trungs' death into a national holiday celebrating South Vietnamese patriotism and the virtues of feminism. Madame Nhu singled out the Trungs as models for the role of women in national defense. She even organized a paramilitary women's group around that theme. But the cult of the Trungs did not catch on in South Vietnam either as a national holiday or as a propaganda tool. After the assassination of Diem in 1963, a statue of the Trung sisters erected in Saigon was demolished. The extent to which the North and South drew upon ancient legends like the Trungs for patriotic propaganda testifies to the enduring memory of Vietnam's past.

Bonzes moved around the countryside and helped establish closer ties among once isolated villages.

Buddhism became a potent religious and political force as the centuries wore on. It functioned independently of the official Confucian bureaucracy. Monks lived among the peasants, sharing their poverty and sympathizing with their hatred of Chinese rule. Buddhist influence also penetrated the circles of the Sino-Vietnamese aristocracy because monks, like the Chinese mandarin elite, were men of letters. Knowledgeable in medicine, astrology, scriptures, and philosophy, they were highly regarded by the people. As monks attracted aristocrats to the Buddhist faith, they became political and cultural advisers to Sino-Vietnamese nobles, as well as spiritual guides.

Vietnam casts off China

Many factors finally united the peasants and aristocrats against the Chinese. The upper-class leaders had long recognized that they could not realize their aspirations under the Chinese. They mobilized the peasants by appealing to that which by the eighth, ninth, and tenth centuries, separated rich and poor alike from China: the Vietnamese language, local customs, and the unique mixture of native religious beliefs. The peasants had immortalized the "golden age" of freedom in the kingdoms of Van Lang and Au Lac through legends that were constantly retold. As a result the peasants resisted strict conformity to Chinese culture and kept alive their own way of life. As their political influence increased the bonzes also promoted national independence and helped forge the crucial alliance between nobles and peasants. The monks' world straddled feudal court and village, so Buddhist religious beliefs established a common ideological bond between aristocrats and peasants.

Chinese rule, although challenged several more times after Ly Bon, remained secure as long as the T'ang dynasty ruled China (618–907). However, the fall of the T'ang provided an opening for Vietnamese rebels, and the struggle for independence was renewed.

In 931, a Vietnamese leader had expelled the Chinese. After a few years in power he was assassinated by one of his officers, Kieu. The leader's son-in-law, Ngo Quyen, was enraged by Kieu's treachery. He gathered support from both nobles and peasants for a full-scale assault against the traitorous assassin, Kieu. As had happened before and would happen again in Vietnamese history, Kieu appealed to China for military help. It was not long before advance columns of Chinese troops reached Vietnam, led by the heir apparent to the imperial throne of China. By then, however, Ngo had already killed Kieu and was preparing for the Chinese onslaught.

The crucial battle took place on the Bach Dang River, a tidal waterway. Like his forerunner, Ly Bon, Ngo had a keen sense of strategy. Aware of his army's shortcomings in arms and men, he resorted to strategem. His troops drove iron tipped pilings into the river bed so that at high tide they would be hidden just below the water's surface. At high tide, Ngo engaged the Chinese in battle on the river and ordered his troops to feign retreat. The Chinese, lured on by the trick, pressed after Ngo's retreating boats. Then the tide began to ebb. At that moment, Ngo's men turned their boats around and drove the Chinese boats against the spikes. Their vessels impaled, the Chinese suffered heavy losses. The imperial heir apparent was taken prisoner and later beheaded.

The battle of Bach Dang in 938 has become as famous in Vietnamese history as the battle of Lexington and Concord in America's struggle for independence. It dealt a fatal blow to Chinese colonial power and prevented Vietnam from falling back into Chinese hands. The fame of the battle belongs to Ngo. He used the classic tactic of feint and strike, for which Vietnamese guerrilla fighters have become renowned. Ngo put an end to Chinese domination, liberated Vietnam, and set the stage for the rise of a new and independent Vietnamese state.

General Ngo Quyen leads the legendary battle at Bach Dang, near present-day Haiphong, where Vietnam won its independence from China in 938. Spikes hidden by high tide pierced and sunk Chinese ships when the tide ebbed.

The Building of a Nation

Vietnam's victory over the Chinese at Bach Dang in 938 ushered in a new era of independence. Over the next five hundred years, six different dynasties would struggle with the major problems of governing a country devoted almost entirely to agriculture. The fortunes of those families rose and fell on their abilities to provide adequate land for peasants and to build the dike and irrigation systems sufficient for the growing of rice, the country's principal source of food and wealth. The pattern that emerged reflects two important aspects of Vietnamese history. First, the governments that lost peasant support were inevitably overturned by insurrection and widespread social unrest; and second, rebellion and revolution became a common and even accepted instrument of political and social change for the Vietnamese. In the nineteenth and twentieth centuries, a number of Vietnamese political groups—Nationalists, anti-French Colonialists, and Com-

munists—have emphasized Vietnam's revolutionary tradition to justify their political movements and attract support for them.

As successive dynasties grappled with domestic affairs, Vietnam also had to deal with serious foreign threats. From the north, China made repeated attempts to reconquer Vietnam. Except for another brief Chinese occupation in the fifteenth century, the Vietnamese were always able to muster the men and resources to defeat their powerful northern neighbor. Since resisting Chinese aggression required the strength of collective action, the Vietnamese began to stress national unity as the key to preserving their nationhood and independence. Under the banner of a unified Vietnam, the North Vietnamese justified this century's war against South Vietnam.

A conflict of a different kind, a war of ideas, also took place after Vietnam drove out the Chinese. Two major ideologies, Confucianism and Buddhism, vied for supremacy in Vietnam. Their dispute raged over the very practical question of which ideological group could best govern the state and provide for the needs of a population consisting mostly of peasants. Vietnamese peasants were not concerned with abstract social or political issues but with the basic

problems of irrigation, land distribution, and security for their villages. Things have not changed much for the Vietnamese and their governments. When Vietnam, still a land of peasants, was divided in 1954, the ideological battle between North and South focused chiefly on the best ways to deal with these same problems.

The "Kingdom of the Watchful Hawk"

Having fought for the ideals of independence, the tenth-century Vietnamese faced the challenge of translating them into effective government. However, the times were treacherous as a number of warring feudal lords tried to divide Vietnam among themselves. Meanwhile, Vietnam's peasant farmers, who had battled the Chinese for peace to till their rice fields and feed their families, were subjected to several decades of anarchy.

Vietnam's historical annals record that it was a peasant, Dinh Bo Linh, who saved his country from chaos. As a youth, he led his own gang of warriors, who looked upon him as their protector. Later he joined the service of one of the powerful lords. After

Preceding page. The powerful Ly emperors, one of whom is depicted here, brought stability to Vietnam during its early years of independence in the eleventh and twelfth centuries. This statue sits in a Buddhist pagoda, commemorating the revival of Buddhism under the patronage of the Ly.

Dinh Bo Linh, astride a buffalo on the right, organized peasants against twelve warring feudal lords who divided Vietnam in the tenth century. Dinh Bo Linh united the country in 968. Here, a young Bo Linh brandishes a sword and plays at battle with his fellow buffalo herders.

Too Close to China, Too Far from Heaven

For two thousand years, China sometimes played a decisive role in Vietnamese affairs. This Chinese illustration shows representatives of China relinquishing their control of Vietnam to the French in 1884.

For a thousand years Vietnam has maintained an uneasy independence in the shadow of its great neighbor to the north. The Vietnamese have accepted the Chinese as overlords to whom tribute is owed, while looking to them for aid and protection in times of crisis. But China's desire for buffer states at its borders, and Vietnam's fierce resistance to assimilation within the Chinese Empire, have made for an ironic, if consistent, relationship.

Although Vietnam had traditionally struggled against Chinese imperialism, when faced with the threat of French domination in the latter part of the nineteenth century, Vietnamese officials pleaded with China to come to their aid. For more than ten years the largely Chinese Black Flag pirates fought for the Vietnamese government against the French. In 1883 full-scale war broke out between China and France. With the latter's victory a year later, China was compelled to relinquish the imperial seal of Vietnam.

But if China no longer maintained a formal protectorate over Vietnam, the centuries-long relationship between the two countries endured. Over the next sixty years, at least three important Vietnamese nationalist parties found shelter in China. The last of these, the Vietminh, acted as intelligence agents for the Chinese against their common Japanese foe and then emerged from southern China to seize control of Vietnam in August 1945.

After World War II, China provided training and supplies to Vietnamese forces in their renewed resistance to the French. Ho Chi Minh's North Vietnam again looked to China in the early 1960s, this time for military aid first to frustrate the Americans and finally to defeat the South Vietnamese.

But if China expected Vietnam to return gratefully to its traditional satellite role, it was sadly disappointed. The Vietnamese still retained their ancient suspicion of Chinese domination. Moreover, their increasing reliance on Russian support now placed them squarely on Russia's side in the Sino-Soviet split. By early 1979 the two recent allies were at war. Citing persecution of Chinese merchants in Vietnam and provocative military activity along their common border, China launched some fifty thousand troops against its southern neighbor. Chinese infantry and armored divisions poured through Friendship Pass, the main route for most of the $10 billion in aid China had provided Vietnam to help defeat the Americans only a few years earlier. The Chinese, claiming this taught the Vietnamese a "lesson," quickly retreated, leaving intact the distrust and hostility of both sides.

"The Vietnamese are indeed not a reliable people," complained one eighteenth-century Chinese emperor. "An occupation does not last very long before they raise their arms against us and expel us from their country. The history of past dynasties has proved this fact." In 1978, Vietnam's deputy foreign minister, Nguyen Co Thach, put it more bluntly: "China changes allies as often as people change underwear. ... Vietnam is nobody's dog."

A sandstone figure of one of the Indian goddesses worshipped by the Chams, ancient rivals of the Vietnamese. The Chams, now an isolated minority in southern Vietnam, reflected the extensive religious and cultural influence of India in Southeast Asia.

his lord's death, Bo Linh, with the aid of friends and volunteers, defeated the other lords and founded a unified kingdom that he called Dai Co Viet—"Kingdom of the Watchful Hawk."

Bo Linh also managed to keep China at bay without going to war. He persuaded the Chinese to accept Vietnam's independence in exchange for a payment of tribute three times a year and acknowledgment of China's overlordship. Bo Linh realized that Vietnam would never enjoy the military or economic resources to ignore China's power. For Viet-

nam and other countries along China's borders, this arrangement was based on a Chinese-centered system of international policy. It determined the pattern of Chinese-Vietnamese relations until the French arrived in the nineteenth century. Still, China would always be waiting to intervene in Vietnam whenever political turmoil arose there.

Vietnam's march to the South

While seeking peace with China, the Vietnamese were attacked by their southern neighbor, Champa, a great seafaring kingdom founded by Indian merchants on the Annamese coast near modern Hue. Since the beginning of the Christian era, the Chams—pirates, nomads, and merchants—had sailed the waters of the South China Sea. Now the Chams, a people racially distinct from the Vietnamese, were after the rich agricultural lands of the Red River Delta.

The Vietnamese not only repulsed the Chams but responded with an expansionist policy of their own. Victories over the Chams in 1044 and 1061 moved Vietnam's southern frontier below the seventeenth parallel. To settle newly won territory, colonies of Vietnamese peasant-soldiers pushed into the southern coastal plains and gradually displaced the remaining Cham inhabitants.

These victories were only the opening round in a fight to the death that would last until 1471. In that year, with each side using the most ruthless means to exterminate the other, the Vietnamese overwhelmed the Chams and ravaged their capital, Indrapura. They slaughtered forty thousand Chams and took more than thirty thousand prisoners. The last Cham king was executed and Vietnam annexed Champa's remains. Today, the once proud Chams constitute a minority in Vietnam, the victims of a long-standing racial and cultural prejudice.

For the Vietnamese, conquering Champa was only the beginning of an aggressive policy toward their neighbors which continues to this day. In their untiring struggle to expand their territory, the Vietnamese have acquired a sense of national destiny, a desire to be the dominant country on the Indochinese peninsula. Their history is one of a people winning land, a process the Vietnamese call "slowly munching silkworms." Seen in this context, Vietnam's invasion of Cambodia in 1978, its hegemony over Laos, and its conflicts with Thailand are merely contemporary episodes in a long history of warfare between the Vietnamese and neighboring states.

Buddhists and Confucians vie for power

Vietnam's successful campaign against Champa was aided by a long period of internal political unity. From the eleventh to the fifteenth centuries, two powerful families ruled Vietnam, the Ly (1010–1225) and the Tran (1225–1400). The Ly family rose to power with Buddhist support, and many Ly emperors became ardent Buddhists. Since the ouster of the Chinese colonial administration and its Confucian officials, Buddhism, which attracted both aristocrats and peasants, formed the strongest religious and political force in the country. Soon almost the entire ruling class of officials and educators in Vietnam was composed of Buddhists.

Despite their continuing devotion to Buddhism, the Ly emperors found that they could not rely solely on the Buddhists as their political and administrative arm. By nature, many Buddhists were unsuited to the highly competitive and worldly nature of politics. Buddhism asserted that all worldly affairs were vanity and taught the renunciation of material duties. The monks, who sought to free themselves for the spiritual pursuits of "self-awakening" and "enlightenment," were ill at ease in the day-to-day conflicts of public life.

Vietnam's emperors looked to China for a model of government and chose the Chinese-style Confucian bureaucracy, which they had experienced first hand under Chinese colonial rule. In developing a Confucian-trained civil service, they laid the foundations of Vietnamese government that lasted until the French conquest of Vietnam in the late 1800s. In 1075, competitive examinations were inaugurated for nine ranks of mandarins, civilian and military. To learn the teachings of Confucius required a thorough indoctrination in the culture of China. Candidates for the civilian mandarinate studied Chinese language and writing and classical Chinese literature, poetry, and philosophy. Prospective mandarins studied these seemingly irrelevant subjects because they were trained as generalists who could act as models of behavior and morality for the people, not as specialists in a particular profession.

The long-term inheritance of these Chinese studies was a static educational system and an elite bureaucracy separate in training and outlook from the Vietnamese peasant majority. Mandarins eventually became hostile to social changes that might threaten

This western rendering shows a military mandarin in ceremonial dress. Civil and military bureaucracies, staffed by Confucian mandarins, gradually came to dominate Vietnam's government. Military mandarins enjoyed less prestige than their civilian colleagues, and to this day educated Vietnamese prefer the higher status of a civilian career to a military one.

their status or to new ideas that might alter their outlook. So when the Vietnamese encountered westerners in the eighteenth and nineteenth centuries, they were generally hampered in responding to foreign ideas, religions, and technology. Failure to understand the West eventually made Vietnam tragically vulnerable to western imperialism and superior technology.

Military mandarins had less prestige than their civilian counterparts, since Confucianism considered a military career inferior to a civilian one. They had to pass physical as well as intellectual tests and underwent something like an ROTC program that included rigorous physical training. Only after passing tests in physical fitness and the use of weapons were they subjected to a review of military tactics and history.

Thousands of eager students crowded the regional test centers. They pitched tents for shelter in large fields. At night a roll call was taken to make sure that only eligible candidates were admitted to the testing areas. The exams began at dawn. Mandarins monitored the students from the tops of watchtowers to prevent cheating. Some of the old examination grounds were used as airfields during the Vietnam War.

Few of the many candidates for degrees at any level were able to pass these grueling exams. Only about two thousand of the highest degrees were awarded during the exams' 844-year history. The thousands of unsuccessful candidates were no better off than before. But everyone realized the difficulty of qualifying for a degree, so there was no shame for those who failed. The system even allowed a student several chances to pass. The emphasis on degrees and education continues in Vietnam today, where earning academic degrees for status is frequently seen as an end in itself.

Scholars without degrees still had to make a living. They supported themselves by drawing up deeds and by presenting petitions to mandarin officials. They also kept village tax records, practiced medicine, or tutored. Even without a degree and formal status as mandarins, these "village scholars" served as important unofficial links between uneducated villagers and the state administration. It was not unusual, however, for ambitious village scholars to use their influence among the peasants to build a local political power base. As spokesmen for village interests, they were often able to gather wide popular support for rebellions against high taxes or other oppressive government measures. Later, under the French, many village scholars who refused to participate in the colonial administration played a similar role in organizing resistance movements.

The mandarinate also brought privileges to the degree holder's family. Sons of the highest mandarins were exempted from military service, taxes, and the mandatory labor that so many others endured. In fact, the rise of families on the social and political ladder depended only to a limited degree upon their wealth, land, or individual efforts. Although wealth could buy the education necessary to pass the mandarin exams, education and position in the bureaucracy determined one's status.

The decline of the Buddhists

In the early stages of Vietnamese Confucianism, no serious conflict arose between Confucians and Buddhists. As the Confucians solidified their political position, however, they waged an aggressive campaign against Buddhist beliefs. The Confucians accused the Buddhists of oppressing the peasants under religion's guise by pressing impoverished peasants into serf labor on their vast tracts of monastic land.

By the fourteenth century, Buddhist monks, under growing criticism, steadily withdrew from the affairs of court to the solitude of their pagodas and monasteries. Ceding their influence in national politics to the Confucians, they soon limited their activities to religious instruction in the villages. As the power of the Buddhists diminished, talented young men increasingly chose a career in the Confucian mandarinate as a ladder to advancement. The relatively restricted role of Buddhism in Vietnam today reflects the extent to which the Confucian establishment suppressed Buddhism centuries ago.

But Buddhist political influence did not disappear entirely. Buddhism remained popular among the people, and monks retained a powerful hold on the religious and social life of the villages. Its influence in Vietnam has persisted to the present day. Since the beginning of the Vietnamese war, Buddhist leaders, especially in the South, have unified various sects and formed a common central organization with both religious and political associations. In later years, Buddhists formed an opposition party to the Catholic regimes of Ngo Dinh Diem and Nguyen Van Thieu in South Vietnam. They organized protests against Diem's preferential treatment toward Catholics. The protests soon erupted into violent confrontations between Buddhist and Catholic factions. Such turmoil has been a traditionally divisive element in Vietnam and has undermined attempts at political unity.

Mandarins build a bureaucracy

The emperor's mandarin officials oversaw the affairs of the village. They supervised the construction and repair of dikes and planned the building of canals

The Buddhist Factor

On June 11, 1963, a Buddhist monk, Thich Quang-Duc, set himself afire in Saigon to protest the oppressive regime of South Vietnamese President Ngo Dinh Diem. People around the world reacted with shock and horror to this spectacular event. One American called it "an act of savagery, violence, and fanaticism, requiring a condition of mental imbalance."

But to the Vietnamese, and especially to Vietnam's sizable Buddhist community, the monk's dramatic suicide had a powerful religious and political significance. The Buddhists traditionally believed that self-immolation was the act of a person free of physical needs and prepared to enter upon a completely spiritual existence. Fire served as the rite of passage to an eternal state of blessedness and peace. Politically this act of purification was designed to shame the government by contrasting the monk's virtue with the corruption and repressiveness of Diem's regime.

Thich Quang-Duc's suicide aroused international concern about South Vietnam's political situation. Within Vietnam it crystallized widespread discontent against the restrictions and controls brought about by the war and provoked a tumultuous movement of popular protest. Thus Buddhists, as they had been so many times before in Vietnamese history, were thrust into the role of providing moral and political leadership for the people and representing their interests to the government.

Although a religious minority in South Vietnam, Buddhists wielded an authority rooted in the ancient pagodas of the countryside. With the fiery death of Thich Quang-Duc, Buddhism became a critical political and social element in Vietnam for the remainder of the war.

Having calmly lit his gasoline-saturated robes, the Buddhist bonze, Quang-Duc, 73, burns to death in a main intersection in Saigon. Surrounded by three hundred fellow monks and thousands of other Vietnamese observers, the old man committed suicide in protest against what he called government "persecution of Buddhists." The incident intensified opposition to the regime of Ngo Dinh Diem.

The Vietnamese general Tran Hung Dao, a master of guerrilla tactics, defeated invading Mongols in the thirteenth century. Immortalized by generations to follow, his spirit is still invoked as a guardian against evil.

and irrigation systems. The mandarins' role in the community was not to enforce an impersonal, absolute law formulated by a bureaucracy far removed from the villages. Instead, their sometimes frustrating task was to adapt Confucianism to the circumstances of everyday village life. Confucianism was, in many ways, a rule by man rather than by law. Maintaining harmonious relations within a community was more important to the mandarins than a strict literal interpretation of the law. Ideally they mediated and settled disputes in accordance with local custom and the facts of a particular case, and their decisions usually declared neither party completely right or completely wrong.

The mandarin system was by no means immune to corruption. Mandarins frequently misused their power in the community to extort bribes from those seeking decisions to their advantage. Thus the scale of justice was all too often tilted in favor of wealthier members of the community at the expense of poorer peasants.

The mandarins also introduced a universal military draft. Compulsory military service reflected Vietnam's growing sense of national identity: The army was called to fight for the entire country, not for the private interests of feudal lords as had been the case in the past. Every community had to register all male inhabitants for the draft. Because of the importance of agriculture, soldiers were permitted to serve in the military service for six months each year, spending the other six in the rice fields. The wisdom of this traditional Vietnamese policy was lost on South Vietnamese leaders and their American advisers in the 1950s and 1960s. The South Vietnamese Army drafted men away from their villages for full-time military service, thus seriously disrupting the economic cycle of village agriculture. This resulted in high desertion rates and animosity toward the government.

Chinese attack Vietnam

In 1257, China, ruled by the Mongol emperor Kublai Khan, decided to test the mettle of Vietnam's national army. Just as the French would in the nineteenth century, Kublai Khan recognized the strategic importance of Indochina's east coast for the control of the spice routes between east Asia and India. He soon tried to force the Vietnamese into submission. The war between China and Vietnam continued on and off for twenty-seven years. Vietnam was never seriously threatened until 1284 when the Mongols attacked with an army of five hundred thousand men.

The Vietnamese emperor had expected the attack and sent Tran Hung Dao, Vietnam's best general, to protect the northern frontier. Tran Hung Dao could mobilize only two hundred thousand troops, and at first, the Vietnamese retreated after losing several battles to the Mongols. The discouraged Tran emperor then went to Tran Hung Dao and announced his intention of surrendering. But Tran Hung Dao was not cowed. He bravely replied: "If your majesty wishes to surrender, please first cut off my head." This helped to restore the emperor's confidence.

"Kill the Mongols"

Tran Hung Dao mustered every resource at his disposal. He rebuilt his troops' morale through intensive training and sent out a proclamation of defiance to the Mongols, which has since become famous in Viet-

The Guerrilla Legacy

Communist General Vo Nguyen Giap, Vietnam's modern war hero, followed Tran Hung Dao's teachings on guerrilla warfare against the French and the Americans. Ho Chi Minh nicknamed Giap "Volcano Covered with Snow" because of his mood swings between hot temper and iciness.

The military teachings of Tran Hung Dao, Vietnam's ancient master of guerrilla warfare, are as revered today as they were in the thirteenth century when he defeated five hundred thousand Mongol invaders. Tran Hung Dao's tactics have become a classic feature of Vietnamese military strategy. He taught his army to assemble only at the site and time of battle, using a feint-and-strike maneuver to ambush superior forces and to harass enemy supply lines. His troops used their knowledge of local terrain—jungles, mountains, and rice fields—to establish inaccessible hideouts, weapons caches, and bases. Tran Hung Dao trained even his largest units to operate like guerrillas, avoiding major engagements whenever possible and wearing down the enemy through exposure to tropical heat and disease. Later Vietnamese generals who followed Tran Hung Dao's example were also successful. But no student of Tran Hung Dao has become more famous than

General Vo Nguyen Giap, North Vietnam's military mastermind.

General Giap has often acknowledged that he learned many of his "tricks" from Tran Hung Dao. He first demonstrated his expertise in Tran Hung Dao's tactics during the war against the French. In October 1947, when the French launched a major offensive to wipe out Ho Chi Minh's Vietminh, Giap frustrated their every move. He withdrew his forces into the dense jungle and wooded areas of northern Vietnam, refusing to allow his soldiers to do battle with the better-equipped French. The French columns, for all their vehicles, tanks, and heavy artillery, were prisoners of the narrow mountain roads. Giap, meanwhile, deployed his troops along the roads to harass the columns with mines and barricades and to lure increasingly restless French troops into ambushes. Eventually shortages of food and fuel, as well as jungle heat and malaria, took a heavy toll

on the French. By 1948, what French commanders had called the "greatest military action in French history" had ground to a halt, a dismal failure. All the French gained from their gigantic effort was a bitter taste of the kind of guerrilla strategy that would ultimately carry the Vietminh to victory.

Giap's use of Tran Hung Dao's tactics against the French foreshadowed a similar and equally successful insurgency war against the combined military strength of the United States and South Vietnam. To some it seems that the Americans and South Vietnamese had ignored the strategies employed by Giap against the French. But they could have looked even further back—to Tran Hung Dao—for an understanding of Vietnamese guerrilla tactics tried and tested for over seven hundred years.

namese annals of war. Incited by the proclamation, Vietnamese soldiers tattooed the words "Kill the Mongols" on their arms.

The Vietnamese army carried out a superb defense, using tactics adapted to their inferior numbers of troops and weapons. Squads of guerrillas harried the Mongols and cut their supply routes. Tran Hung Dao lured the Mongols southward to expose them to Vietnam's natural allies: tropical heat and disease. A student of history, he decided to make Vietnam's last stand along the banks of the Bach Dang River, where three hundred and fifty years earlier Ngo Quyen had used underwater spikes to defeat the Chinese. Tran employed an identical strategy, and history repeated itself. Iron-pointed spikes were again hidden below the surface of the water at high tide and the invading navy drawn in. When the tide ebbed, the Mongol boats were pierced and sunk. Those who remained of the enemy were harassed and killed as they retreated toward China.

With the victory, the Vietnamese became one of the few peoples to repel the Mongol hordes. Tran Hung Dao also became one of the most revered Vietnamese heroes. From his deathbed, he gave the Vietnamese emperor a lesson in dealing with a vastly superior foe. He sent a message to the emperor that no Vietnamese government has forgotten without peril: "The army must have one soul like the father and son in the family. It is vital to treat the people with humanity, to achieve deep roots and a lasting base."

Disunity cripples the country

By the midfourteenth century, the Tran dynasty had lost its vigor and was vulnerable to a coup. Vietnam had been ravaged by mountain tribesmen, and several expeditions against tough Laotian raiders had ended in failure. On the domestic front, royal incompetence precipitated an overwhelming economic crisis. Corrupt emperors allowed greedy mandarins to extract exorbitant taxes from poverty-stricken peasants. Decadent court life also outraged the people and drove honest officials out of government service. The emperors indulged in extravagant feasts and entertainments while a series of natural disasters pushed already hard-pressed peasants to the breaking point. Members of the royal family even married one another, a violation of sacred Vietnamese taboos.

The country's weakened condition provided the perfect opening for an opportunist like Ho Qui Ly, one of the emperor's chief ministers. Ho pulled the political strings that strangled one emperor and forced another to abdicate. He also terrorized the court mandarins, forcing them to serve him and executing those who refused. In 1400 he dethroned the last Tran emperor and declared himself ruler of the kingdom. Meanwhile, Tran loyalists, resentful of losing their privileges and power at court, conspired in hopes of destroying Ho and restoring the old monarchy.

China invades Vietnam

China was keeping a watchful eye on the course of events in Vietnam. By now the Chinese had overthrown the Mongol dynasty and were united under the powerful Ming emperors. In 1407 China, seeking to avenge its defeats in the tenth and thirteenth centuries, invaded Vietnam with two large armies. Ho, a first-rate general, was ready for them. He stationed his forces along the Red River, confident that his troops could repel anything that China threw at them.

The Chinese, however, held an extra weapon that proved mightier than the Mongol hordes. They were in contact with dissident factions within Vietnam, mostly Tran loyalists, and had promised to return the old dynasty to power if the dissidents collaborated. As a result, the Vietnamese showed little spirit in the ensuing battle, and the Chinese won. Ho was captured, and after an interlude of five hundred years China controlled Vietnam. The Tran and their accomplices paid a heavy price for their collaboration because the Chinese broke their promises. After defeating Ho, the Ming denied Tran claims to the throne and returned Vietnam to colonial rule.

Under the Ming, the Vietnamese were subjected to a regime as harsh as anything they had known during the earlier thousand-year occupation by China. According to Vietnamese accounts, Chinese masters drove labor gangs into the mines to extract gold ore, which was shipped to China. Peasants were sent out to scour disease-ridden jungles for rare woods and spices and to dive for pearls at the bottom of the sea.

Economic exploitation was accompanied by ruthless measures to deprive the Vietnamese of their nationhood. Alarmed at Vietnam's vibrant national spirit, the Chinese carried away its literary and historical archives in order to erase all memory of the past. Many of the country's scholars and technicians were removed to China and replaced by Chinese carpetbaggers. The Ming governors even issued identity cards for all Vietnamese citizens.

Vietnam strikes back

"We have sometimes been weak and sometimes powerful, but at no time have we suffered from a lack of heroes." This is a sacred motto of the Vietnamese people. Le Loi became one of Vietnam's greatest heroes by leading the triumphant movement of national resistance against the Ming. Le Loi, a wealthy landowner, was outraged by China's exactions on the people. He organized a center of resistance in his native village of Lam Son, attracting many followers with the revolutionary slogan, "He who wants to live joins the resistance, he who wants to die accepts service under the Ming." Nguyen Trai, a popular writer of political tracts and poetry, served as his comrade in arms. Nguyen Trai's works became the

Elephants, used triumphantly by the legendary hero Le Loi against the Chinese in 1426, traditionally served as vehicles of warfare in Southeast Asia. These South Vietnamese soldiers are off to war in 1962 mounted on elephants able to charge at a speed of fifteen miles per hour.

rebels' most powerful weapon, rallying support to the cause of freedom and transforming Le Loi into a legendary hero.

Proclaiming himself the "Prince of Pacification" in 1418, Le Loi embarked on the awesome project of evicting the Chinese. Like resistance leaders against the French five hundred years later, Le Loi confronted the problem of staging a full-scale revolt while the country was occupied by a foreign power.

Despite the odds, Le Loi organized a sizable guerrilla army to harass provincial authorities. Following the example of Tran Hung Dao, Le Loi began his campaign by attacking only outlying posts and supply columns, never exposing his guerrillas to the superior might of the Chinese army. Le Loi's plan was to wear down the Chinese with ambushes, star-

vation, and disease. The Chinese provincial forces soon became wary of venturing outside their towns and fortresses. During the day Chinese soldiers patrolled the countryside, but at night the villages and roads belonged to the rebels. Five hundred years later, French and then U.S. forces would face an identical situation in their own counterinsurgency efforts.

Le Loi's resistance movement produced small but persistent uprisings throughout the country. Le Loi then sent tactical units into the Red River Delta to foment revolt among the peasants. There in 1426 he won decisively over the Chinese with a distinctly Indochinese weapon: elephants. China's horses were no match for Le Loi's charging elephants. The Chinese lost all their artillery and fell back to a few fortified places. After a series of negotiations, peace was finally concluded between Vietnam and China in 1428.

Generations of Vietnamese poets and historians, down to the present day, have heaped praise upon Le Loi, a legendary master in the art of guerrilla warfare. His achievements will not go unsung, for in contemporary Vietnam the veneration accorded Le Loi is second only to that given to Ho Chi Minh.

The fruits of revolution

The charismatic patriot Le Loi became emperor in 1428 soon after the Chinese had evacuated the country. Vietnam, however, had no time to revel in its independence for the scars of war were everywhere. Wide stretches of rice land lay abandoned. Disease and starvation reigned, and social disorder laid waste the countryside.

Le Loi tried once more to solve the persistent problem of masses of landless peasants. He knew that unless the peasants could earn a living he would not have a stable regime since peasant taxes provided the chief source of government income. Le Loi used the traditional Vietnamese method of enacting land reforms and reducing social unrest. He ordered a redistribution of land among the entire population, but there is no evidence of the extent to which his land reforms were implemented.

Vietnamese land reform programs intended to reduce social tensions have always been plagued by unequal distribution and, ultimately, by the accumulation of large estates by powerful landlords. The Communists under Ho Chi Minh gained popular support among the peasants by taking radical steps to eliminate traditional class differences, to break up the land monopoly of the rich by seizing all private estates, and to insure land redistribution on an equal basis. For the South Vietnamese governments, however, land reform was a nagging problem that was never resolved despite U.S. pressure.

The family and the state

The Le emperors' efforts to reinforce Confucian values produced Vietnam's first comprehensive set of laws, the Hong Duc Code, which remained in force until the eighteenth century. Designed to safeguard the emperor's authority, the code protected the family, the cornerstone of the Confucian state, focusing

of sons denouncing their parents before "peoples'" tribunals, however, still remains a shocking spectacle to most Vietnamese.

In the South other factors have tended to weaken family ties. The attraction of city life in Saigon and elsewhere has lured many young people away from their villages and their families. Western influences, especially American, have also contributed to the breakdown of traditional family authority. Nevertheless, nepotism in the South Vietnamese government and military ballooned to scandalous proportions during the 1960s and 1970s. Appointing relatives all too often produced incompetent administrators and military officers and impeded the effectiveness of South Vietnam's war effort.

A Le dynasty emperor being carried in state.

especially on filial obligations and marriage rites.

Even though the Confucian state honored the family as the core of society, the Le emperors constantly worked to check family influence. They knew that many families, having paid for the studies leading to their sons' degrees, might seek favors in return when they entered the bureaucracy. The Le emperors imposed a system of restrictions to prevent officials from using their office for personal interests. For example, no official could marry a woman with family ties to the region under his jurisdiction.

Although the emperors endeavored to control nepotism and family influence, they faced a losing battle. Obligations to the family, extending even to remote cousins, have traditionally taken precedence in Vietnam over obligations to the state. Developments in twentieth century Vietnam, however, have somewhat altered the primary role of the family in society. The North Vietnamese, espousing Communist ideology, have attacked these time-honored family bonds as counterrevolutionary. The sight in North Vietnam

Civil war: Vietnam is divided

The corrupt sixteenth-century successors of Le Loi could not govern the country. Vietnam had no fewer than eight emperors between 1502 and 1527, while powerful generals fought among themselves to gain control of the kingdom. Mac Dang Dung, a fisherman who had risen to prominence with the aid of powerful friends, finally seized power. He put the Le emperor to death and, in 1527, proclaimed a new dynasty.

One Le supporter, Nguyen Kim, took refuge in the mountains near the Laotian border. There he set up a government in exile in 1532 which was nominally headed by a descendant of the Le. Nguyen Kim was later poisoned by a prisoner in 1545 while advancing against Mac Dang Dung; Kim's son-in-law, Trinh Kiem, then took command of the Le army. Trinh defeated Mac, and in 1593 the Le dynasty was formally restored to the throne. The Le would rule Vietnam until late in the eighteenth century, but only in name. Trinh and his successors usurped imperial power, keeping the Le emperor only as a figurehead.

Trinh's father-in-law, Nguyen Kim, had a son, Nguyen Hoang, who persuaded Trinh to let him leave Hanoi and become governor of a sparsely settled province near Hue. By 1620 Nguyen Hoang's son and successor thought his support strong enough to cut ties with Hanoi and refuse to send any more taxes to the royal court. From then on the Nguyen family ruled the South independently of the Trinh-controlled kingdom in the North.

The Trinh had no intention of giving up the South without a fight. Seven times between 1627 and 1673 the Trinh tried to regain the South, but the Nguyen won every time. The Trinh's powerful army literally ran into a wall when they invaded Nguyen territory. The Nguyen, relying on the narrowness of the south coastal plain, constructed two twenty-foot-high walls, one six, the other eleven miles long. These walls divided Vietnam along the seventeenth parallel, foreshadowing the division of the country on that same parallel after the Geneva Conference in 1954. The Trinh could never breach these walls, and Nguyen armies repelled Trinh armies up to five times larger than their own. The Trinh were also handicapped by fighting on unfamiliar terrain in a torrid climate while the Nguyen defended their own villages and rice fields. Trinh aggression ceased in 1673 in stalemate. Both sides agreed to a truce, which designated the Linh River as the border between the two territories.

The march to the South continues

While the Trinh governed the old country in the North, the Nguyen were actively building a new one in the South. During the seventeenth century, Nguyen settlers and colonists moved south toward the enormous and fertile Mekong Delta. The delta still belonged in name to the Khmer kings of Cambodia, but the age of Khmer glory had passed. Cambodia had never even exploited this rich delta.

The colonization of the South by the Nguyen was a turning point in Vietnamese history. As they entered the delta, Vietnamese pioneers emerged from Annam's narrow coastal plains into a wilderness vaster than any they had ever seen before. Having broken with the North and set up an independent regime, the Nguyen were now able to concentrate their energies on creating a new kingdom. With expansion in mind, they built their administration around a core of military officials who supervised colonies of peasant-soldiers. These colonies became the main instruments of settlement.

A steady flow of refugees from the North, fleeing Trinh tyranny, provided the Nguyen with an ever-fresh source of pioneers. For impoverished northern peasants, the South offered wider spaces to settle and cultivate, greater freedom of movement, and more substantial opportunities to earn a living. The land a man cleared became his; this traditionally was the dream of every peasant.

As their people settled foreign territory, Nguyen rulers worked to prevent the alien Cham and Khmer cultures from tainting the Vietnamese way of life. They built schools and required the Vietnamese language to be used in literature and in official documents. In many cultural ways, the Nguyen domain became almost a copy of the northern kingdom.

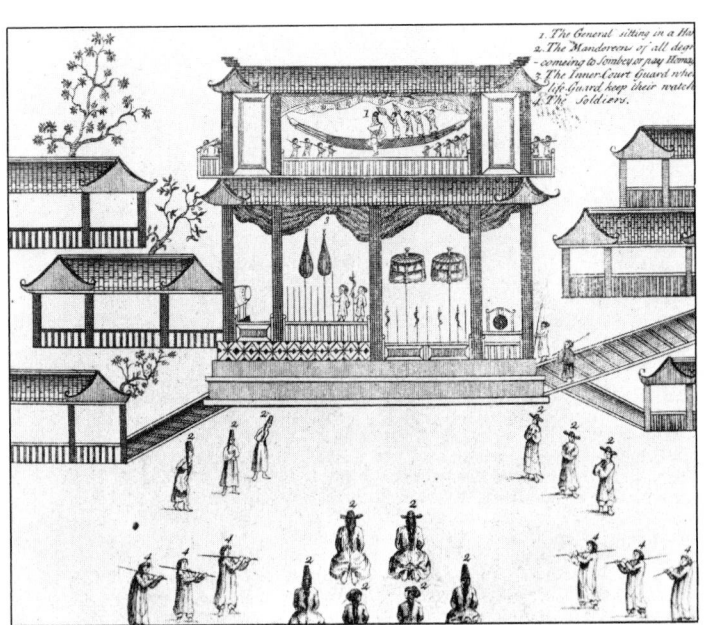

The court of the Chua or "general," the Trinh ruler of Tonkin. The Trinh usurped the power of the Le dynasty whose emperors remained as figureheads through the late eighteenth century.

More fundamental influences, however, kept the two halves of the country culturally similar. The settlers came in large family groups and naturally wanted to retain traditional discipline, customs, and religious beliefs. Also, the daily chores of draining swamps and clearing jungles required close cooperation, insuring that the patterns of village life would be carefully reproduced.

Frontier life had its unique effect on southerners. Southern landholdings tended to be larger than in the North, where the ancient land policies restricted the size of individual plots. In the South the size of a peasant's land was restricted only by the amount he could farm and pay taxes for. Tight-knit family relations also slackened as a result of increased mobility. In the South the eldest son no longer had to limit his ambitions to inheriting the family house and his share of land, as in the North. He could strike out to establish his own legacy. Frontier families were often too busy fighting for a new home to observe strictly the traditions of ancestor worship, such as keeping a genealogy book, saying ritual prayers at the family altar, and gathering on the anniversary of an ancestor's death. Southerners eventually created new traditions that seemed unfamiliar to their northern brothers. Before they could substantially exploit the fertile Mekong Delta, however, they were visited by representatives of a new and foreign civilization—the "barbarians" of Europe. The Europeans would soon challenge both the Trinh and Nguyen for the riches of Southeast Asia.

Vietnam in contact with the West

When Marco Polo of Venice returned from his visit to Kublai Khan in the Far East in the thirteenth century, he brought with him more than spices, tea, and spaghetti. He also gave to Europe the dream of harvesting the immense riches of China. For two hundred years after Polo's voyage, Europeans traveled by land to seek the vast riches of the Orient. But in the fifteenth century, westerners, with the aid of new navigational equipment, took to the seas, eventually discovering alternate routes to the East.

The port of Faifo, near modern Da Nang. The Portuguese opened a trade center here in the seventeenth century with the hope of developing a Vietnamese port along the trade route to China.

The riches of China proved alluring, and soon major European powers were engaged in a bitter struggle to corner the Far Eastern market. Because of its proximity to China, Vietnam—a land that otherwise might have been ignored by European traders—became an important pawn in the struggle. Throughout the seventeenth and eighteenth centuries, and even after France gained control of Indochina in the nineteenth century, Europeans would make a series of vain attempts to use Vietnam as an entry to the more lucrative markets of the Orient.

The first westerners began to arrive in Vietnam in the midst of the Trinh–Nguyen feud in the seventeenth century. Portuguese traders landed at the port of Faifo, near modern Da Nang, where they met Chinese and Japanese merchants already transacting business. From their base of Macao, established in 1557, the Portuguese hoped to expand trade with China.

The Nguyen used the Portuguese to their advantage. With Portuguese assistance, the Nguyen built an arsenal for producing heavy guns. Regular shipments of arms from Portugal also enabled the Nguyen to partially offset the numerical superiority of the Trinh. In 1637 the Portuguese opened a trade center at Faifo but abandoned it after the Nguyen tried to restrict their activities. The Portuguese had angered Nguyen authorities by ignoring local laws and customs and by cheating the people.

Dutch merchants, who had already established trading ports from India to Indonesia, came next. The Dutch, competing with Portugal for trading rights in Vietnam, sided with the Trinh against the Nguyen. Twice Nguyen forces severely damaged Dutch fleets

in league with the Trinh. To avenge their defeats, Dutch forces raided the southern Vietnamese coast and beheaded every peasant they could capture. This availed them little. By 1700 the Dutch, disappointed in their expectations of profitable trade, had left Vietnam for good.

What the Europeans, to their dismay, failed to understand was that Vietnam, unlike China, India, or even Champa, did not have fully developed domestic or international commerce. The Vietnamese had always been too preoccupied with agriculture to develop a substantial trade economy. Since Vietnam's growing population consumed all of its most important product, rice, there was no surplus for trade with other countries. Demand for foreign luxury goods was confined to a small wealthy class.

Confucianism also retarded the growth of trade in Vietnam. Confucian ideology held the merchant profession in contempt, in part because merchants could control a large portion of wealth in a basically poor society. Both educated mandarins and hard-working peasants considered merchants middlemen who profited from the labor of others while producing nothing.

This had serious implications for the future. It hindered the development of a middle class in Vietnam. Without such a class, Vietnamese society is divided between peasants and the rich even today. The South Vietnamese government attempted to develop a modern, democratic form of government. But the education, health, and income differences between peasants and the upper class were almost impossible to narrow.

Missionaries in Vietnam

Although European traders sailed from Vietnam with little to show for their efforts, they left behind missionaries who were to play an important role in Vietnamese history. The success of the first Catholic mission at Faifo, established by Portuguese Jesuits in 1615, prompted a mission to Trinh territory, led by a Frenchman, Father Alexandre de Rhodes. The gifted and dedicated Rhodes quickly mastered the native language and within six months could preach in Vietnamese. He wrote a catechism in Vietnamese and published a Vietnamese–Latin–Portuguese dictionary.

Rhodes' works were the first to be printed in *quoc ngu*. The new script had been invented by Portuguese Jesuits so that they could write Vietnamese in Roman letters. This new method of writing eventually freed the Vietnamese from the difficulties of memorizing the Chinese ideograms.

Rhodes' preaching was immediately successful. He reported that in two years among the Trinh he baptized almost seven thousand people, some of noble rank. Although many Vietnamese were receptive to the teachings of the missionaries, Catholic intolerance of polygamy and local traditions of spirit worship hindered mass conversions. Also, the mandarins were as hostile to Catholicism as they had always been to Buddhism. They argued that Christian dogma was dangerous because it stressed the importance of the individual. The mandarins pointed out that placing individual spiritual and moral concerns above those of the family and the state was not only immoral but subversive.

The influence of Alexandre de Rhodes on Vietnamese history extended far beyond religion. Rhodes had joined the Portuguese-led Jesuits because of their papal mandate to head missionary work in the Far East. But the young cleric emerged as the first spokesman for French political and commercial interests in the area. When he returned to France from Vietnam in 1645, Rhodes began a campaign to increase the French presence in Vietnam. He was concerned that France's rivals, England and Holland, might gain the upper hand in the area, thereby denying the French access to the trade routes with China. With the aid of the French court and the permission of the pope, Rhodes organized a new mis-

Mixing piety with politics, the Jesuit missionary Alexandre de Rhodes converted thousands of Vietnamese to Catholicism while collaborating with French merchants and politicians to enhance the French position in Vietnam.

Peasant-soldiers like this one filled the ranks of the Tay Son brothers' revolutionary armies. The Tay Son were sons of a rich man, but their eighteenth century mobilization of peasant support succeeded in ousting the Trinh rulers in the North and the Nguyen in the South.

sionary society in 1662 to minister to the young Catholic community in Vietnam.

The new French clergy quickly developed ties with merchant traders and French politicians eager to gain important trade advantages in Vietnam. French fortunes in Vietnam nevertheless quickly took a turn for the worse. Both the Nguyen and Trinh realized that Catholicism was serving foreign political and commercial goals. By traveling between the two warring kingdoms, missionaries aroused the suspicion of both that they were engaging in espionage. In 1639 the Nguyen ordered all foreign missionaries expelled and burned all Catholic books. The Trinh, under mandarin pressure, also took vigorous steps to halt Christian evangelism. One Trinh ruler issued a statement declaring, "a subject owes all his allegiance . . . to the state and his sovereign." His successors condemned Christianity and prohibited preaching by Catholic priests.

Soon the emperors employed more violent means to discourage Christians. Many missionaries and converts willing to defy Vietnamese authorities were sentenced to death and execution. Alexandre de Rhodes personally witnessed the brutal execution of a young Vietnamese Christian named Andrew by government authorities:

A soldier coming up behind him pierced him [Andrew] with his lance, which emerged at least two palm's length at the front. . . . The same soldier, having pulled out his lance, drove it a second time with redoubled force as if seeking his heart. That didn't even shake the poor innocent, which seemed utterly amazing to me. Finally another soldier, seeing that three blows from the lance hadn't brought him down, gave him his scimitar across the neck, but accomplishing nothing, he struck another blow that so severed his throat that his head fell to the right, held on only by a bit of skin. But at the moment his head was separated from his neck I heard very distinctly the sacred name of Jesus—which could no longer come from his mouth—issue from the wound, and the instant his soul flew to heaven, his body fell to earth.

Tay Son rebellion

Near the end of the eighteenth century, a revolution broke out because of social unrest in both the Trinh North and the Nguyen South following the uneasy peace that had been established between them. Anarchy prevailed, and large numbers of troops were used to suppress revolts. In the struggle between Trinh and Nguyen lords, the peasants paid heavily in lives, high taxes, and the destruction of their farms. As always, greedy landlords capitalized on the peasants' misery by acquiring more land, and starvation became a common fate.

The revolution begun in 1773 was led by the three Tay Son brothers. Although these brothers belonged to the wealthy class, they started a broadly based social uprising that swept quickly across Vietnam. Desperate peasants and highland tribesmen supported them, as did many Buddhists and disaffected mandarins.

The three brothers, Ho Nhac, Ho Lu, and Ho Hue, launched their campaign in the South and defeated Nguyen troops sent to stop them. The Trinh, ready to take advantage of Nguyen troubles, dispatched an army against their old adversaries. Trinh troops forced their way past the once-impregnable Nguyen walls and seized the Nguyen capital of Hue. They were satisfied with their victory and went no further. Meanwhile, the Tay Son were free to operate in the South and sent an expedition to the Mekong Delta. The force captured Saigon and murdered the reigning Nguyen prince and his immediate family. Only his young nephew, Nguyen Anh, escaped.

"The Virgin Mary is Moving South"

From the earliest days of western contact with Vietnam, the role of Catholicism in Vietnamese society extended beyond religion. When it became clear that Catholics would remain a distinct minority within the country, the Catholic missionaries did not hesitate to turn to politics to further their ends. Most striking, of course, was Pigneau de Behaine's support of the future emperor, Gia Long, from 1783 to 1799. By throwing his influence and, he hoped, that of France behind Gia Long, Pigneau tried not only to gain concessions for Vietnam's Catholics but also to secure the throne of Vietnam itself for a Catholic successor—Gia Long's young son, Prince Canh.

When the French ultimately gained control over Vietnam beginning in 1863, they offered special treatment for the long-persecuted Catholic minority. The French aided the Catholics by awarding them higher positions in the new colonial bureaucracy, more grants of land, and most of the scholarships for higher education. Even in the granting of French citizenship, conversion to Catholicism was an important consideration. These policies, begun by the French missionaries, led to a subtle division within Vietnamese society.

It was against this backdrop that the United States began the slow process of involvement in Vietnam. In 1950, long be-

fore most Americans were aware of Vietnam, a prominent Catholic clergyman with strong missionary interests, Francis Cardinal Spellman, used his political contacts in the hopes of seeing a Catholic at the head of an independent Vietnam. Operating behind the scenes much like his French predecessors, Spellman introduced a Vietnamese politician, virtually unknown outside his country, to influential Americans like Senator John F. Kennedy. That Vietnamese politician, Ngo Dinh Diem, became South Vietnam's first president.

When the Geneva Conference convened in 1954, American representatives took a special interest in the Catholic minority. They insisted on and received a three-hundred-day period of free movement between the North and the South. During this period more than six hundred thousand Catholics traveled south of the demarcation line. Many were undoubtedly motivated by the message contained in leaflets dropped by American planes: "The Virgin Mary is moving south."

Once Diem had solidified his power, South Vietnam's million and a half Catholics continued to receive preferential treatment. Catholics often gained exemption from the necessary physical labor to be shared in the building of strategic hamlets. In land redistribution programs Catholics received the safest and best

South Vietnam's Catholic president, Ngo Dinh Diem, kisses the ring of Bishop Joseph F. Flannelly at St. Patrick's Cathedral, New York, in 1957. Shepherded by Francis Cardinal Spellman in the early fifties, Diem met American VIPs and gained American favor as the man to lead an anti-Communist Vietnam.

land near the coast, while the rest of the people had to accept inferior locations. Not surprisingly the mood of the Buddhist majority became increasingly rebellious.

Ultimately the Buddhist protest led to the coup that ended the Diem regime. The successive governments that followed Diem tried to attain a balance between Catholic and Buddhist forces, but stability was found again only in the regime of President Thieu, himself a Catholic. His regime, like that of Diem, was weakened by the continued use of political repression as much against his Buddhist as his Communist opponents.

When the first Buddhist monk burned himself in protest in the streets of Saigon, it shocked most Americans. But the grievances of the non-Catholic majority had been building, not only since Diem had taken power but for an entire century. For it was exactly one hundred years earlier, in 1863, that the French had first conquered Vietnam and begun the self-defeating process of religious discrimination.

Rid of the Nguyen in the South, the youngest Tay Son brother, Ho Hue, moved northward and took Hanoi, the Trinh capital, in 1786. He and his brothers presented themselves as champions of the people and as defenders of the poor. This rallied many peasants to their cause. A Spanish missionary reports that the Tay Son moved through villages announcing that "... they were not bandits, but envoys from Heaven, that they wanted to see justice prevail and to liberate the people. . . . They preached equality in everything. And faithful to their doctrine, they robbed mandarins and the rich of their properties, which they distributed to the poor."

After taking Hanoi in 1786, the Tay Son were essentially masters of all Vietnam. However, a group of mandarins opposed to the Tay Son asked China's Manchu rulers for help. The Chinese responded by invading Vietnam in 1788 with two hundred thousand men, but Ho Hue, who had proclaimed himself emperor of all Vietnam, North and South, repulsed them with an army of one hundred thousand men and 100 elephants. After Ho Hue's triumph, China formally recognized his government.

Tay Son rule, with its strong nationalist overtones, moved away from Chinese Confucian traditions. The Tay Son relaxed Confucian restrictions on trade to encourage Vietnamese to take an active role in commerce. Also, the Vietnamese language replaced time-honored Chinese at the court in Hanoi. In fact, the Tay Son movement had a distinctly anti-Chinese character. During the fall of Saigon in 1782, Tay Son troops pillaged and burned Chinese shops and massacred ten thousand Chinese inhabitants. They hoped to destroy the commercial monopoly of Chinese traders in Vietnam, whose wealth the natives resented. (Similar anti-Chinese feelings have surfaced again in Vietnam since the end of the war. In the last few years, thousands of Chinese merchants and shopkeepers have been forcibly driven out of Vietnam by the Communist government.)

As emperor, however, Ho Hue was unable to solve Vietnam's social problems, which constantly endangered the stability of his regime. He held out the prospect of a real social revolution, but in the end the people were disappointed. Promised reductions in taxes and forced labor requirements, as well as the breakup of the land monopoly of wealthy landlords, were never implemented. In 1792, before Ho Hue could address these problems, he died.

One year later, his brothers and supporters, Lu and Nhac, were also dead, and Ho Hue's ten-year-old son was unfit to govern the country. Without a strong leader, the country was beset by renewed peasant revolts and civil unrest.

Vietnam's Early Feminist

Ho Xuan Huong, the major poet of the Tay Son era, was a woman of extraordinary talent and spirit. Like all Vietnamese women, she was barred from the Confucian educational system, but her learning and intellectual accomplishments rivaled those of the most outstanding mandarins. She became an outspoken supporter of social and political rights for women, using satiric poems often with blunt sexual language to sting the male establishment. Her favorite targets were those Vietnamese institutions—the mandarin bureaucracy, Buddhist priesthood, marriage, and the schools—that severely restricted the participation and ambitions of women. She sharply criticized polygamous marriages, a common practice in Vietnam and compared the role of a wife in such a marriage to that of an unpaid laborer:

One rolls in warm blankets,
The other freezes:

Down with this husband sharing!
You're lucky ever to have him,
He comes perhaps twice a month,
Or less.
Ah—to fight for this!
Turned to a half-servant, an unpaid maid!
Had I known
I would have stayed single.

To avoid the pitfalls of marriage, Huong even wryly praised pregnancies outside of marriage and recommended the single-parent family.

The eternal guilt is borne completely by you, young man.
The results of our love I, the concubine, ask to carry.
And I do not care if the months of public opinion disagree with me.
Only people who become pregnant while lacking husbands are good.

French intervention and the Vietnamese struggle for unity

At the time of the Tay Son rebellion in the 1770s, France was nearly recovered from the Seven Years War with England, which had erupted in 1757 and resulted in French losses on battlefields in both Europe and Asia. As France again turned its attention to the Far East, its newly organized French East India Company regarded Vietnam as the last chance to avert English domination of the profitable trade with China. The French also recognized the strategic importance of Vietnam as a base from which to harass trade between British India and China and to strangle it in the event of war. Once more, the initiative for French intervention in Vietnam came from French missionaries, not diplomats and generals.

The missionary who accepted the challenge was Pigneau de Behaine. Pigneau arrived in the Far East in 1765 and two years later was named to head French missions there. He was able to play both roles required of a great French missionary: the artful diplomat and the fearless general. In 1777 Pigneau met the fifteen-year-old Nguyen Anh, the only surviving heir to the Nguyen throne, and helped him escape from the Tay Son. In his seesaw battle with the forces of the Tay Son, Nguyen Anh, the future Emperor Gia Long, avoided any commitment to the French. But in 1783 Nguyen forces collapsed and Saigon fell to the Tay Son. As a result, Nguyen Anh empowered Pigneau to negotiate a treaty with the French government for aid and entrusted his young son, Prince Canh, to the Frenchman as a sign of commitment. The prince would be taken to France and educated as a Catholic.

At the French court in Paris, with the young Prince Canh in tow, the missionary's quest for Vietnamese aid met with a warm reception. While the exotic prince delighted the frivolous court society of the French monarchy's last years, the foreign office

Summoned by mandarin officials (far right) loyal to the Le emperor, the Manchu army came from China in force to help quell the Tay Son uprising in 1788. Mounted on elephants, Tay Son troops repulsed the Chinese cavalry. This Chinese engraving, made in 1789, depicts the Manchu invasion in lavish detail.

dreamed of a presence in the South China Sea that would destroy British trade with China.

The result was the Versailles Treaty of 1787 which granted French men and arms to the Nguyen in return for unhampered French trade in Cochin China. Leaving Prince Canh in Paris, Pigneau returned to the Far East with not only a copy of the treaty for Nguyen Anh's signature but also a private letter from the foreign office to military officials in Pondicherry, the most important French port in India. Unknown to Pigneau, the letter he carried authorized military officials in Pondicherry to veto the entire mission if they opposed it. They did.

To the negative attitude of his fellow Frenchmen in Pondicherry, Pigneau is said to have responded, "I shall make the revolution in Cochin China alone." Exchanging the monocle of the diplomat for the baton of the general, Pigneau raised his own military force and returned to Vietnam in 1788. He was too late. Tay Son resistance was already crumbling and was even further weakened by the deaths of the three Tay Son brothers in 1792 and 1793. In Europe, meanwhile, the outbreak of the French Revolution in 1789 had wrenched France's attention away from foreign matters and guaranteed that Pigneau could not look homeward for more support. All that Pigneau's French troops in Vietnam could do was help the Nguyen forces develop naval tactics, which finally allowed them to crush the Tay Son. With Pigneau's strategic guidance, Nguyen Anh's navy defeated the Tay Son fleet, and a Nguyen army seized Hue in 1802. Nguyen Anh's victory was complete. For the first time in history, Vietnam was firmly united all the way from the Gulf of Thailand in the South to the Chinese frontier in the North.

Angkor: A Wonder of the World

"One of these temples—a rival to that of Solomon and erected by some ancient Michelangelo—might take an honorable place beside our most beautiful buildings. It is grander than anything left to us by Greece or Rome. ..." These lines were written by the French naturalist, Henri Mohout, who introduced Europe to the magnificent Khmer temples of Angkor Wat during the nineteenth century.

When the great Khmer kingdom of Angkor was founded at the beginning of the ninth century, its first ruler sited his capital in northwestern Cambodia near the Great Lake (called Tonle Sap by the Khmers). Using slave labor, Khmer kings built gigantic reservoirs, intricate canals, and sturdy dams. Soon a complex network of canals linked every town in the kingdom. Large ships sailed up the Mekong into the Great Lake and transferred their cargoes to smaller boats that could reach the most inaccessible areas. These hydraulic systems provided a ready source for irrigation, and the Khmers developed a flourishing agriculture.

Water also provided the hydraulic power and means of transport to develop the Angkor capital city. To glorify themselves, the kings erected increasingly elaborate temples there. The most famous of the Angkor monuments, the complex of Angkor Wat, was constructed by the Khmer King Suryavarman II in the twelfth century.

Planned as a burial vault for the king, Angkor Wat is one of the largest and most impressive religious structures in the world. Surrounded by a moat, it covers more than half a square mile and represents the highest achievement of Khmer art and architecture. Its central structure once stood 130 feet high. The temple rises in three successive tiers on top of which are five towers. The most remarkable feature of the temple compound is its sculptural ornamentation, adorning thousands of feet of wall space.

This type of pyramid or "temple-mountain," which was also used for other monuments at Angkor, represented Mount Meru, the legendary abode of the Hindu gods. Hindu culture was spread in Cambodia by Indian merchants traveling through Southeast Asia to markets in China, Vietnam, and the East Indies. The Khmer kings styled themselves "Kings of the Mountain." When a king proclaimed

The main gate to Angkor Thom, the largest Angkor temple complex, is guarded by two lines of stone giants. The roadway leading to the gate is lined on one side by demons (above), on the other side by gods (right).

Two women sit beside the moat at the main entrance to Angkor Wat (left, above). The monument's central pyramid, about seven hundred yards away, is barely visible (center, to right of square tower).

The outside world has received little news of the magnificent temple-city of Angkor since Khmer guerrillas took over Cambodia in 1975. Angkor, a city where more than five hundred thousand people once lived and worked, has been abandoned since the thirteenth century, slowly enshrouded by the tropical forest. Recent reports speak of serious damage to Angkor from artillery, theft of art treasures, and neglect. Here, the central pyramids of Angkor Wat, the greatest of the Angkor temples, loom over several visitors (left).

Four tevodas, or celestial women, decorate an Angkor city wall (right). The carvings are modeled on the features and fashions of the beautiful women that surrounded the Khmer kings.

The Bayon, the religious and geographic center of Angkor Thom, was the last great Khmer monument (below). The vast temple consists of more than fifty towers, each graced by four smiling faces.

himself divine according to the cult of the Indian gods Vishnu or Shiva, the temple-mountain became his spiritual home as well.

Other structures adorn the ancient Khmer capital. Even larger than Angkor Wat is Angkor Thom (which means large city), with its awesome centerpiece, the Bayon. Both were built by Emperor Jayavarman VII in the late twelfth century.

By the thirteenth century the Angkor empire began to disintegrate. Many causes have been suggested for its decline, from a series of costly border wars to the enormous expenses of building the Angkor temples. The construction of so many huge stone structures may have driven overtaxed and overworked peasants to rebellion.

Whatever the reasons, by the nineteenth century Angkor had disappeared so completely from people's memory that few believed it still existed. Over the centuries the people had abandoned the Angkor province to the always advancing jungle. By 1933 when French archaeologists initiated a major restoration project at Angkor, the city's temples, shrouded by dense jungle growth, had almost vanished from sight. Many of the monuments were subsequently restored to their former grandeur, but were damaged during the 1970s when Communist Khmer Rouge guerrillas occupied the ancient city. After 1975, when the Pol Pot regime began its reign of terror in Cambodia, Angkor fell into further disrepair, caused both by vandals and the encroaching jungle. Vietnam's invasion of Cambodia in 1979 brought in a slightly more moderate government, which renewed restoration efforts at the city. But both the future of Suryavarman's temple-mountain and that of the Khmer people remained uncertain.

The faces adorning the Bayon pyramids bear an expression called "the smile of Angkor." The portraits, perhaps representing regional Khmer government officials, communicate the omnipresence of the Supreme Being.

The French Conquest

The victory of Nguyen Anh and the unification of Vietnam came at a crucial juncture in Vietnamese history. Only the outbreak of the French Revolution in Europe had saved Vietnam from French domination during the chaotic period of the Tay Son rebellion. But the new dynasty established by Nguyen Anh would not escape renewed French demands for trade and religious toleration.

To meet the French challenge, Vietnam's rulers drew on the country's long Confucian heritage. When Vietnam had emerged from Chinese colonial rule in 938, Confucian doctrine had held the young nation together. In absorbing Chinese culture, the Vietnamese had also assimilated China's policy of isolating itself from foreign influences. Vietnam, however, lacked China's immense size, power, and self-sufficiency. Simply "thinking big" would not enable Vietnam to ward off western encroachment. China's own experience in the nineteenth century, when the court

at Peking was increasingly forced to turn real power over to western nations, ought to have warned the Vietnamese that Chinese-style isolationism could not save their country. China, opened up by the British opium trade, was itself slowly succumbing to western aggression.

But Nguyen Anh and his successors failed to learn from China's experience. Rather than taking steps to modernize Vietnam in preparation for the confrontation with the West, they decided that only complete isolation from the West could preserve Vietnam's independence. For them, isolationism represented a withdrawal behind the cultural walls of Confucianism to keep out foreign influences and the forces of change.

Vietnam's Confucian heritage was a major source of the country's strength, but it also contributed to its downfall. By the midnineteenth century Vietnam seemed, politically and economically, to be the most firmly united and the most powerful country in Indochina. Yet Confucianism posed insurmountable barriers to Vietnam's defense against the West. Vietnam was destined to be ruled once more by foreigners. The unity and power created by Nguyen Anh would be reduced to a memory—but a powerful memory inspiring future generations of Vietnamese.

Vietnam's last dynasty

Nguyen Anh proclaimed himself emperor in 1802 and moved his capital from Hanoi to Hue. He called his kingdom Vietnam—previous regimes had called the country Annam. He took a new name, Gia Long, and founded the last Vietnamese dynasty, called the Nguyen. Its reign did not end until the abdication of Emperor Bao Dai in 1955.

As Vietnam entered the nineteenth century, its future looked bright. The country had a heritage of almost nine hundred years of independence and a powerful tradition of national pride. Now Vietnam was unified once more, larger and more populous than ever. As virgin territory in the South was developed, it seemed likely that food would become abundant for all and new land would be available for settlement.

Gia Long tried to restore Vietnam's economy. He repaired highways and built new ones, the most im-

portant being the Mandarin Road from Saigon to Lam Son near the Chinese border. The Mandarin Road symbolized the new unity of the country. It linked the frontier South—the Mekong Delta—with the old kingdom of the North—the Red River Delta. The Vietnamese little suspected that within seventy-five years their country would be divided once more by the French and remain so for a century.

Gia Long also tried to undo the disastrous effects of almost thirty years of warfare upon the peasants. The Tay Son had attracted broad support by promising extensive reforms in landholding, forced labor, and taxes. There were also many abandoned lands because so many young men had been drafted for military service, and others had been forced to leave their homes and become refugees. Under the Tay Son, dams had been poorly maintained, causing severe floods. Gia Long instituted a vast program of public works for the construction of dikes and canals. He also built public granaries in order to ease rice shortages after poor harvests.

Successive Nguyen emperors worked to wipe out the ancient abuses of the wealthy landlords who hoarded rice land, even abolishing all large estates held by princes, nobles, and high officials. But these reforms, aimed to reduce the power of feudalism, did little to relieve the peoples' ills. Vietnam still had too many rich landlords ready to exploit poor or landless peasants. Like so many agricultural reforms in the past, they remained largely in the planning stage.

The Nguyen emperors also undercut their own social reforms. They forced peasant artisans to build luxurious palaces and magnificent temples at Hue. Their public works projects required such masses of laborers that even some existing rice land was abandoned. Often these laborers toiled the whole day into the early evening and even stood guard for the rest of the night. Frequently this led to death from starvation or sheer exhaustion.

Nguyen foreign policy: Vietnam and its neighbors

The basis of Nguyen foreign policy, like that of its predecessors, was the necessity of preserving friendly relations with China. After ascending the throne, Gia Long dispatched envoys to Peking to request approval of his reign. In 1804 the envoys returned bearing the official seal recognizing Nguyen rule. Soon after, the "Celestial Messenger," as the envoy from Peking was called, was escorted from the frontier with pomp and an armed contingent of Vietnamese troops, preceded by elephants arrayed for battle.

Southward the Nguyen continued the expansionist policy of their ancestors. Not content with having seized the southern region from the Chams and Khmers, they vied with Thailand for control of the rest of Cambodia. Neither was able to take Cambodia, so in 1845 they worked out a diplomatic compromise. Unable to defend its borders, Cambodia agreed to recognize the joint overlordship of Vietnam and Thailand. The Vietnamese also seized Laotian territory along the Mekong River. Only the French colonial rule and the Vietnam War halted Vietnam's attempts to dominate the entire Indochinese peninsula.

The mandarins return to power

Gia Long implemented his program through the traditional corps of mandarin officials, who had been stripped of honors and property by the populist Tay Son. In their anti-Chinese propaganda, the Tay Son had depicted the mandarins, who epitomized Chinese influence in Vietnam, as being unsympathetic to the national aspirations of the Vietnamese people. But under Gia Long, Confucian education and the mandarin bureaucracy made a rapid recovery.

Gia Long retained the services of four Frenchmen who had enlisted with Pigneau de Behaine when he consolidated his power in 1802. Pigneau himself had died in battle in 1799. The Frenchmen were each given the title of "high mandarin." But the emperor's appointments of the four French mandarins did not indicate a prowestern policy. His friendship for the Frenchmen did not extend to France, the country they hoped to represent.

Gia Long laid the foundation of the new imperial regime, but it was his son, Minh Mang, who established a strong central government. Like his father, Minh Mang, who ruled from 1820 to 1841, believed that the first priority in conducting the affairs of state was to train competent officials. Total Confucian orthodoxy became the goal of his regime, and the number of bureaucrats increased significantly. The emperor knew that the mandarin educational system had become rigid over the centuries and was no longer a practical method for training the country's future rulers. He publicly deplored the limited nature of the subjects studied in schools. But he did little to reform the educational system. Students continued to master the history, literature, and traditions of China.

The message of Emperor Minh Mang (1820–1841) to outsiders, was "westerners go home." A traditional Confucian, he was angered by the political activities of Catholic missionaries and ultimately ordered ten of them executed.

Both Gia Long and Minh Mang, deeply influenced by their Confucian backgrounds, decided that Vietnam's national interest required strict isolation from the West. In fact, on his deathbed in 1820, Gia Long warned Minh Mang against showing any preference to any western country. As a result, Vietnam was unprepared either to learn from the increasingly aggressive western powers or to resist their colonial designs.

Minh Mang battles the missionaries

Minh Mang's strident Confucianism linked the Catholic issue with the controversy over western trade. Out of gratitude to his former French allies, Gia Long had never persecuted Christians, unlike his predecessors. He once said he wished that the pope had not condemned ancestor worship, barring forever a reconciliation between Confucianism and Christianity. Soon after succeeding his father, Minh Mang, however, outlawed the Catholic religion. He suspected

Europe and the King of Siam

The King of Siam's uniform symbolizes the western ways adopted by the rulers of Siam (modern Thailand) in their struggle to retain independence from France and England.

By the end of the nineteenth century only one country on the Southeast Asian peninsula had successfully retained its independence: Siam. To the west, Burma and the Malayan principalities had fallen under British domination. Vietnam, Cambodia, and Laos were incorporated into the French Indochina Union.

Even the wisest policy of the most gifted rulers had less to do with Siam's independence than the accident of Siam's location. The British colonies lay to its west; the French to the east. Both England and France recognized that any move by either into Siam would be construed by the other as a threat. Neither power acted to destroy Siamese independence.

Yet Siam (which did not take its contemporary name, Thailand, until the beginning of World War II) also had unusually flexible and sensible rulers. After facing enormous pressures from European powers in the seventeenth century, Siam shut its borders to the West until 1830. During this period of isolation, Siam, in a pattern remarkably similar to that of Vietnam, extended its influence southward and like Vietnam, Siam became one of the world's greatest rice exporters. But unlike Vietnam, Siam used its agricultural wealth to develop governmental institutions capable of responding to the pressures of the West. By the 1820s Siam was displaying its diplomatic flexibility. When a series of civil disorders broke out among the Malayan princes, Britain dispatched a warning to Siam to refrain from intervening. The Siamese heeded the warning, and Britain left Siam alone.

In the 1850s Siamese independence was guaranteed. In 1855 England succeeded in concluding a commercial treaty with Bangkok that opened up its ports to British commerce. In 1856 Siam offered the same concessions to the French. This ability to treat the rival powers equally helped preserve independence. Treating the French and English equally also involved "feeding the tigers." Siam was forced to cede to the two European powers over one hundred thousand square miles of territory which it claimed.

But as the Chinese discovered, concessions to foreign powers alone could not guarantee sovereignty. The age-old Siamese governmental control of trade hampered the new ways of doing business. So the nineteenth-century Siamese reformed their bureaucracy, passed European-influenced commercial laws, and adopted western tariff policies. These steps made foreign trade easier and so removed a major cause for European intervention. The new laws also placed the Siamese treasury on a sounder footing.

The openness of the Siamese court to European influence is perhaps best illustrated by the employment of an Englishwoman, Anna Leonowens, as governess to the royal children. The story of her service in Bangkok was later published as *Anna and the King of Siam* and was the basis of the Broadway musical, *The King and I*.

collusion between missionaries and western traders, who had begun using military means to gain economic control of Asia.

Nguyen officials reinforced anti-Christian feeling by sending hundreds of petitions to Minh Mang requesting that he forbid Christian proselytizing. The mandarins considered the beliefs and practices of Christianity superstitious. The mandarin bureaucracy also began to see its moral and social authority undermined by activist missionaries. Besides promising relief from suffering and eternal salvation, the priests attracted converts from among the hard-pressed peasant villagers by offering material benefits as well. Missionaries angered the mandarins by stepping in to resolve village disputes. This gave Christian villagers the means to settle cases without having to submit to the whims of the mandarins, who frequently demanded expensive gifts to decide a suit. As a result, the mandarins resented the missionaries' rising prestige, which threatened their status in the community.

Vietnam rejects modernization

The prevailing antimissionary mood among the emperors and their Confucian officials intensified hostility toward the West. Gia Long had imported western military hardware and expertise to defeat the Tay Son, but he turned a deaf ear to advocates of even modest cultural westernization.

But there were a few proponents of westernization among Vietnam's educated classes. By 1850 several Vietnamese scholars traveled abroad in Europe, China, and Japan and returned with proposals for the modernization of Vietnam. One of these men presented fifteen proposals to the Vietnamese court. He recommended, among other things, cooperating with western powers, teaching modern sciences in the schools, reforming the administration, and publishing newspapers. He also suggested that European experts be invited to Vietnam to assist in modernizing agriculture, developing commerce and industry, and reorganizing the army.

None of these far-sighted reformers, however, could persuade the emperor and his mandarins. The mandarins isolated the emperor from all innovative schemes and kept him ignorant of the modernization of Thailand and Japan. Since the central government controlled all publishing and the mandarins controlled the government, public expression of alternative viewpoints was severely limited.

This 1840 French drawing of the execution of three priests in Annam tells a bloody tale of martyrdom. The Vietnamese rulers' violent treatment of missionaries led to French military retaliation.

England's Asia

One of the most astonishing episodes in history is the story of the gradual British domination of Asia. The small European island, half a world away, did not even begin its Asian adventures until long after Portuguese, Spaniards, Frenchmen, and Dutchmen had already staked out claims in Asia. England was getting its own house in order.

By 1688 England became the first major state in European history to place its finances on a firm footing. Rather than wring every last penny out of an impoverished peasantry to support the government, the English taxed the wealth of the country, the landed gentry. This fiscal policy permitted the English to build their navy and to finance and fight the wars necessary for overseas expansion.

Though founded as early as 1600, the British East India Company, the major tool of British imperialism in Asia, did not assume a major role until after 1688. In 1698 the company founded the British settlement in Calcutta, destined to become—after London itself—the second capital of the British Empire. For the next half century the company battled with the French to gain supremacy in India. In the Seven Years War (1757–1763) the French lost Pondicherry, headquarters of their own East India Company, and saw their other ports neutralized. Clive's famous victory at Plassy in 1757 insured British success. Four more times before 1815 the English seized Pondicherry, each time returning it to the French at the conclusion of the war.

In Asia, English rule was represented not by the British government but solely by the privately owned British East India Company. Its Board of Control appointed the Court of Directors, ruling in Calcutta. This private "government" in Calcutta in turn appointed its own ambassadors to various Asian ports. So the representatives of this private corporation carried out diplomatic negotiations, concluded treaties, and even used its own troops.

But representatives of the company abused their independence, and in 1773 and 1784 Parliament restricted the company's political freedom (while not curtailing its commercial activities). Parliament now assumed responsibility for appointing the governor general and for overseeing the company's political policies. British subjects in India were placed under British law, with a supreme court established to maintain order.

Having assured themselves of the dominant position in India, the British took various steps to secure India's borders. They began by absorbing Burma, to the east, into India in two steps. To guard against the expansion of the Russian empire from the north, they then secured the "buffer" states of Afghanistan and Persia (now Iran) by installing on their thrones monarchs totally dependent upon the British. To insure safe trade between India and China the British moved against Malaya and in 1819 declared Singapore a colony directly under Parliament.

Singapore's strategic location controlled the narrow Straits of Malacca that provided the best route between Calcutta and China. It also provided England with a naval base in the event of war in the South China Sea. Thus, Singapore became an Asian Gibraltar—and more. Singapore was close enough to China to attract Chinese traders and quickly became one of the busiest ports in Asia. It thus became the long-sought depot where British trade with China could take place outside of the control of Chinese officials.

The British next struck at China itself. The most lucrative trade between British India and China was in opium, a trade technically banned by the Chinese government. In 1841 the British decisively defeated Chinese troops in the "Opium War." As a result, England won sole rights to distribute opium legally to the Chinese population. In addition, Britain acquired a new crown colony—Hong Kong. The French proved helpless as the British made the Indian Ocean and the South China Sea English lakes. From the court at Peking to the isolated tribes of northern Laos, goods for sale bore the label, "Made in England."

By 1850 the British navy was unsur-

England's Asian Empire at Its Height

British Empire

British Protectorate

Dates indicate British acquisition

— British Empire boundaries

— Modern boundaries

Modern names used throughout

passed. Britain's firm political base in India had turned it into an Asian power of the first order. Its bases in Singapore and Hong Kong provided a nearly impregnable line of defense. It followed a clear policy of protecting its commercial interests above all other considerations, and its staff of civil servants and diplomats had much experience in the four corners of the world and possessed high professional standards.

By contrast the French had virtually no Asian territory and no bases. Their commercial enterprises were hardly developed. They lacked experienced diplomats and relied instead on missionaries whose work of religious conversion often created more distrust than cooperation. No wonder that in 1855, on the eve of the French conquest of Indochina, a French diplomat was forced to acknowledge that in the Orient "fear of the English is the beginning of wisdom."

Thus, by the midnineteenth century, the Nguyen rulers found themselves at a dead end. The failure of their reforms and the increased power handed over to the mandarins had alienated vast numbers of peasants. Furthermore, their antimissionary policies appeared to many peasants to be directed against those who tried to help them. By rejecting all proposals to modernize Vietnamese society the Nguyen left themselves virtually impotent against the power of the West. Only the reservoir of nationalist feeling, nurtured over two thousand years, remained to do battle against the French as they renewed their attempt to create in Vietnam their long-sought Asian colony.

France returns to Asia

The antimissionary policy of the Nguyen ultimately provided France with its opportunity to intervene in Vietnam. France, hindered by political instability at home, was slow to take advantage of the situation because problems of a handful of priests thousands of miles away paled in comparison to France's domestic upheaval in the early 1830s. The revolution of July 1830 drove the French Bourbons from power. Their successor, the July Monarchy of Louis Philippe, prince of Orléans, was greeted with total hostility by Europe's conservative leaders. To avoid complete isolation, Louis Philippe's government achieved a rapprochement with England. Friendship with England meant taking care not to arouse British suspicions in the Far East. Once again, all that was left France in Asia was missionary work.

Minh Mang's continued harassment of Christians made the priests' work difficult. But when in 1837 and 1838 he executed ten missionaries for engaging in political intrigue he had to back down. France protested the treatment of its missionaries, and in an unprecedented move, Minh Mang sent a deputation to Calcutta, Paris, and London to quiet European concerns. He begged Europe's leaders to declare Vietnam off limits to missionaries: If no churchmen went to Vietnam, he argued, there would be no confrontations. But Minh Mang's argument failed to convince France.

When the emperor died in 1841, his successor,

Thieu Tri, further moderated Vietnamese anti-Christian sentiments. His policies, however, could not avert a decade of gunboat diplomacy by France in support of its missionaries. France secured the release of five jailed missionaries in 1843 when gunboats sailed into Tourane, later called Da Nang. In 1847, after two French missionaries were condemned to death but pardoned and deported to Singapore, French naval officers boarded and disabled two Vietnamese warships. Fearing imminent attack, the French bombarded the stationary ships, killing many Vietnamese. That same year Thieu Tri died. His successor Tu Duc proved more anti-Christian and antiwestern. French foreign policy was inconsistent, reacting to the independent initiatives of missionaries rather than following any rational plan conceived in Paris.

In 1848 the July Monarchy came to an end after France's third revolution in sixty years. Its successor, the Second Republic, was uninterested in Asia and in any case had little power to achieve much abroad. So Vietnam received a short respite from French pressure.

But in 1849 the French elected Louis Napoleon, nephew of Napoleon Bonaparte, as president of the Second Republic. By 1852 Louis Napoleon had dismissed the republic's parliament and declared the "Second Empire," crowning himself Emperor Napoleon III. The Second Empire, proclaimed Napoleon III, would restore France to its rightful glory. Hue shuddered, and with good reason. Under its new emperor and new imperialist policies, France would win its first colony in Southeast Asia.

Louis Napoleon's imperial dream

Fulfillment of France's imperial dream took more than a decade after Napoleon III first claimed his title. The early foreign policy of the Second Empire suffered from bumbling incompetence. In 1856, faced with increased pleas for help from missionaries, the French foreign office began a diplomatic campaign in the Far East which proved to be a last effort to gain satisfaction in Vietnam without taking over the country. The mission began in Siam, where France signed a commercial treaty. The French consuls failed to bring gifts for the Siamese, angering the court at the outset. Seemingly unaware that Siam considered Cambodia its vassal state, the French then told Bangkok that they intended to negotiate directly with Cambodia and seize a Cambodian island. Siamese anger must have turned to bewilderment when the

Captain John Briggs, the first person to reach Vietnam sailing under the American flag. Almost nothing is known of his voyage, but it did not encourage others to follow him. More than fifteen years lapsed before another American arrived.

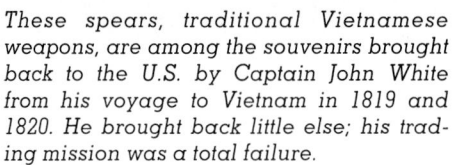

These spears, traditional Vietnamese weapons, are among the souvenirs brought back to the U.S. by Captain John White from his voyage to Vietnam in 1819 and 1820. He brought back little else; his trading mission was a total failure.

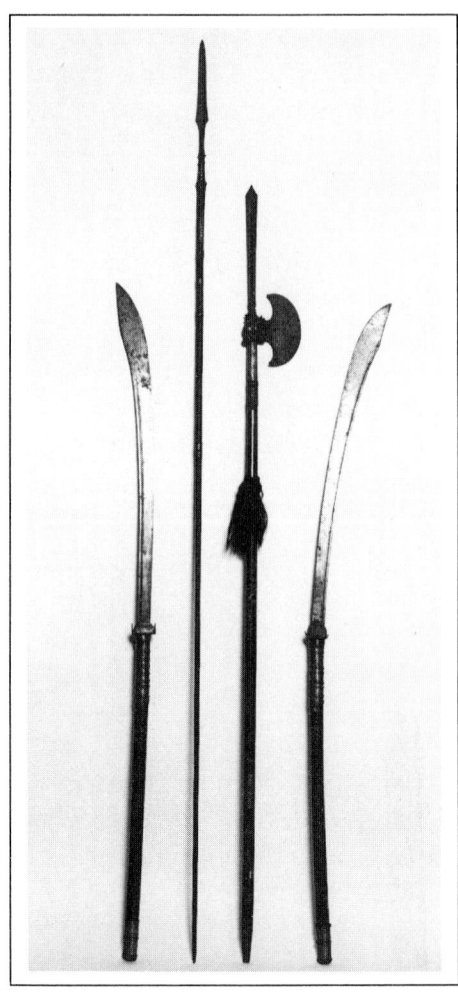

Americans in Vietnam: The First Encounters

It did not take the newly created United States of America long to imitate older European nations in developing trade relations in the Far East. The trading opportunities of the former British colonies had been restricted by the monopoly of the British East India Company. But when the United States became independent in 1783 it was left free to develop its own relationships with Asian nations. In 1803 Captain John Briggs of the United States Navy became the first American to land on Vietnamese soil. Little is known of his journey, but it is unlikely that he achieved much success. More than fifteen years passed before another naval officer, John White, sailing from Salem, Massachusetts, reached Vietnamese waters in 1819.

White left an extensive journal detailing his experiences in Vietnam and describing his failure to negotiate trade agreements for Vietnamese sugar. He was contemptuous of the delaying tactics and obstructionism of the Vietnamese mandarins, unaware that they were under orders to discourage trade with western powers. Like most Americans, then

and now, he found Vietnamese food unappetizing and was struck by the unclean conditions in Saigon. His reactions to Saigon, Vietnam's growing frontier city, were not unlike those felt by Europeans exposed to America's unsettled West. Ultimately he left Vietnam with an empty ship and recovered his losses only by purchasing cargo in other Asian ports.

A more formal mission to Vietnam was initiated by the American government in 1832. Captain Edmund Roberts, arriving with a letter from Secretary of State Livingston, written on behalf of President Andrew Jackson, attempted to gain an audience with Emperor Minh Mang in the hopes of arranging normal diplomatic relations between the two countries. The American mission was treated with great ceremony, feted at an elaborate banquet (they complained about the food), but not introduced to the emperor. The Vietnamese annals report that Minh Mang refused to grant the mission an audience because the letter from President Jackson failed to meet the stringent requirements of Asian protocol. Jackson had addressed

the emperor as "Great and Good Friend" rather than by name, as Vietnamese custom dictated. Given the emperor's policy of isolation from the West it is unlikely that the mission would have been successful in any case.

With these diplomatic failures, the Americans, like the British, gave up hope of establishing any satisfactory trade relations with Vietnam. As did the European powers, Americans participated in the gunboat diplomacy of the 1840s and 1850s. In 1845 Captain Percival, commanding the USS *Constitution*, arrived in Tourane Harbor to demand the release of an imprisoned French missionary. Percival refused to believe the Vietnamese promise to hand him over to the French and ordered the shelling of the harbor. With this futile gesture, Old Ironsides left Vietnamese waters en route to more noble missions. But Americans, like the Europeans before them, had been impressed with the qualities of Tourane Harbor. When Admiral Perry completed his famous voyage to Japan, he urged President Polk to acquire an American

port in Asia, suggesting Tourane. Polk, however, replied that the establishment of American sovereignty on Asian soil would be "incompatible with our system of government."

Knowledge that the American system of government differed from those of Europe slowly became apparent to Asian rulers, including the Vietnamese. When the French temporarily seized Hanoi in 1873, Emperor Tu Duc sent an ambassador to the United States, feeling that this democratic country would defend Vietnam against European imperialists. The envoy was well received, but when the French voluntarily evacuated Hanoi, U.S. assistance was no longer needed.

A decade later, however, the French again occupied Hanoi, this time permanently. The French became embroiled in a war with the Chinese, who had answered a Vietnamese call for aid. Initially, when neither side was able to gain a decisive edge, the Vietnamese and Chinese asked the United States to arbitrate the future of Vietnam. Any possibility that the U.S. might become the ultimate savior

The USS Constitution shelled Tourane in 1845. In the only known photograph of "Old Ironsides" under sail, the ship is seen off the coast of Virginia years after the South China Sea voyage.

of Vietnamese independence was dashed when the French refused to agree to American mediation. The French were certain that American opinion would go against them.

When the French ultimately secured their position in Vietnam, the United States adjusted to the new situation as they had to other European conquests in Asia and Africa. America soon became one of the leading trading partners with French Indochina. Shortly after the beginning of the twentieth century, the United States gained possession of the Philippine Islands. America had joined the Europeans as an Asian power with its own Asian interests and its own Asian policy. The stage was set, but it was still more than a half century before the curtain was to rise.

French asked them to help persuade the Vietnamese to negotiate in good faith—without knowing that Vietnam and Siam were bitter enemies.

With this "preparation," the French sent a naval squadron and diplomatic mission to Tourane. A Vietnamese mandarin would later say of the failed mission, "The French barked like dogs, but later ran away like goats." The naval force arrived first and immediately shelled Tourane Harbor. The diplomats, however, were caught in a typhoon and were unavailable to take advantage of the naval attack. When the diplomats finally arrived five months later, the naval force was gone, forced to resupply. By then the negotiating team had no means to force concessions from Hue and left in failure. The damage to French prestige was equaled only by the suffering the preposterous expedition brought to French missionaries.

Napoleon III then decided it was time to reassess his Indochina policy. In 1857 he appointed a commission to recommend further action. This panel would change Vietnam's destiny: Its members suggested the formation of a "protectorate" over Vietnam at an "opportune moment." They argued for the need of a French port in Southeast Asia, pointing out that Vietnam was not an area of English interest.

Scarcely had Napoleon III received these recommendations than a new crisis erupted in Vietnam. In the fall of 1857 a Spanish missionary, Monsignor Diaz, was executed. Missionaries begged Napoleon III, defender of the nation's prestige and its faith, to intervene. The Paris foreign office demurred. Having heard that Vietnamese defenses were being strengthened, they believed that a substantial force would be needed to force negotiations. The foreign office also doubted the missionaries' reports of riches to be won.

Despite all this, Napoleon III decided to intervene. A week later the Spanish government eagerly accepted his offer to join France in avenging Diaz's execution.

The French move in

But even at this last moment, Vietnam's fate was tied to that of its great neighbor to the north. Napoleon first ordered Admiral Rigault de Genouilly, the commander of the expedition, to the Far East to lead the French half of a joint military mission with England. The French and English hoped to remove the last obstacles to trade with China. In 1858 a combined naval force sailed up the Arrow River threatening to raid Peking unless China relented on the trade issue. The Chinese eventually gave in, even granting Europeans a diplomatic quarter in Peking in 1861.

China thus remained the big prize in Asia, even as the French prepared to unleash their military power against Vietnam. In the nineteenth century Vietnam's problem—to echo the lament of Mexican peasants—remained what it had been for two thousand years: Vietnam was too close to China, yet too far from heaven.

Before a satisfactory treaty with China could be reached, however, Genouilly sailed for Vietnam, intending to attack Hue. Genouilly's problems began almost as soon as he entered Tourane Bay on August 31, 1858. Like many French and American military commanders to follow him a century later, Genouilly suffered from inappropriate military equipment, misleading intelligence reports, and a poor understanding of the people he was about to confront.

To begin with, the French vessels were too large to navigate the river from Tourane to Hue. In addition, missionaries had provided Genouilly with "intelligence" reports indicating that Hue would surrender at the first sign of force, that Vietnamese Christians would rise against the authorities, that the natives would labor for the French, and that mandarin control over the Vietnamese had slipped. None of these proved true, and the imperial Vietnamese forces massed near Tourane stood silent as they watched tropical disease take its toll on the French stranded in the harbor.

After heated debate between Genouilly and his unperceptive missionary advisers, the admiral disregarded a final piece of advice. The missionaries had finally urged Genouilly to sail against the monsoon winds and attack in the North, where Christians were more numerous. Instead, Genouilly dispatched one missionary to Hong Kong to secure reinforcements and sailed south, with the monsoon, to attack Saigon.

On February 17, 1859, the citadel at Saigon fell to the French. Genouilly issued an enthusiastic dispatch to Paris lauding the riches of the Mekong Delta. He also reported that hopes of finding native collaborators should be dismissed. Just as they had when faced with similar situations in the past, the Vietnamese refused to negotiate despite the occupation of Saigon. With the mission apparently bogged down, Genouilly was replaced by Admiral Page in October 1859.

France wins its colony

Page quickly endorsed his predecessor's analysis: The Mekong Delta was well worth more effort. He recommended annexing Saigon and the surrounding territory. Until Page announced his new objectives, Napoleon III had almost decided to scrap the entire campaign. The French had made no progress toward gaining their most minimal goals, let alone establishing a protectorate over Vietnam. With the new admiral's adjusted plans, however, the mission was saved. France's "opportune moment" was at hand.

Admiral Charner and three thousand French troops arrived in Saigon in February 1861 to relieve Admiral Page's garrison. In July Charner claimed Saigon for France. Vietnamese guerrillas harassed the French, but by 1862 France was firmly in control of the three provinces surrounding Saigon: Dinh Tuong, Gia Dinh, and Bien Hoa. Hue continued fighting, sure that disease and guerrilla warfare would turn back the French. French losses were high and Paris sent no reinforcements.

Suddenly Emperor Tu Duc agreed to peace in June 1862. Civil war had broken out in Tonkin led by supporters of the old Le dynasty, forcing Tu Duc to sacrifice the South to retain his throne. The peace treaty giving France the three provinces and the island of Poulo Condore, a $4 million indemnity, and religious liberty was ratified April 14, 1863. In addition, Tourane and two other ports were opened to French ships. Finally, France was granted power to veto any other foreign alliances that Hue might attempt to conclude. The Spanish, for their efforts, received half of the $4 million.

France finally had its Asian port. But Saigon had become a shadow of what it once was. In 1860 the population of Saigon-Cholon had been nearly two hundred thousand. When the French assumed control most people fled, and the population declined to twenty-five thousand. The mandarins fled to the provinces still under the control of Hue. French administration of the territories was almost nonexistent: There was little left to administer. With his new holdings turning to ghost towns, Napoleon III considered renegotiating the treaty with Hue. But any hope of rebuilding Saigon through a new treaty ended when France learned that Hue was attempting to install a pro-Vietnamese pretender on the Cambodian throne.

The French viewed this attempt to turn Cambodia against France as a threat to the three occupied provinces of southern Vietnam. Moreover, France had signed a treaty of protection with Cambodia in 1863 and viewed that country as falling within its sphere of influence. The new French governor general of Saigon, Admiral de la Grandière, met the challenge in 1867 by occupying three western provinces, Vinh Long, Chau Doc, and Ha Tien. French power was now consolidated from Saigon to Phnom Penh, and Napoleon III discarded any thoughts of revising the earlier treaty. Although its latest conquest was not ratified until 1874, France's occupation of the South was complete: Cochin China became a French colony.

Napoleon III would have little time to reap the benefits of his new dominion. Only four years after the

In 1858 the misadventures of the French ship, Le Coq Gaulois, brought it to Tourane (Da Nang) under Admiral Genouilly. Hue was the ship's destination, but the waterway from Tourane to the imperial capital could not be navigated by large vessels. Tropical heat and disease ravaged his stranded fleet.

colony's formation, France experienced another revolution and change of regime. Napoleon III's empire fell with his defeat in the Franco-Prussian War in 1870. After a period of destructive civil war, the Third Republic was formed by a fragile coalition of conservatives. In keeping with its precarious hold on French power, the new republic followed a policy of extreme caution in Asia. New initiatives would come from the French navy, acting independently of Paris and already in control of Cochin China.

The French turn north

The first of the naval adventures began in 1873, when a French merchant of some disrepute, Jean Depuis, started delivering armaments to southern China. Depuis had secured permission from Vietnamese authorities to deliver the arms via the Red River, usually closed to western ships. Officials in Paris, ever cautious, had approved the mission but advised Depuis that it was undertaken entirely at his own risk. Depuis made his shipment, returning to Hanoi with a new contract to provide salt to China's Yunnan Province. When Depuis attempted to deliver the salt, Vietnamese authorities blocked the ascent up the Red River, having no wish to see it used as a French highway. Depuis refused to abandon his attempt and, despite the warning from Paris not to expect help, sent a plea to Saigon for support. Hue, too, had sent word to Saigon: Remove the troublesome merchant.

The new governor general of Cochin China, Admiral Dupré, saw in the double request a chance to fulfill France's long-standing hope of controlling northern Vietnam. He dispatched to Hanoi a young captain, Francis Garnier, hero of the 1866 Mekong River expedition into China. (See Picture Essay.) Accompanied by only a small force, Garnier was ostensibly ordered to dislodge Depuis. But under secret orders from Dupré, Garnier was to find some small pretext to open fire and capture the Hanoi citadel, forcing Hue to negotiate.

Arriving in Hanoi in mid-October, Garnier took offense at "the insufficient quarters for his men." To remedy this "insult," Garnier bombarded the Hanoi citadel and declared the Red River open to international traffic. On October 20, 1873, he captured the citadel, while pro-French forces—mostly Vietnamese Catholics—occupied many key coastal points.

Paris greeted news of Garnier's exploits with an immediate uproar. The Chamber of Deputies renounced the mission. Dupré, in Saigon, disavowed any foreknowledge of Garnier's intentions and sent as negotiator to Hue a certain M. Philastre, noted for his sympathetic attitude toward the Vietnamese. A month after Garnier occupied the Hanoi citadel, he was killed in battle by Chinese pirates aiding the Vietnamese government.

Philastre, arriving in Hue on January 29, 1874, ordered the French strongholds evacuated. On March 15 he concluded a treaty with Hue. France received much more than expected from the fiasco. Under the agreement, France renounced any intention of acquiring Tonkin. In exchange, the Red River was opened to international traffic, French control of all six provinces of Cochin China was finally acknowledged, and the Hue government was required to ask France for assistance in the event of a foreign crisis.

Emperor Tu Duc's actions following the signing of the treaty showed what he thought of the agreement and of France's claims to dominion over his country. He revived the traditional practice of sending tribute to China as if to emphasize, and threaten France with, that country's protectorate over Vietnam. The losers were Vietnamese Christians—over twenty thousand were reportedly killed as French collaborators.

France conquers Vietnam

If Vietnam was devious in upholding the treaty, the French simply turned their backs on the agreement. France's foreign policy took a bold turn in 1879 when popular forces finally won an election and took control of the Third Republic from the conservatives. The new republican leaders enjoyed the strongest domestic support of any French government in the nineteenth century, and the confidence of their foreign policy reflected it.

With the support of the new government, Le Myre de Vilers, now governor general of Cochin China, in 1883 dispatched a force to Hanoi led by Captain Henri Rivière. His mission: to occupy Hanoi and force the Hue government to grant France a protectorate over Vietnam. The pretext: none. Like Garnier, Rivière quickly seized the citadel in Hanoi and other coastal cities. Like Garnier, Rivière was killed by pirates soon after his victory. But the effect on Paris was the opposite of what Garnier's had been ten years earlier. Even before news of Rivière's death reached Paris, the Chamber of Deputies had appropriated funds to support a full expeditionary force. In August this force began the twelve-year pacification of northern Vietnam. Emperor Tu Duc had already died in July 1883. His mandarins reported that the emperor passed away "with curses against the invader on his lips," a victim of sorrow at seeing "foreigners invade and devastate his empire."

The years following Tu Duc's death were dominated by war and intrigue. After his death, rule was shared by two regents. Three of Tu Duc's successors died under mysterious circumstances, almost surely the victims of the regents' desire for power over Vietnam. Despite their ruthlessness, the regents in Hue retained the presence of mind to call China, Vietnam's age-old protector, to the aid of Vietnamese sovereignty. China's renewed interest in Hue's affairs gave France a new enemy, and in 1883 war broke out between the two countries over control of Tonkin. French forces took nearly a year to convince the Chinese that Tonkin belonged to France.

With the peace concluded between France and China in June 1884, China relinquished the Imperial Seal of Vietnam. The court at Peking had kept the seal as a symbol of ancient Chinese suzerainty over Vietnam. With great fanfare the French consul in Hue shattered the seal and with it the fragile links which had tied Vietnam and China together for two thousand years. For the first time the fate of Vietnam would be completely out of the hands of the Chinese.

French consolidate power

But Vietnam was hardly able to enjoy this development. Rather, more and more authority over Vietnam fell to France. Under a treaty forced upon Hue, the French military could occupy any part of the kingdom, France could determine the fiscal affairs of Vietnam, and all foreign loans required French approval. When the third of Tu Duc's successors died at the hands of the regents, the French insisted that they approve the selection of the new emperor. With France's blessing a thirteen-year-old boy, Ham Nghi, was selected. At Ham Nghi's investiture, the Vietnamese witnessed the most blatant of French insults. French envoys shocked the court by entering the palace through the center gates—gates previously used only by Vietnam's old protectors, the ambassadors of the Celestial Kingdom of China.

But French control of Tonkin was not yet secured and perhaps never would be. Faced with a series of insults to the Vietnamese royal family, the court at

Francis Garnier (above) and Henri Rivière suffered tandem fates, ten years apart: Each died at the hands of pirates while trying to sack Hanoi. Rivière, at least, had his country's support for his mission. Garnier's earlier venture was decried at home.

Hue began to understand the true nature of French "protection." In July 1885 Hue decided that all-out war against the French was the only alternative. Vietnamese troops, numbering, according to the French, thirty thousand, mustered in the Hue citadel to attack the French resident general, General de Courcy, and his one hundred and fifty men. Despite the overwhelming odds, de Courcy routed the Vietnamese army. But the court had already fled to the mountains, issuing an edict calling for a popular rising against the French. For ten more years the Vietnamese engaged French troops in guerrilla wars in the jungles, mountains, and villages of Tonkin. The struggle against foreign domination, a struggle which for centuries had shaped the destiny of the Vietnamese people, had been renewed.

The Mekong River Expedition

When the French established sovereignty along the banks of the Mekong River in 1863, they had acquired their first colony in Asia. But they were, if anything, further from their goal of establishing in Vietnam a base from which they could tap the trading riches of China. It did not take them long, however, to recognize a potential river way into southern China in the uncharted, but generally northward, course of the Mekong River. In 1866 Governor General de la Grandière appointed an expedition to find the source of the Mekong, thought to be in some remote mountainous region of western China. De la Grandière hoped to determine whether the river provided a navigable waterway to the Chinese border.

The resulting expedition had all the adventure of the search for the source of the Nile River in Africa. De la Grandière's choice of commander of the expedition was an experienced and respected French naval officer, Doudard de Lagrée. His second-in-command was a younger, tempestuous officer, Francis Garnier, who had been one of the leading advocates of the expedition. The group departed from Phnom Penh on June 5, 1866, and eight days later arrived at the first of the Mekong's many rapids, the Sambor Rapids near Kratie in northern Cambodia.

After six days of struggle, often carrying their boats along the shore, the explorers determined that the rapids were unnavigable, even for steam-powered craft. Commander Lagrée decided that the mission would not lead to expanded commerce and could only be of geographic and scientific significance, matters of secondary importance to the welfare of his men. Garnier, however, still hoped that a way could be found to navigate the Mekong and thereby bring the riches of China to the new French port of Saigon. The initiative in planning the expedition increasingly fell to the more determined Garnier.

Lagrée's men had tremendous respect for their leader, which held the group together during its travel through the exhausting climate and harsh terrain of northern Laos. But it was Garnier's determination that brought them into China and eventually to the valley of the Yangtze River, the first Europeans since Marco Polo to view the great Chinese river so far from the sea.

Shortly after it crossed the Chinese border, the explorers gave up hope of following the Mekong to its source. Instead, they turned east for the port of Shanghai, and ultimately home. Lagrée fell victim to a fatal tropical disease, and his body was respectfully borne by the men for an honorable burial on the "French soil" of Saigon.

But even in its hour of failure the expedition begot another dream. Garnier was the first to notice that the small rivers east of the Mekong did not, as logic might suggest, flow back into that great river. Rather they flowed eastward, indicating the presence of yet another major waterway. That other river turned out to be the Red River, flowing down from southern China into Vietnam's Tonkin Delta. If the Mekong did not provide a river way into China, thought Garnier, perhaps the Red River would. But in 1866 the Tonkin Delta lay beyond French power, in the still independent northern portion of Vietnam. Seven years later Garnier led his final mission, at the cost of his life, in an attempt to bring that river under French control.

Under Colonial Rule

After the middle of the nineteenth century the various European powers tried to impose their values and culture on the rest of the world, and the era of imperialism began. They did so with little foreknowledge of the impact they would have upon their new subjects. Imperialism often involved shameless exploitation of the labor and wealth of foreign lands. This was particularly true in east Asia, where peoples with a strong sense of nationhood and civilizations in many ways more "developed" than that of the West took great pride in their history.

French imperial rule in Indochina often showed imperialism at its worst. By imposing their own standards and values upon Vietnam's traditional society, the French cut that society loose from its ancient moorings.

One result of French rule in Vietnam stands out among all others. The French found Vietnam a country of *landowning* peasants; less than a century later they left it a country of *landless* peas-

ants. The suffering that accompanied this process affected every aspect of Vietnamese life. The transformation into a landless peasantry, more than anything else, haunted the Vietnamese and provides the essential backdrop for modern Vietnamese history.

This dispossession did not come about solely because the French were greedy or corrupt. It was also the result of good French intentions that failed. Most important it came about because the French unleashed forces which rewarded and protected those Vietnamese who ruined and despoiled their countrymen.

The civilizing mission

The colony established in Cochin China in 1863 was not France's first. By 1848 Frenchmen had already begun colonizing Algeria. In the next fifteen years a distinctly French theory of colonization emerged, captured in the phrase *mission civilisatrice*, or civilizing mission. If the French had indeed achieved the highest level of civilization, as they sincerely thought, then it was obviously their moral duty to raise other peoples to that level. The result was the official French colonial policy of "assimilation."

In Cochin China in 1863, and later in the rest of Vietnam, this meant that the Vietnamese were regarded as children, to be brought up in the exact image of their French "parents." The style of the parenthood was severe: "Father knows best." The Vietnamese were to have no choice but to become Frenchmen.

The French called their colonies "France, Overseas," meaning that the colonies were to become part of the sacred soil of the motherland. As its goal French colonial rule envisioned granting to Vietnam the status of one or more French *départements* (roughly the equivalent of American statehood). Perhaps someday Vietnamese, wearing their berets, would pass their evenings sipping wine at sidewalk cafes, engaged in animated conversations in the French language. This is only a slightly exaggerated version of what the policy of assimilation meant. It was destined to fail.

The colonial policy of the French was quite different from that of the British. From the moment that Parliament assumed full responsibility for India in 1859, the English announced that their eventual goal was an independent India, at some distant and unspecified date. The British were, at least in theory, permissive parents. They would set an example for the native Indians, from which they could draw knowledge and guidance in developing their own ability for self-government. But the Indians were not destined to become Englishmen. Rather, so the theory went, they would remain Indians, enriched by the experience of British rule.

Some of the French administrators in Vietnam actually believed the British theory rather than their own. Although it never supplanted the official assimilationist theory accepted in Paris, it was sufficiently strong in the colonies to earn its own name: "associationism." Some associationists simply acknowledged that it was impossible to govern according to official assimilationist theory. Others disliked the idea of brushing aside all Vietnamese tradition and hoped that the valuable part of it would be retained to mix with French experiences. In practice, both theories collided equally with the reality of colonial rule: It was imposed with the use of force and only force could sustain it.

From the outset of French rule in Vietnam, this dependency on force violated Confucian political theory. Whereas Confucian government was based on basic virtues following proper ritual and conduct, French rule was based on superior arms. The French rulers displayed none of the virtues which in the eyes of the Vietnamese would have legitimized government.

As a result, after Hue agreed to cede the first three provinces of Cochin China to the French, the mandarins simply fled or retired to their homes. The administration of Cochin China therefore required immediate reform. After 1867 the six provinces ruled by the French were divided into twenty-four districts. Each was headed by an inspector of native affairs drawn from the French military personnel assigned to Vietnam. The French, unlike the British, lacked a professional colonial service. These military governors

France builds the Indochina Union

France's conquest of Vietnam proved its most important, but not its only, colonial acquisition in Southeast Asia. By 1893 France also controlled the entire eastern portion of the Indochina Peninsula, including the modern countries of Vietnam, Cambodia, and Laos.

The French conquest of Cambodia dates from 1863, and in many ways was a continuation of a centuries-old Vietnamese policy. In acquiring Cochin China, France also inherited Vietnam's claims of overlordship over Cambodia. For a hundred years Vietnam and Siam had quarreled over Cambodia, each of them gradually absorbing more of Cambodian territory. If the French had not come, Cambodia would probably have ceased to exist as an independent nation. But the French imposed their will on Cambodia and Siam. Using the old Vietnamese claims, in 1863 they forced King Norodom of Cambodia, not yet installed on the throne, to sign a treaty of protection. Siam objected, and scattered fighting ensued between the French and Siamese.

King Norodom, meanwhile, made plans to have himself crowned in Bangkok, in hopes of asserting his independence against France. But the French literally took him prisoner and crowned him themselves in Phnom Penh. In 1867 the situation was finally stabilized by a treaty between France and Siam. Siam acknowledged the French protectorate over Cambodia and received in exchange the three western provinces of Cambodia. King Norodom never forgave the French for dismembering his country. These provinces were returned to the newly independent Cambodia by the Geneva Convention in 1954.

Cambodia proved to be a difficult land for the French to "protect." King Norodom, under constant pressure by French advisers, agreed to a number of reforms but never carried them out. While many of these reforms were obviously overdue, such as the abolition of slavery, Norodom was fearful lest the reforms destroy Cambodia's traditional culture. By 1877 Cambodia had changed little under the French protectorate.

The French governor general of Cochin China and Cambodia, Le Myre de Vilers, looked to recent Cambodian history for a possible solution. Noting that in the 1830s and 1840s Vietnamese peasants had totally "vietnamized" eastern Cambodia and had done much to develop the economy of Phnom Penh, he suggested to Paris that the French encourage a mass migration of Vietnamese into Cambodia. He believed that within fifty years the "natural superiority" of the Vietnamese would dominate the Cambodians, and administration of the country would pose no more problems.

The French encouraged this migration, but never to the extent suggested by Le Myre de Vilers. Rather they decided to wait for King Norodom's death. Finally, in 1904 they were able to install his more pliable half brother Sisowath on the throne and begin the long-delayed process of insuring French domination of Cambodia.

The French conquest of Laos, like that of Cambodia, was based on Vietnam's traditional claims of suzerainty over the Laotians. But unlike its claims to Cambodia, this suzerainty was a dead letter by the time the French arrived on the Laotian border, after establishing the protectorate over northern Vietnam in 1883.

French interest in Laos was largely geographic. Noting English advances into northern Burma, Laos' northwestern neighbor, the French feared that their colonial rivals would use Laos to find a land route to southern China. (French fears were not entirely unfounded as the Burma Road to China of World War II fame proved.) The French, in addition, still entertained hopes of using the Mekong River as a route to China and wanted to secure control of the entire course of the river. Ultimately, the sparsely populated Laotian territory would provide a needed buffer between English territory in Burma and the more valuable French holdings in Tonkin.

In 1893, having deployed their military to the gates of Bangkok, the French forced the Siamese to recognize their claims, and the French protectorate of Laos was established. Because of its isolation and poverty Laos scarcely felt the effects of French domination. The independent Laos of the Geneva accords of 1954 was largely the traditional society that the French had found a century earlier.

In order to provide for uniform administration of these territories, the French created the Indochina Union in 1887. After the inclusion of Laos in 1893, the union consisted of five administrative areas, each theoretically equal although ruled under differing conditions. Vietnam contributed three of the units: the colony of Cochin China, where the French ruled directly with their own administration, and the protectorates of Annam and Tonkin, where a native administration continued to exist but increasingly under the power of the French. The protectorates of Cambodia and Laos formed the other two units.

Hanoi served as the capital of the entire union, with the governor general of French Indochina serving simultaneously as resident superior of Tonkin. The lieutenant governor general served as resident superior of Cochin China in Saigon. With French commercial interests concentrated in the South and with the large French bureaucracy serving there, governors general often had a difficult battle to maintain control over Saigon. Residents superior also sat in the capitals of the other three administrative units: Hue in Annam, Phnom Penh in Cambodia, and Vientiane in Laos.

served for only short terms until their military assignments ended. They seldom gained much knowledge of the people they ruled.

Vietnam's new profession

After a few futile efforts to create a bureaucracy educated in the language and history of Vietnam, the French gave up and tried to rule their subjects in the French language, which few Vietnamese could understand. Although the administration later tried to require Frenchmen to learn Vietnamese as a prerequisite for civil service, this effort proved a failure. A government survey in 1910 revealed that in all of Vietnam only *three* Frenchmen were sufficiently fluent in Vietnamese to carry on the complex business of administration. Since few Vietnamese learned more than a smattering of French, a blow was all too often a substitute for a word.

A new native profession arose from France's efforts to overcome the language and cultural barriers: the Vietnamese interpreter. Many of the early interpreters in Cochin China were Catholics who had picked up some French from the missionaries. Later, chauffeurs, houseboys, and others who had learned enough French to communicate in their work also took up interpreting.

Most French administrators felt comfortable with these Vietnamese who "knew their place." Having acquired a rudimentary knowledge of the French system, these Vietnamese became the "culture brokers" in the dealings between the two races, the essential middlemen between the French and the Vietnamese. Their position gave them many opportunities to manipulate the process for their own personal gain at the expense of their fellow Vietnamese. Indispensable and able to ingratiate themselves with the French, they got away with almost anything. These middlemen appeared over and over again during the French occupation. These were the "dependable Vietnamese." If one of their victims did try to complain to the authorities, how could he do it except through the middlemen?

In creating the culture brokers, the French worsened a persistent problem of the traditional Confucian bureaucracy—the identification of the civil servant as a member of a distinct class, separate from the rest of the people. This legacy produced a serious problem for both Vietnams after 1954, as each strove to create bureaucracies trusted by the masses.

Often a culture broker became "village secretary,"

because he could understand French decrees and communicate with French administrators. In Tanan Province in 1895 the French discovered that a village secretary had given peasants tax receipts for amounts far less than they had actually paid and had pocketed the difference. Using the forced labor intended for public works, he had built ten guardhouses on his own property. For guards he had recruited the local militia, paid from the public treasury. When French surveyors came to the village to record the owners of property, he told the peasants that the surveyors were there to steal their property. He ordered them to refuse cooperation. The peasants depended upon him rather than on legal titles for their property.

Corruption was usually uncovered only when competing interests within the village had the resources

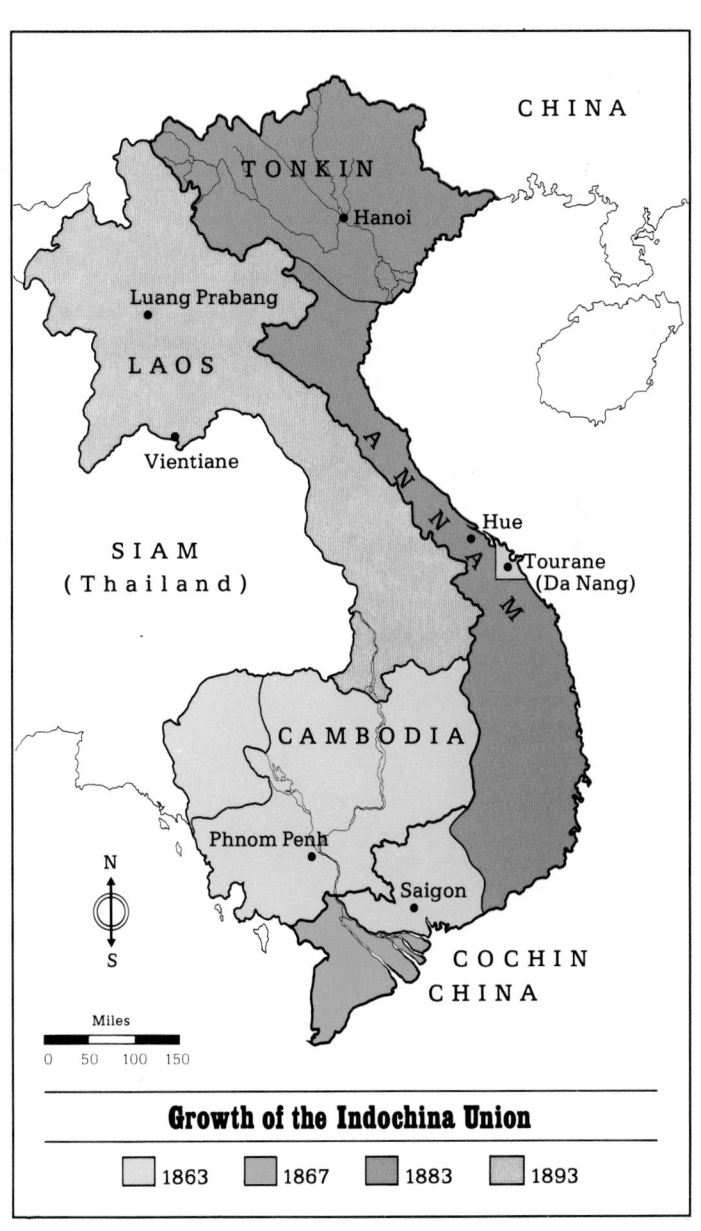

Growth of the Indochina Union

⬜ 1863 ⬜ 1867 ⬜ 1883 ⬜ 1893

to bring their complaint to somebody high up in the French administration. In such cases justice was usually rendered. But often the middleman was able to create alliances with the local notables and thus protect himself against a complaint to higher authority. In 1917 a culture broker who had learned a little French during a few years primary schooling entered a village in Cochin China and married the daughter of a notable. With his knowledge of the western alphabet he was recruited to become mayor, largely a clerical position.

He was subsequently discovered embezzling from the village treasury, but his father-in-law saved him from punishment by repaying his theft. He was forced to resign as mayor, but the village had to retain him on the Council of Notables, since he was the only person able to write in Roman script. He later applied for the higher post of assistant district chief. The French overlooked his past record as an embezzler and chose him over more respected competition. He had the connections.

A bureaucrat's dream

France's inability to develop a competent foreign service allowed the middlemen to play an important role in the French administration. The French lack of competence extended, with a few notable exceptions, to the very top colonial officials. Admiral de la Grandière served as the third governor general of Cochin China until 1868. During the next eleven years, before the beginning of civilian government, nine successive military men served as governors general. This naturally caused a constant shifting of policies. Without experience in colonial administration, the naval officers were unsuccessful in following the official assimilationist policy, if only because the French colonial bureaucracy was too small to do the job.

However, the first civilian governor general, Le Myre de Vilers, who had extensive experience in Algeria, actively attempted to put into effect the assimilationist policy. He introduced the French legal

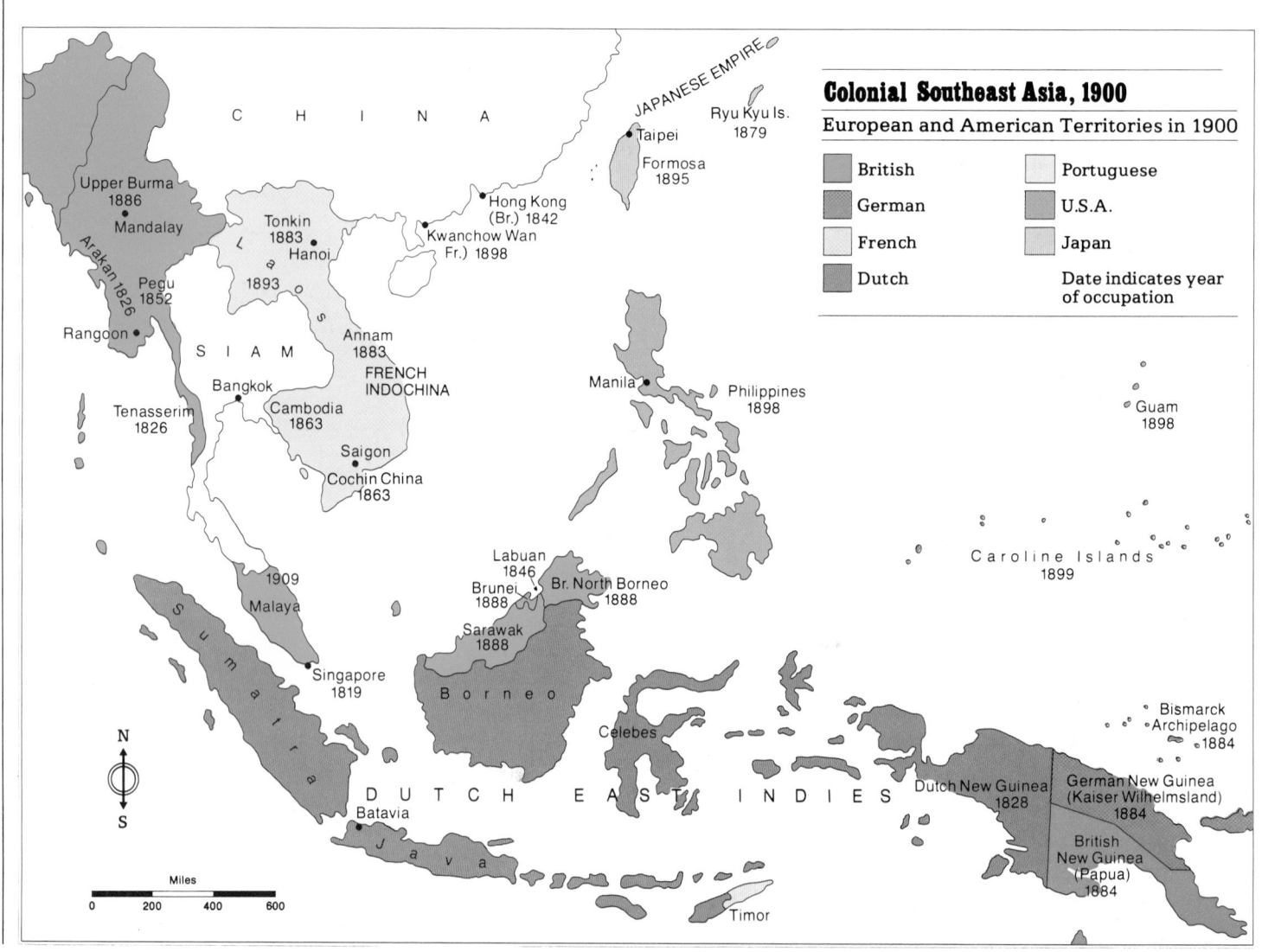

Colonial Southeast Asia, 1900

European and American Territories in 1900

- British
- German
- French
- Dutch
- Portuguese
- U.S.A.
- Japan

Date indicates year of occupation

and educational system at the expense of Vietnamese traditional practices. Although neither of these efforts proved successful, his formation of the Colonial Council of Cochin China left an important mark on Vietnam.

The Colonial Council, instituted in 1880 under instructions from Paris, was designed to begin educating the Vietnamese in democracy. The council included ten Frenchmen, six elected directly by the 1,150 French residents of Cochin China and four selected from the governor general's privy council and the Chamber of Commerce. The Vietnamese were represented by six members, elected indirectly by village notables, a process that afforded culture brokers ample opportunity to wield their influence.

Until 1900 the Vietnamese played a very minor role in the council's meetings. They were referred to as "representatives of the conquered race." They drew more criticism than encouragement whenever they tried to speak French, the official language of the council. Still, membership on the council had its re-

wards for the Vietnamese representatives. Those not wealthy when elected soon became so. They were favored with substantial land grants approved by the council, and their children won many of the few educational scholarships provided by the French.

For several reasons the Colonial Council became little more than a rubber stamp for the plans of the French bureaucracy in Indochina. First of all, Vietnam never successfully attracted a substantial number of French settlers. In 1900 the bureaucrats made up three-quarters of the total French population. As late as 1937 there were fewer than twenty thousand residents who had been born in France. Of these, more than 40 percent had been in Vietnam for less than five years. It was thus relatively easy for the

In the front yard of his Vietnamese home, a French official in charge of artillery poses with his family and his Vietnamese "boys"—as all male domestics were called—for a farewell portrait before his return to France. He stayed three years; few colonial residents stayed more than five.

The car "shakes the earth and flutters the passers-by" complains a popular Vietnamese slogan. Out for an afternoon of touring, this French driver keeps his Vietnamese companion at his elbow for communications with the local population. The French bureaucracy's illiteracy in Vietnamese remained high throughout the colonial period.

With service fit for kings, French sightseers are carried by Vietnamese in litters at Do Son, a picturesque seacoast village fifteen miles southeast of Haiphong.

The Way the French Lived

Those few hardy Frenchmen willing to endure Vietnam's torrid climate were able to lead a life of luxury that would have been impossible for most in France. Using the profits they gained from the exploitation of Vietnam's economy and the availability of cheap labor, they were able to re-create the lifestyle of wealthy Parisians. For the colonialist, at least, Vietnam truly became the "jewel of the empire."

The French were more than willing to share their cultural diversions with those few Vietnamese who could afford them. The ferris wheel at a fair in Hanoi was popular with both French tourists and wealthy Vietnamese (right).

Another "luxury" of French colonial life: French patrons inside a Vietnamese brothel.

TONKIN

Chère Cécile je t'embrasse bien et Louis aussi et Émile embrasse Ma tante Marie pour moi et pour Louis Pierre Levasseur

1473. - Exposition de Hanoï. - La Grande Roue

87. TONKIN - Haïphong — Téatro

30 A. TONKIN — Hanoï - Cathédrale

Haiphong, like Saigon and Hanoi, boasted its own theater (above).

The French colonists did not suffer from loss of cultural comforts of home—they re-created them. A postcard sent home by a French visitor shows an impressive view of the Saigon theater.

A monumental example of the importation of French architecture is the Hanoi Cathedral (right). Several Vietnamese pagodas were leveled to make room for this neo-Gothic structure. The builders spared one pagoda—the haven of a legendary French priest fleeing persecution at the hands of the Vietnamese.

French patrons dine on the terrace of the Continental Hotel, a major attraction of Rue Catinat, the center of French fashion and lavish fares that helped earn Saigon the title, "Paris of the Orient."

A Vietnamese print provides a satiric view of French dancing. Lively French dancing style startled the usually modest Vietnamese, many of whom thought the French bounced when they danced. The name of this bar, "Nhay dam," suggests that its main attraction is "jumping" French women.

bureaucrats to build a political machine to control the six seats allocated to French citizens.

In addition, the lack of strong leadership at the top of the bureaucratic hierarchy—both in Indochina and in Paris—gave the career bureaucrats further opportunity to enhance their powers. The rapid turnover in the military leadership in Cochin China was matched in Paris. Between 1881 and 1893 the Paris ministry responsible for the Indochinese colonies changed six times. In March 1893 the newly created Ministry of Colonies took them over.

Finally, the policy of assimilation required the use of officials knowledgeable about French practices—that is, almost entirely Frenchmen. The result was an inflated bureaucracy. In 1925 a full 50 percent of the colonial budget was used to pay bureaucrats' salaries. By then there were as many French officials for the 30 million Indochinese as there were British officials for 325 million Indians.

Vietnam became a colonial bureaucrat's dream. French officials not only administered but also controlled the apparatus which approved funds, granted promotions, and reviewed the bureaucracy itself. The French Inspection Service, which periodically examined the administration of the colonies, reported substantial abuses in a report to Paris in 1885. Among the items reported were the embezzlement of 400,000 francs by one French official, immorality among French teachers, and lack of any supervision of the Vietnamese workers in public works.

The report also complained about unqualified personnel exiled to Indochina because their incompetence had been proven elsewhere. In addition, the inspectors noted the financial advantages given to favored persons, poor prison service, a tax burden that encouraged tax evasion, and secret budgets, unauthorized by the government, for which taxes were collected and sums spent without any accountability. In sum, the report described Cochin China as "a true colony of exploitation," in which the interests of the natives were sacrificed to those of the Europeans.

The failure of reform

While even the most competent of the French governors general could not reduce bureaucratic corruption, this did not mean that they were unaware of the need for reform. The best governors general at least tried to develop a more efficient government and to do what they thought was best for the Vietnamese.

Sometimes what a governor general thought was best proved disastrous for the Vietnamese. Paul Doumer, governor general between 1897 and 1902 and often regarded as the most competent ruler, undertook a massive reorganization of the colonial government. He established a separate budget for his office so that it could operate independently of the Cochin China Colonial Council. He also established modern governmental departments.

But Doumer's idea of efficient government included oversight of all native Vietnamese officials, thereby creating a need for even more French civil servants. Doumer, the enemy of bureaucratic inefficiency and corruption, thus ironically added to the problem.

Likewise, Doumer's attempt to build a modern rail system for Vietnam was achieved at a heavy price to the Vietnamese. The main railroad line linking Saigon to Hanoi and eventually continuing into the south China province of Yunnan proved to be a commercial failure. It was built with a loan of $60 million, creating a public debt that had to be repaid by future generations of Vietnamese taxpayers. The cost in human terms was even greater. One out of every three peasants working on the Hanoi–Yunnan line died on the job.

At other times, the good intentions of governors general were frustrated by the entrenched interests of French colonialists. The power of these colonialists was most vividly seen when Alexandre Varenne took up his position as governor general in 1925. Varenne greeted the Vietnamese with the first promise by a French official that ultimately Vietnam would be given its independence. The outcry among the French residents was so strong that Varenne was forced to retract his statement three months later.

Finally, well-intentioned governors general often had to face the opposition of the leading officials in the Paris Ministry of Colonies. Thus when Jules Brévié, a noted reformer, left for Vietnam in 1936 the ministry stripped him of important powers. He was no longer able to appoint his own subordinates in Vietnam, and bureaucrats were given permission to correspond directly with officials in Paris, rather than through the governor general's office.

This intransigence by French interests, both in Vietnam and in Paris, was to cost France dearly. Brévié was the last governor general to favor meaningful reform of the relationship between France and Vietnam until 1954—after the French defeat at Dien Bien Phu.

Developing the Vietnamese economy

Steam boilers, imported from France, go into place at a cotton factory in Haiphong in 1899. As a rule the French inhibited economic development that would compete with French industries.

Vietnam changed rapidly under the impact of colonial administration. Colonies, it was believed, should enrich the mother country, which in turn meant exploiting the colonial economy. The French enhanced Vietnam's economic potential, but neglected to do much that could have been done and *was* done in other colonies. The most important French accomplishment was to develop the agriculture of the area in southern Cochin China known as Transbassac, that is, the area beyond the Bassac River.

In 1863 this land consisted largely of untillable marshy soil. The French made it arable by building a network of canals. The dredged earth from the canals was used to fill in the marshlands bordering them. The canals not only served as the most important means of transportation in the Transbassac but also aided in irrigating the rice during the dry season and in draining off excess water during the rainy season. These efforts helped make southern Vietnam one of the world's great rice-exporting regions.

But French economic development was aimed largely at increasing trade between Vietnam and France. Little was done to industrialize the country. This was no oversight by the French but a deliberate policy. The French sought in Vietnam a trading partner, not a competitor. An improved transportation network was designed to ease the spread of French goods throughout Vietnam. The French literally prohibited the development of industries which would compete with those in France.

For example, Vietnam became one of the leading exporters of raw rubber but had only two small rubber-processing factories with a total of 150 workers. It was forced to import almost all of its finished rubber products. British India, by comparison, imported none. The Vietnamese imported 46 million cotton suits annually (for a population of 30 million Indochinese); British India produced 80 percent of its own finished cotton goods. Every part in the railway system in Vietnam, from crosstie to locomotive, was imported; British India produced its entire railway system except for locomotives. The French antiindustrialization policy not only required that a substantial part of Vietnam's wealth be spent on imports but also diminished any possibility that Vietnam could develop a self-sufficient economy, expanded beyond subsistence agriculture.

The power of the Bank of Indochina

Much of the power to determine the economic direction of Vietnam belonged to the Bank of Indochina. The bank, which was established in 1875, was the only major financial institution in Vietnam. It was set up by a consortium of French banks, led by the Bank of Paris which owned 50 percent of its stock. It possessed a near monopoly in the granting of credit, a necessity for almost any business. The bank was thus able to gather around it a large group of friends whose businesses depended upon the bank's good will. Even the government required credit from the bank to undertake its enormous public works programs.

Not surprisingly, the bank translated its economic control into political power. The members of the Colonial Council, both French and Vietnamese, were among the bank's strongest supporters. The bank also used its close connections with the Bank of Paris to influence the French Chamber of Deputies, particularly among the members responsible for colonial questions. With its large financial interests in the French colonial regime and its power in Paris, the bank became one of the leading advocates of continued French rule of Vietnam after World War II.

Ultimately, the Bank of Indochina's influence was felt in almost every corner of the country. A prospering peasant who desired to expand his landholdings required credit arrangements with the bank. A middle-class Vietnamese who might want to open a restaurant would surely turn to the bank to get his business off the ground. The bank used its power to enrich itself. Its initial capital investment in 1875 of 8 million francs had grown to 25 million by 1946. At the same time it paid more than 350 million francs in dividends.

With most of its stockholders living in Paris, it is not surprising that the Bank of Indochina worked to protect French industry from Vietnamese competition. In fact it was among the strongest opponents of Vietnamese industrialization. Instead it encouraged investment in industries that were no threat to those in France. Rice, rubber, and coal thus became the three largest export industries of Vietnam.

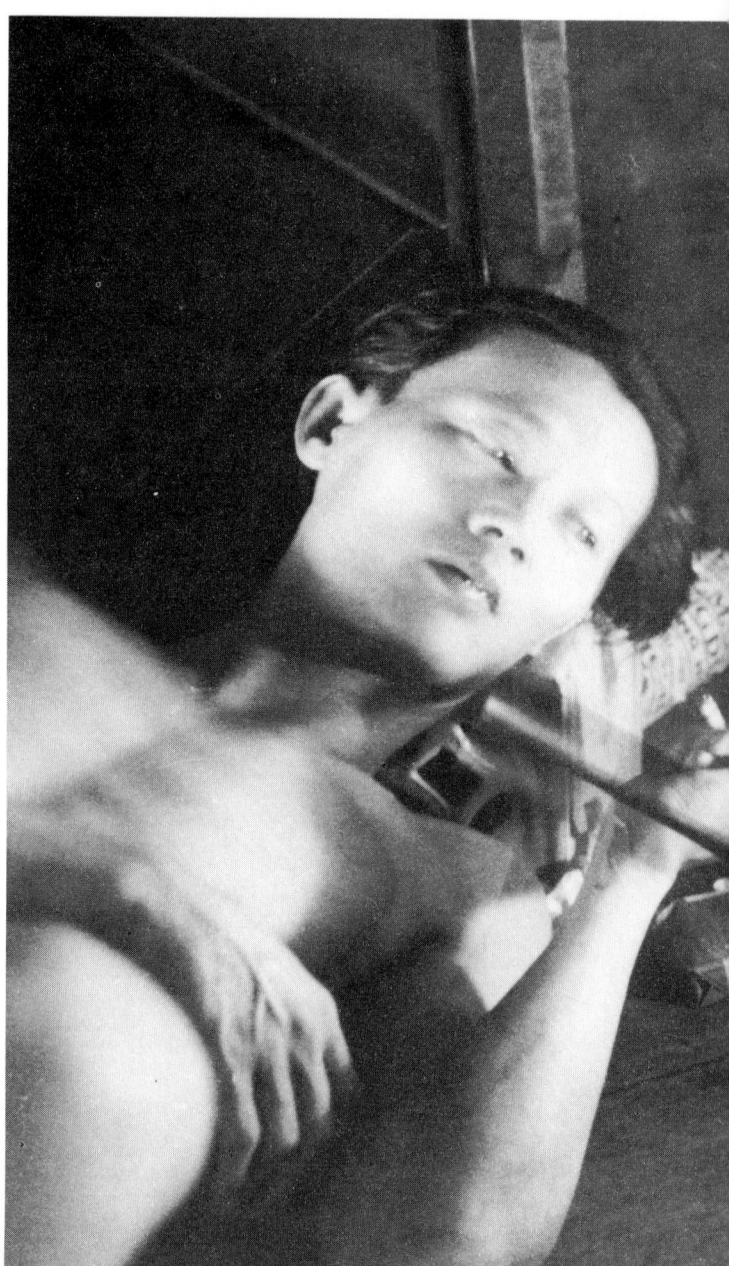

Vietnam's exports

Rice remained by far the most important "industry" in Vietnam from the beginning to the end of the French colonization. The "rice bowl" of the Red River Delta exported almost no rice and was barely able to feed its own population. But in Cochin China the following figures comparing rice cultivation in 1880 and 1937 tell the story:

Area under cultivation	Up 421 percent
Rice exports from Saigon	Up 545 percent
Population of Cochin China	Up 267 percent

The exportation of rice outstripped the increases in land and population. This resulted in part from French attempts to increase productivity, both by improving farming methods and by introducing better strains of rice.

The increased production of rice ironically contributed to much of the tragedy of Vietnamese history in the twentieth century. It caused the Japanese during World War II to covet the rich Mekong Delta as a rice bowl that might help feed an army and population engaged in all-out war. Later, North Vietnam realized that it would never be able to feed its population on its own without the excess rice from the South.

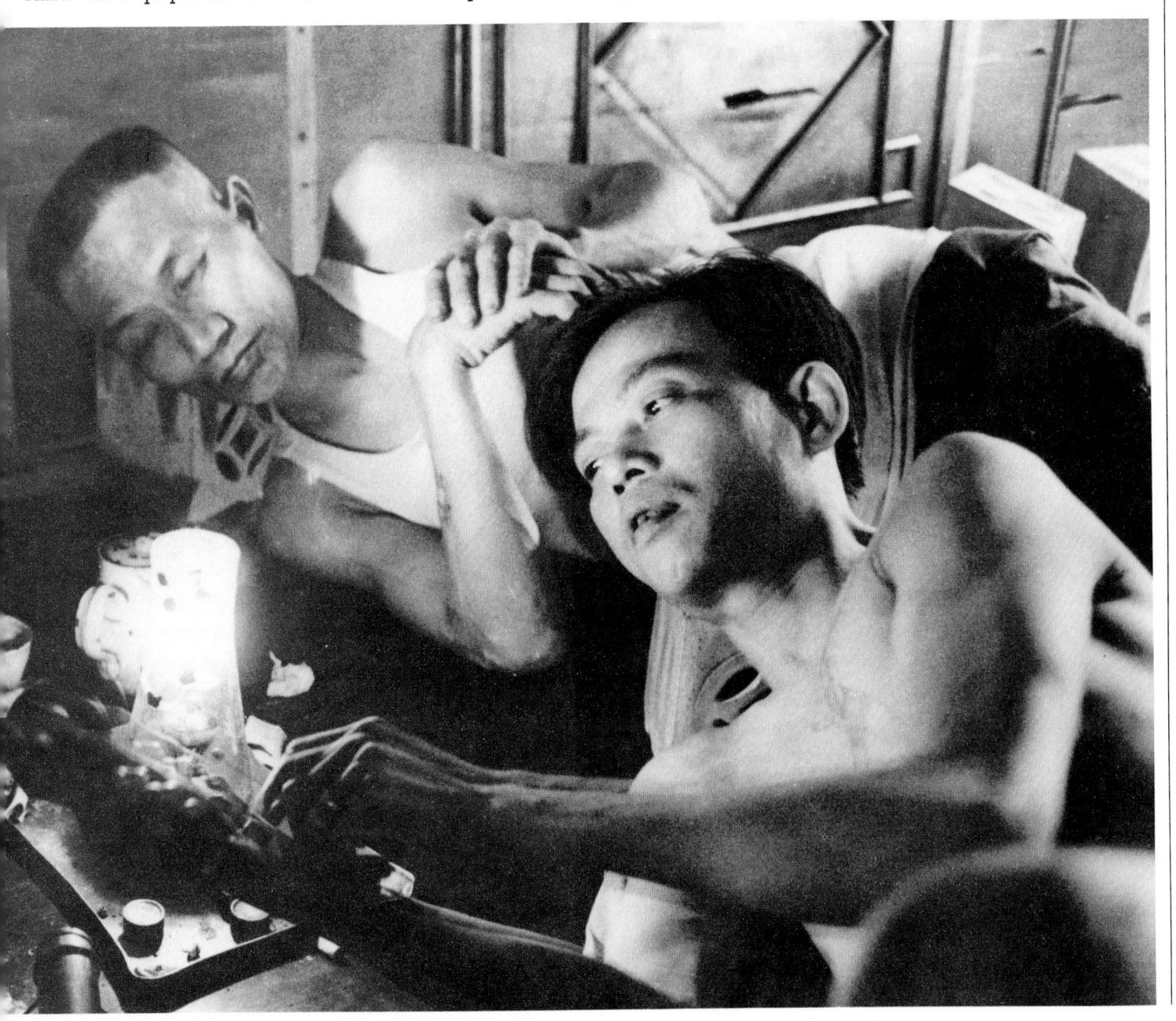

On the wooden benches of an opium den, Saigon opium smokers indulge in the "gift" of the French. The French colonial government made opium sales, traditionally forbidden by Vietnam's emperors, into a profitable monopoly.

The French Connection– The Habit GIs Brought Home

An almost omnipresent commodity in the Vietnam Americans came to know, opium—and its derivative, heroin—was a substance largely foreign to precolonial Vietnam. The British and French introduced opium to Vietnamese society, transforming the "Golden Triangle" of Laos, Thailand, and Burma into the major site of opium poppy cultivation in Southeast Asia. The establishment of French opium "factories" in Saigon and elsewhere made France's monopoly on the drug one of its more lucrative colonial investments.

During the twentieth century the Vietnamese witnessed a steady growth in the narcotics trade, while various international crime organizations struggled with the French for control of the drug's distribution. When the French left, the opium remained.

By the mid-1960s, when American troops began to arrive in Vietnam in large numbers, the "Golden Triangle" was producing two-thirds of the world's supply of heroin. Two rival syndicates, the Shan tribe of northern Burma and a remnant of the Kuomintang army of Nationalist China, maintained control over the region through an extra legal "common market" in the drug.

Narcotics abuse among American soldiers remained a relatively minor problem during the first years of U.S. involvement. But in the late sixties and early seventies heroin usage skyrocketed. By 1971, according to Defense Department estimates, 28 percent of American troops in Vietnam had experimented with opium or heroin. Beleaguered GIs found that the extremely pure local product, which could be purchased for as little as two dollars a fix, enabled them to escape from the monotony and bone-wearying despair of jungle warfare. "Everybody does it," one official in the army's drug abuse program explained. "Vietnam is a bad place and most people want to get through it as quickly and painlessly as possible." The heaviest heroin abuse occurred among white, middle-class

trolled by the brothers of General Tran Thien Kheim, President Thieu's premier.

Many American GIs found the opium left behind by the French an inexpensive way to forget the often nightmarish war. These GIs paid as little as two dollars a "fix" for the opium they are smoking.

draftees with no previous histories of hard drug use. "These kids are a cross section of what the selective service was picking up throughout America," a drug counselor said, "and that is what really shatters you."

The heroin epidemic eventually prompted military authorities to move against drug suppliers. Their efforts bore little fruit, however, as the opium trade was directed by South Vietnamese officials in high government positions. When U.S. drug prosecutors attempted to crack down on heroin smuggling into Vietnam itself, they learned that the Vietnamese customs service, notorious for its indifference to the vast influx of opium, was con-

U.S. drug enforcement efforts were also made more difficult by the Americans' own complicity in the opium trade. In previous years the U.S. military command had ordered Green Beret units to purchase certain opium products in order to establish good relations with pro-South Vietnamese growers. For much the same reason, the Central Intelligence Agency had lent its planes to the anti-Communist Kuomintang for use in its heroin-trafficking enterprise.

In 1972 the Pentagon announced that it had made great strides against drug abuse in the armed forces. But heroin

habits would plague many veterans for years to come. Among the many legacies left to Americans by the French in Vietnam, none proved so deadly as the snow-white powder the Vietnamese call *bach bien.*

Rice exports increased partly at the expense of the native Vietnamese. Per capita consumption of rice did not increase substantially under French rule and may actually have decreased. To the peasants it seemed clear that increased production was doing them little good. Peasants, especially in the North, were still eating only subsistence diets and at times died of starvation, while Chinese middlemen and French exporters became wealthy from the bounty of Vietnamese soil.

The development of the second leading industry, rubber, was entirely the work of the French. The French introduced the rubber tree into the central highlands and gave vast grants of land to Europeans. Between 1916 and 1930 the land under rubber cultivation increased five times to 250,000 acres, divided into 630 plantations. Exports rose almost as rapidly. On the eve of World War II the United States was purchasing one-half of all its rubber from Indochina. By 1940 six companies owned 90 percent of the plantations, and one single company owned 45 percent. All six companies were entirely French owned. By contrast one-half of the rubber lands in British Malaya and in the Dutch Indies was owned by natives.

The Vietnamese workers of the rubber plantations were largely recruited from the over crowded North and signed to three-year contracts by labor contractors operating in the villages. Deserters, who were numerous, could be returned by force. Few chose to remain after three years. One out of every twenty rubber workers died of malaria. Not until 1931 did improved health standards, particularly draining of the mosquito-breeding swamps, make the area safe for labor.

Almost precisely the same situation developed in northern Tonkin and Laos, the center of Vietnam's coal industry. By using better techniques and greater knowledge of geology, the French were able to re-open old mines. The coal industry became even more concentrated than rubber: Two companies produced 92 percent of the total output and one company alone 71 percent.

Labor conditions were equally bad. The mountainous area of Tonkin posed malarial danger to the delta peasants equal to that of the central highlands. Abuses by labor contractors were even greater. Under the system operating in the mines, the wages of the recruits were paid to their contractors, who in turn gave only a portion to the worker. The workers had little power to force the contractor to pay the pre-arranged sum, usually a mere twenty or twenty-five Vietnamese cents per day. Not until 1927 did the French introduce labor protection laws designed to end the abuses of labor contractors and requiring that a portion of the miners' salaries be placed directly into a savings account.

Government monopolies

The private companies were not the only monopolies operating in Vietnam. The government maintained its own monopolies in opium and alcohol. Government monopolies were not unusual in nineteenth-century Europe. They artificially increased the price of goods then considered necessities and always aroused complaints. In Vietnam, however, they induced drastic results.

The opium monopoly was the most notorious. Traditionally the Vietnamese had imposed a death penalty for its sale. In the midnineteenth century this was relaxed slightly to permit the sale of opium among the Chinese, whose welfare was not the government's concern. But when the French occupied Cochin China they set up a monopoly in opium sales. In Cochin China the French leased this monopoly to the existing Chinese dealers for a substantial license fee. This removed even the supposed "virtues" of government monopolies: uniform quality and price. Instead the Vietnamese who tragically became addicts were forced to buy their opium from corrupt, professional Chinese dealers. The normally silent Vietnamese representatives to the Colonial Council pleaded for an end to opium sales. But the French members unanimously refused to abandon the lucrative trade.

After the subjugation of Tonkin and Annam, the French secured a similar monopoly there. Opium sales eventually brought the government more than 1 million piasters annually, about 1 million U.S. dollars. These receipts made a contribution to the Indochinese budget which would equal $5 or $10 billion if applied proportionally to the current U.S. budget.

As evil as the opium monopoly was, the alcohol monopoly more directly affected the majority of Vietnamese. Alcohol was a necessary part of most religious rites. In religious ceremonies, the Vietnamese would take a small sip of rice wine and place the remainder before the ancestral altar. They thus insured the well-being not only of family spirits but also of all the other spirits and genies who could affect their lives. Thousands of peasants had augmented their meager income through private alcohol production.

Under the French all private distillation became illegal; this financially ruined the peasants. The French raised the price of alcohol, levied fines against bootleggers, and made the village notables responsible for enforcing the laws.

The French also established the much-hated "village consumption quotas." If a village did not consume its quota of alcohol, French authorities assumed that illegal stills must be operating and accordingly fined the village notables. The discovery of an illegal still on a peasant's property was considered sufficient evidence to prove guilt. In a village dispute one party would often "plant" a still on his opponent's property and then bring it to the attention of the customs authorities. Naturally, only "connections" and "well-greased palms" were a dependable defense in such cases.

The alcohol monopoly also wrought a disastrous secondary effect on the well-being of the peasants, especially in the Tonkin Delta. Traditionally, most peasants had used part of their rice crop to produce small amounts of alcohol. The residue of rice mash was one of the principal fodders used in pig raising.

Under the government monopoly, the peasants could sell this rice to official distillers but did not get back the rice residue. The subsistence level of the peasants was so low that they had no substitute for the rice mash. There remained nothing to feed the pigs. The result was a dramatic decline in the amount of pork, the most important source of meat in the Vietnamese diet.

Together the government monopolies, including the government-run salt trade, were a particularly odious form of taxation and represented one of the most important grievances of the peasants against the French. The monopolies were also a constant reminder of the intrusion of the French rulers into Vietnamese lives. They vividly portray that what a foreigner considers civilization often means misery for the native people. The same is true of two other institutions that the French attempted to reform in accordance with their own values: education and justice.

Candidates assemble for mandarin examinations in the North. Classical Confucian training, taught and followed by mandarins since the Chinese occupation, disappeared under the French. The last mandarinate examination was held in 1919.

403. TONKIN — Nam-Dinh
Lettrés au Concours

French education

Before the French came, Vietnam claimed a highly developed system of education, revered even by the humblest of peasants. But to the French, aspiring to educate the Vietnamese to become Frenchmen, the old system was intolerable. Educational reform took on especial importance for the French.

In 1874, after a decade of failed reform, the French closed the existing schools. In each administrative unit they established village schools of three years at local expense. The best students were to be sent to Saigon for three additional years of study, ultimately to learn the French language.

These new schools replaced the traditional education centered around the Chinese classics, taught through Chinese ideograms. Lessons were now taught in the Romanized *quoc ngu*. In 1878 the French decreed that only *quoc ngu* and French could serve as official languages.

The French had both practical and philosophical reasons for their promotion of *quoc ngu*. The missionary-trained teachers employed by the French were illiterate in the Chinese classics and could only teach in *quoc ngu*. But more important were the philosophical reasons. The French wanted to counteract the Confucian ethical system and the importance of the mandarins embodied in classical Chinese education. They also believed that a knowledge of the Romanized *quoc ngu* was the first step toward making French the first language of Vietnam.

Yet in 1882 only one-third of the villages had primary schools. The twenty-four thousand enrolled students represented at most 10 percent of the school-age population. On the eve of World War II, less than one-fifth of all school-age boys attended classes.

Even these statistics are misleading. In many cases, the only day students spent in the classroom was the day on which the inspector made his tour. Teachers were routinely "tipped off" about impending visits. The teachers were often drafted into doing administrative work for the village, so schools would be closed for long periods of time. One French estimate indicates that only one-tenth of the tax moneys collected by village notables for local education was actually spent for that purpose. The rest was simply pocketed.

The causes of this failure were varied. To begin with, the French never overcame the Vietnamese resistance to the French style of education. The Vietnamese did not transfer their respect for classical Confucian education to the western approach. Instead they complained that the new education lacked a moral component. Confucian education had been cosmological, teaching a student his place in the universe, his relation to his family, his village, his coun-

Vietnamese workers, like these rice huskers of "Paper Village" near Hanoi, suffered under France's colonial land policies. For these peasants the small broken pieces of rice kernels they were allowed to keep were more important to their subsistence than their meager wages.

try, and to the spirit world. French education did none of these things.

Beyond this resistance lay the unwillingness of the French to support financially a system of universal education capable of accomplishing the immense task of assimilation. The quality of the teachers was low. Houseboys and cooks took places as teachers only because they knew a little French. They lacked the training, age, wisdom, and morality that had made the village teacher in traditional Vietnamese society a person esteemed as an equal to the notables.

The French were successful in raising *quoc ngu* to the first language of the country. Education in classical Chinese died out. The last examination for the mandarinate was held in the North in 1919. One French observer, commenting in 1905 on the new system of education, wrote, "Traditional Annamite society, so well organized to satisfy the needs of the people, has in the final analysis been destroyed by us."

French justice

The effort by the French to introduce their legal system also faced problems. The early French administrators opposed the traditional Vietnamese legal code instituted by Emperor Gia Long. Certain aspects of the Gia Long Code simply did not conform to the consciences of nineteenth-century Frenchmen. For example, the Vietnamese code granted a divorce because of the sterility of the wife. Lack of children was sufficient proof. Because French judges *knew* that it was difficult to determine which party was sterile and were reluctant to discuss such issues in open court, they refused to enforce this provision. Still, the early French administrators in Cochin China permitted the Gia Long Code to guide them. The French did not suffer from evil intentions but from an inability to understand Vietnamese. They had to depend as usual on middlemen, who translated each case to a presiding French officer.

The first civilian governor general of Cochin China, Le Myre de Vilers, immediately reformed this system. He stripped the native affairs inspectors of their judicial powers and created a separate judiciary charged with enforcing the French legal code. He decreed that all future French judges must know the Vietnamese language. But six years later, in 1886, only *one* magistrate had met the test. In 1917 Governor General Sarraut initiated similar judicial reforms in Tonkin and Annam.

Whether one of the judicial systems—the traditional or the French—was better, the clash between the new and the old created problems. The Vietnamese objected to the new French practice of separating administrative from judicial functions. They were accustomed to quick justice, based on the immediate accessibility of the local mandarin. They objected to precisely what the French (and most westerners) considered a virtue: the remoteness of judges from the actual case.

The Vietnamese also objected to many of the "humanitarian" reforms initiated by French judges. The French objected to the use of corporal punishment for minor crimes and instead levied fines or sentences of a few days in jail. A poor Vietnamese, however, often far preferred a quick caning, painful though it was, to a monetary fine or a few days of labor lost in jail. It was again a case of the French instituting well-intentioned reforms with insufficient knowledge of the social context or their ultimate effects.

Such was the nature of French colonial rule. A general administrative system was controlled at all points by Frenchmen but staffed increasingly with Vietnamese more interested in getting rich than in fair government. A policy of uneven economic development discouraged the growth of an industrial economy but provided substantial wealth to Frenchmen in rice, rubber, and mining. A system of state monopolies became a financial burden to the peasants. An educational system actually gave education a bad name. And a judicial system, in the name of "higher civilization," made the attainment of justice almost impossible. By themselves they were sufficient to destroy traditional Vietnamese society. But when these "reforms" violated the most basic of all Vietnamese values—"The law of the emperor ends at the village gate"—they created a revolution.

French colonial rule and the Vietnamese village

The village was the central institution of Vietnam, both in traditional society and under French administration. No aspect of French rule had a greater impact on the village than the land policies put into effect by the administration. The imposition of a westernized legal code and judicial system played a major role in shaping those policies. The traditional Vietnamese legal codes made scant mention of property or of its buying and selling. The most successful

Vietnamese emperors tried to preserve small land-holdings and prevent the creation of large estates. Seldom would a mandarin grant a creditor the land of a peasant when debts went unpaid. In other words, land was not viewed as simply another commodity of value to be bought and sold or exchanged.

French land policy, on the other hand, encouraged the concentration of land in the hands of a few. Western law made it possible for European colonists and native Vietnamese to challenge the ownership of another's land in courts of law, to force peasants to hand over their land in repayment of debts, and to make a legal deed, rather than custom and usage, the basis of property ownership. Such laws provided ample opportunity for culture brokers, who understood these new laws, literally to steal the land of millions of peasants. In addition, the French belief in the efficiency of large-scale farming led to a conscious policy of creating large estates for a small number of wealthy individuals, both French and Vietnamese.

Creation of large estates

By the treaties of 1863 and 1874, which recognized the French rule of Cochin China, the colonial administration inherited from the Hue government the possession of all unoccupied lands. The French were thus able to offer substantial estates free to Europeans in the hope of attracting permanent colonists. Although some Vietnamese received land grants, the vast majority went to Europeans. And the tax laws always favored the European settlers.

The result of such policies was that by 1901, 717 Europeans owned over 880,000 acres of land (creating an average estate of 1,200 acres). They held much of this land for purely speculative purposes, not developing it themselves. They showed no inclination to make the investments necessary to modernize and mechanize agriculture. Rather, the traditional method of a single peasant family tilling a small plot of land remained the norm. The only difference was that now the peasant family tilled for an owner who often lived in Saigon rather than for itself.

Despite the advantages and encouragement given to French applicants for land concessions, there were many opportunities, both legal and shady, for native Vietnamese to acquire large estates. Having become convinced that a large number of Frenchmen would not seek their fortunes in Vietnam, the government issued a decree in 1882 that made it possible for anyone to stake a claim to free land. A claimant first had to register his claim, with a rough sketch of its boundaries, at the provincial capital. He would lose his right to the claim unless the land were cultivated and taxes paid by the end of the second year. Since a peasant family was capable of cultivating only a small plot of land on its own, this law would not have led to the creation of large estates. But some Vietnamese, especially the middlemen, applied less honest means to accumulate property.

There were several patterns by which peasants could be swindled out of their land. An unscrupulous culture broker might stake a large claim on the frontier of cultivated land. Peasants would arrive to farm the land and not have the knowledge or financial ability to register their claims in the provincial office. When the rice was ready to be harvested, the culture broker would reappear and show his claim to the land. The peasants were given the choice of leaving the land, and their harvest, behind or becoming tenants on the land they had developed.

Another middleman's tactic took advantage of the widespread tax evasion traditional among the peasants. To avoid paying taxes, peasants would simply not register their landholdings. The middleman could then pay taxes on a peasant's unregistered land and claim it. A similar tactic permitted middlemen and village notables, often working in concert, to usurp traditional communal lands. The size of communal lands declined by 50 percent from 1880 to 1930.

Finally, if no other device was available, a culture broker could simply initiate a bogus lawsuit claiming land to which a peasant held bona fide title and whose legal ownership was beyond dispute. The culture broker could win the land because of the peasant's lack of understanding of the suit and financial inability to challenge it in court. While statistics are not available, it is believed that thousands of peasants lost their land in this manner.

The many types of land swindles—most of which might have been prevented by a thorough application of French laws—were possible only because of the negligence of the French. They refused to train and pay a competent bureaucracy. The native Vietnamese civil servants to whom the peasants might appeal were very often the culture brokers involved in the swindles. The French bureaucrats were inaccessible because of the language barrier and unsympathetic because of the machinations of the culture brokers. In addition, many French bureaucrats took the view that what went on between two Vietnamese was of no interest to them.

Many higher officials in the French civil service were aware of what was happening in the villages and, in fact, tried to end the abuses. They understood that western property laws could operate with fairness only when all property was adequately surveyed and a single, official land register drawn up. In 1925 a decree was issued calling for such a comprehensive survey of all lands. But by 1938 only the survey of Saigon and Cholon had been completed, and in more than half of the provinces the work had barely begun. The French were unwilling to make the financial commitment required to protect the property of the peasants. In fact, the low salaries paid to the surveyors provided new opportunities for swindles. A job as a surveyor became known as one where "one can make a killing." Too frequently, boundaries were drawn according to the desires of the highest bidder.

In the same year that the surveying project was begun, the French issued another decree whose effect was to make even more peasants landless. In July 1925 the French decreed that peasants unable to pay their land taxes would forfeit their land. When the worldwide depression reached Vietnam a few years later this resulted in the widespread legal usurpation of land by the wealthier Vietnamese. Typically, the original landowner continued to work the land, but now as a tenant farmer rather than as a peasant-owner.

The formation of large estates was most prevalent in Cochin China, where the availability of large tracts of frontier land made the formation of estates much easier. In the North, land was scarcer and property claims less ambiguous. Culture brokers in Tonkin, however, still had much opportunity to create large estates. French law abolished the Vietnamese prohibition against outsiders buying land in a village. Thus, wealthy peasants were able to accumulate land spread over several villages. Most of these estates were built or extended through moneylending. In Bac Ninh Province, in the 1930s, all of the 250 largest landholders were moneylenders. These Vietnamese owned a total of 25,000 acres of land registered in their names. They also held, through defaulted loans, an additional 35,000 acres that were still registered in the names of the original owners.

By 1930 the concentration of land in a few hands had taken on alarming proportions. The population and cultivated land in Cochin China tripled from 1880 to 1930, but the total number of landholders remained constant. The 2,000 largest landholders (about 0.3 percent of the families) owned 35 to 45 percent of all the land. But the concentration of land was even more dramatic in the Tonkin Delta where land scarcity was an historic problem. In the entire Tonkin Delta there were fewer than 1 million landowners. Approximately 9 percent of them controlled 52 percent of the total cultivated land. But even more dramatically, the 250 largest individual landowners (about 0.02 percent of the families) owned 20 percent of the land.

The landless peasant

The concentration of landholdings resulted in the landlessness of the majority. In Cochin China it is estimated that by 1930 a *minimum* of 55 percent of the peasant families were landless; such might have been the fate for as many as 75 percent. Estimates in Tonkin suggest that about 35 percent of the peasants held tiny plots of land (generally communal land) not capable of supporting a small family of five persons. Another 35 percent of the families were completely landless. Thus, approximately 70 percent of the peasantry were virtually, if not technically, without land.

The status of landless peasants differed somewhat between the North and the South, but their living conditions were virtually the same. They became tenant farmers who owed a landlord a substantial portion of their harvests as rent. These rents generally were calculated to be about 40 percent to 50 percent of a normal harvest, but 70 percent was not unusual. They

A peasant could never afford farm machinery like this tractor, and few wealthy landowners showed the desire of this one to purchase modern equipment. Many once-independent farmers became landless agricultural workers whose labor was cheaper than machines.

suffered severely from a poor harvest after which their only recourse was to borrow from the landlord. They were then bound to the land until the debt was repaid, a virtual impossibility. Many peasants thus became debt-slaves to their landlords unless they abandoned home and family, fleeing the authorities.

Below these rent-paying farmers stood another group even more unfortunate, the hired salary workers. Some worked under yearly contracts, others only when work was available. Daily wages seldom surpassed fifteen to twenty Vietnamese cents. But since these workers were almost always in debt, they seldom saw their salaries. Rather it was applied to their debts. They worked for the one or two free meals that

The Struggle to Survive

Even for relatively well-situated peasants in the North, life under French rule became a continual struggle. For the less fortunate, the landless peasant, the struggle was an impossible one. "Family budgets" for two fictitious but representative peasant families, one "middle-class" and the other landless, describe how close to the brink of disaster the peasant lived.

The middle-class peasant

Hung Phan, a typical middle-class peasant, lived outside of Hanoi with his wife, Hung Huyen, and their two children, Hyop and Hung. The Hung family was luckier than most, since it owned three acres of land; about 90 percent of Vietnam's families owned less land than the Hungs. Hung could produce 1,600 kilograms (3,520 pounds) of rice each year but only if he put his wife and children to work in the rice field. The Hungs used about 1,290 kilograms of rice each year to feed themselves. To supplement their diet and to buy clothes and other necessities, they spent about sixty piasters (about sixty dollars) a year.

Hung could count on an income of approximately forty-eight piasters from the sale of crops other than rice, piglets, and eggs. To balance his budget he would have to sell the unused 310 kilograms of unrefined rice at whatever price was offered by the local merchant. In the market at Saigon (where the price of unrefined rice reflected the profits of each middleman and was thus substantially above what an individual peasant could hope to gain), the selling price exceeded four Vietnamese cents in seven of the fourteen years between 1925 and 1938. The Hungs, and other peasant families like them, could thus balance their budget less than half the time.

The poor landless peasant

The Tran family lived in a small village on the Red River about thirty miles north of Hanoi. Tran Van Hiep had once farmed his own four-acre rice field, but when harvests were bad he could not make ends meet. Eventually, he lost his land to a moneylender, Nguyen Minh Thien, the wealthiest man in the village. Now he and his wife, Tran Van Nhu, and two sons were fortunate to be granted farming rights to one acre of communal land.

In a good year, Tran could earn about fourteen piasters from the proceeds of the small plot's harvest. But Tran had fallen into debt since losing his land, so instead of selling his harvested rice he delivered it directly to Nguyen Minh Thien. His family, including his sons Thi and Long, could provide for their needs only by laboring on Nguyen Minh Thien's large estate.

Their income was meager at best, but never enough to offset necessary expenses. Working about three hundred days each year, together the Trans took in thirty-three piasters. By raising and selling an occasional dog and selling vegetables from their garden, they could increase their income to thirty-six piasters a year, but that amount was still short of their needs. Their annual expenses amounted to about forty-five piasters, broken down as follows:

Food	23 Piasters
Clothes	7 Piasters
Taxes	4 Piasters
Farming needs	7 Piasters
Feasts	4 Piasters
	45 Piasters

Tran had virtually no means to keep his family from falling further into debt. After a few years, he was so indebted to the landlord for whom he and his family worked that they no longer received salaries. Instead, their wages were retained in payment for the debts, and they worked merely for the one daily meal received from the landlord.

Tran fell far enough into debt that he was forced to leave his family and look for work in the mines. There he survived the disease and hard work and was just able to prevent the total disintegration and starvation of his family. In bad years, Tran would be totally dependent upon the relief provided by the French.

But the full financial misery of both the Hung and Tran families was greater than their budgets show. Each would also incur extraordinary expenses because of funerals, weddings, and religious celebrations. Expenses for any of these might reach twenty to forty piasters, for many an entire year's income. Peasants like the Hungs and Trans clearly could not save for such eventualities and would be forced to turn again to moneylenders.

Tran and his family eventually became little more than debt-slaves to their landlord. Meanwhile, it was all that Hung Phan could do to keep his land and prevent his family from being forced into the Trans' situation. Should either family have become involved in a lawsuit brought by an unscrupulous middleman or an aggrandizing local notable, it would have had no means of defending itself. A "minor" inconvenience (such as the need to travel to the provincial capital or being sentenced to three days in jail for irritating a local notable) could have brought ruin. Life for Tran, Hung, and all other Vietnamese peasants under French rule became a losing battle for mere survival. During World War II, when the French relief system broke down, an estimated 2 million peasants died from hunger.

they received in the fields. The more fortunate among them, especially those hired by large estates on a yearly basis, might receive free clothing and shelter.

For the landless peasant, borrowing money became a way of life. But this was no less true of their neighbors who owned only small plots of land. They too almost universally required credit in order to make ends meet. Borrowing and its result, high rates, were not a product of the French colonial rule. On the contrary, Vietnamese emperors had long fought a losing battle to keep interest rates down. Still, traditional interest rates began at a "low" of about 36 percent annually. The old system took into account the likelihood that the debtor would never repay the principal on the loan. Interest rates were thus designed to recoup both interest and principal for the creditor. As has already been noted, Vietnamese mandarins would almost never reward a creditor

---

Outside the mandarin's office, suitors state their business. What went on "under the table" was probably more important than the discussion taking place here. Since mandarins found it impossible to deal with the French bureaucracy and often saw their positions undermined by it, they used their power more for self-gain than for honest government.

with the land of an indebted peasant. Under French law, however, it became increasingly possible for creditors not only to charge high interest rates but also to gain control of the land when the peasant defaulted.

Landless peasants needed loans simply to secure the basic necessities even in good years. Peasants with small plots turned to the loan sharks when harvests failed or when they incurred extraordinary expenses. Such extraordinary expenses, however, were a normal part of Vietnamese life. Funerals, marriages, and other celebrations required substantial outlays of cash.

When the French insisted that tax payments be made in cash rather than in rice, the demand for credit increased. Forced to borrow within their village, peasants found that interest rates were often compounded daily and soared above 100 percent annually. The French, like the Vietnamese emperors before them, tried to find a solution. First the Bank of Indochina was induced to make credit available at 18 percent interest; then cooperative credit institutions called "People's Agriculture Credit" were established with interest at 12 percent. The problem with both solutions was that poor peasants were ineligible to borrow. The Bank of Indochina required the ownership of 125 acres as a prerequisite for securing a loan. The cooperatives required a prepayment for membership. The result of both "reforms" was to make loans available to wealthier landlords. The landlords could then in turn loan the money to needy peasants at high rates, making a nice profit from plans designed to lower interest rates.

Decline of village government

While turning the Vietnamese peasantry into a class of paupers, the French also undermined village government. In place of the traditional values of age, education, and virtue in government, French rule seemed to reward the colonial values of connections, wealth, and complacency. If the old system did not always result in civic virtue, it never lost sight of the Confucian ideal. Under the French, the traditional virtues were not even an ideal.

Several patterns of village political life under the French combined to corrupt the traditional village order. First, notables, at the mercy of French harassment, found themselves unable to deal with the new bureaucracy. Even the lowest French clerk felt superior to the highest Vietnamese official (and until the

1940s always received a higher salary). Notables who tried to protect their villages from bureaucratic harassment were thrown into jail—a particularly humiliating experience in a society where "saving face" was of utmost importance. Many of the notables, freed from governing according to Confucian ways, bought off their superiors and gained autocratic control of villages. The new system also allowed unskilled and ignorant notables to rise by serving wealthy local landowners. Finally, in villages where notables gave up altogether, middlemen took over in their pursuit of riches.

Under the French, village mayors were handed more and more tasks, without pay, according to French custom. And fewer and fewer Vietnamese were willing to accept the added burdens. As a result, the position of mayor went increasingly to those who intended to abuse the job. A similar pattern emerged from French interaction with village notables. If a notable failed to carry out a decree or collect taxes, the French confiscated his property. Naturally, men of property refused to become notables, again opening opportunities for the middlemen.

Inevitably the peasants became caught in a vise. On the one side the French administration cared about little else than raising enough in tax revenues to pay for the colony, no matter how this was accomplished. On the other side stood their fellow Vietnamese: culture brokers, village notables, and wealthy landowners, attempting to build or increase their fortunes as rapidly as possible and fearful of incurring the wrath of the French for failure to raise the required revenue. Tax collection time became an annual crisis as the burden grew almost impossible for the Vietnamese peasants to bear. By 1901 taxes in Vietnam were already substantially higher than those in the colonies of Indonesia, India, or Malaya. They were higher even than those in Japan, a society

Reaping What the French Had Sown

"The law of the emperor ends at the village gate." For a thousand years this ancient proverb has suggested the delicate compromise that existed in Vietnam between the central authority and the autonomy of the villages of the countryside. It was this balance that the French colonial regime destroyed. The result was a landless peasantry and a demoralized local government that attracted not the most virtuous, but the most corrupt.

Almost as soon as the first American political advisers arrived in South Vietnam after the Geneva accords of 1954, they realized that the survival of popular government depended upon the solution to these problems. But they were never able to persuade successive South Vietnamese governments of the necessity of halting the destructive process set in motion by the French.

With the support and encouragement of the Americans, Ngo Dinh Diem, South Vietnam's first prime minister, quickly introduced a wide-ranging program of agrarian reform. But by 1962 virtually nothing had been accomplished.

The reforms failed because Diem sought a village administration loyal to himself, not to the villages. But going further than even the French dared, he abolished the election of village officials in favor of appointments by the central government. It was a solution that only made a bad situation worse. The new officials, including relatives of Diem, obtained huge amounts of the land intended for the poor, while bad administration and enforcement at the local level left no one to represent the interests of the peasants.

Despite continued urging by American advisers, no serious attempt at land reform was made again until 1970, when the government of Nguyen Van Thieu began at last the distribution of lands originally seized by Diem. Within two years four hundred thousand peasants had received titles to new lands. A major feature of this land reform effort was the central role given to village governments in carrying out the program. American pressure had resulted in reforms, including the reintroduction of village elections, which promised a return to traditional village autonomy.

But within a year Thieu began an about-face. Adopting Diem's position, he abolished the newly won autonomy of village officials. Not only did this move sabotage the implementation of the land reform program, it further diminished the popular acceptance of the national government in Saigon.

Trying to deal with the problems created by the French, South Vietnamese leaders repeatedly found themselves caught in a vicious circle. Survival of the government required the good will of the people, but the only real support for these governments came from the landlords and bureaucrats. Popular government required land reform and a reinvigorated village autonomy, but such measures were sure to antagonize the landlords and officials.

In the end, the South Vietnamese leaders chose the landlords and the bureaucrats over the peasants. They emasculated local government and failed to carry out meaningful land reform. As a result, they alienated the people from the central government and ultimately the war effort. Unable or unwilling to solve these problems, the South Vietnamese government reaped the bitter harvest the French had sown, the impoverishment and indifference of their own people.

undergoing rapid government-sponsored industrialization.

The French central government also lacked the sensitivity to local conditions that characterized the traditional system. Taxes were not lowered in times of bad harvests. Such natural disasters led to foreclosure, malnutrition, and even the sale of children, as peasants sought to avoid jail sentences.

French insensitivity to local conditions reached an extreme in Cochin China in 1935, when an epidemic struck the water buffalo. Because the water buffalo was an essential beast of burden in the cultivation of rice, the epidemic had severe financial repercussions, creating higher costs for peasants and reducing harvests. Not only did the French refuse to lower taxes in view of the deteriorating economic situation, they continued to demand payment of the livestock tax on the now-dead water buffaloes. They argued that the buffalo had been living during a portion of the tax year.

In many ways what the Vietnamese peasants experienced in the nineteenth and twentieth century was not unique. Their peasant "cousins" in Europe had suffered many of the same hardships a few hundred years earlier. What the French called civilization—the introduction of modern legal codes, the increased concentration of landownership, and the introduction of a "cash" economy in which possession of money became paramount, rather than the possession of land and goods—were all changes under which European peasants had once suffered.

However, European peasants had received partial compensation in the form of a revitalized society, a process which worked in reverse in Vietnam. Whereas European peasants could look for new employment in industry, the only real alternative for the Vietnamese peasant was banditry. Nor were Vietnamese peasants blessed with a more professional and efficient bureaucracy. Instead, the administration became even more corrupt. The lives of European peasants were improved by the gradual elimination of arbitrary rule by the nobility; in Vietnam the peasants were increasingly exploited by their wealthier neighbors.

Perhaps the most striking feature of French colonial rule, despite the massive French bureaucracy, was the absence of Frenchmen. The typical peasant dealt with the lower members of the bureaucracy: the culture brokers. In the village, the notables and wealthy landowners increasingly became instruments of the French rule. At the very least they operated beyond the supervision or surveillance of the French. A Vietnamese who had *never* once met a Frenchman himself would not have been unusual. In fact, many Vietnamese tried to avoid what was almost always an unpleasant encounter between the two races.

For many—perhaps the majority—of the peasants, their day-to-day misery resulted from what their *fellow Vietnamese* did to them—and what the French permitted them to do. Amazingly, the Vietnamese peasant came to realize that ultimately the French were responsible for all of this. But they never forgot that they had two enemies: the French who ruled them and the Vietnamese who exploited them in the name of the French. The result was that the struggle for independence, common throughout Asia and Africa after World War II, became in Vietnam a social revolution as well.

The French were not the only taskmasters. Wealthy Vietnamese sometimes exploited other Vietnamese perhaps more than the French colonists did.

The Saigon the French conquered in 1863 was a squalid river town, forty-five miles west of the South China Sea.

French capital and the development of the rice-producing Mekong Delta, however, soon transformed the sleepy provincial market into Indochina's major port. On what was little more than a strip of marshland, the French built an elegant new city, its handsome boulevards and squares flanked with flowering trees earning for Saigon the reputation of "The Paris of the Orient."

From the Continental Hotel to the Romanesque cathedral, the Rue Catinat was the heart of French Saigon (opposite page). There, shops displayed the latest in Parisian fashions while white-suited French colonial settlers took their leisure at sidewalk cafes.

When the French departed in 1956, Saigon became the capital of South Vietnam. The city retained its French heritage but changed greatly under the impact of the war. American aid and American soldiers made Saigon a garish boom town, while refugees from the countryside crowded into shanties on the fringes of the city in such numbers that by 1970 Saigon was one of the world's most densely populated urban areas.

Most of the foreigners left after the war, along with thousands of Vietnamese assigned by the government to "new economic zones" outside the city. American signs were torn down and almost all of the bars closed.

Postwar Saigon, renamed Ho Chi Minh City, was still thronged with shops and people, its markets and streets clogged with bicycles, pedicabs, and even a few Hondas. As one American reporter observed after a return visit: "The place is still Saigon—noisy, a bit seedy, and very tough."

Four Cities of Vietnam

Saigon

Much has changed in Saigon since the French left: Here young Vietnamese in American T-shirts ride their Hondas down the Rue Catinat. Only now the same street, which Americans knew as Tu Do (Liberty), has become Dong Khoi (General Uprising), the main thoroughfare of Ho Chi Minh City.

Although known as the pre-eminent French city of Vietnam, Saigon is marked as well by a profusion of Buddhist, Taoist, and Cao Dai temples. Here a group of boys receives religious instruction at the Market Temple in downtown Saigon (opposite page).

Through thirty years of war and nearly as many political regimes, some things remain the same. A Saigonese woman still sweeps the sidewalk in front of her home, as she has done each day for as long as she can remember (above).

In Saigon's crowded central market, traffic jams are commonplace as omnipresent cyclos clog the streets.

Saigon still bears the marks of the American presence. Along the wharf a fleet of abandoned Chrysler taxicabs quietly rusts.

Where once Saigonese could view Hollywood movies, now a billboard advertises a Russian film, Light at the End of the Tunnel.

The French gave Hanoi its modern name, but Vietnam's ancient capital has clung tenaciously to its national heritage.

For eight hundred years, Hanoi was the principal commercial and administrative city of Vietnam. When Emperor Gia Long took up residence at Hue in 1802, Hanoi retained its economic importance, and one hundred years later the French made Hanoi the capital of all Indochina.

As they had done in Saigon, Vietnam's colonial rulers sought to turn the city into a French town. Around the ancient citadel they built wide avenues and imposing public buildings reminiscent of the provincial capitals of France. They also made Hanoi an intellectual and cultural center, establishing universities, theaters, and museums.

Unlike Saigon with its raffish energy and European charm, Hanoi remained essentially a quiet, Vietnamese city. With North Vietnam's independence secured in 1954, Hanoi became the new country's capital. In the years that followed, the city witnessed a rapid industrialization. During the Vietnam War, those factories became a principal target of American bombers, which left in their wake serious destruction.

But thirty years of war accustomed the people of Hanoi to discipline and self-denial. As the Vietnamese rebuilt their city, Hanoi's fancy shopping streets were quiet, the few remaining cafes empty. Instead, her citizens awakened each morning to strains of patriotic music, then bicycled to work down the long French boulevards beneath banners exhorting them to vigilance and sacrifice for their country.

Hanoi

On May Day, long lines of Vietnamese wait to view the remains of Ho Chi Minh at his tomb in central Hanoi. The park surrounding the mausoleum has also become a favorite meeting place for young couples.

A young family enjoys a May Day stroll along streets in downtown Hanoi (above).

An off-duty North Vietnamese soldier cycles home from the Hanoi market.

Food shortages plagued Hanoi during the war, and scarcity continues today. Here housewives haggle over vegetables at the city's large open-air market (far right).

A crowd gathers to follow a match of Chinese, or "Elephant," chess (above). The counters placed on the display board represent elephants guarding the Forbidden City. Sometimes teenagers act as counters, standing patiently on large boards laid out on the grass.

The match itself takes place within a small building on the grounds of the Temple of Literature (left). "This place," reads the inscription beside the doorway, "is reserved as a palace for education."

Founded in A.D. 1070, Hanoi's famed Temple of Literature—Van Mieu—is dedicated to Confucian scholarship (opposite page). This part of the temple, lying beyond the "Lake of the Returned Sword," is known as "Jade Mountain"—Ngoc Son. Among other artifacts, it houses a stone inscribed with the ancient history of Hanoi. Two enormous live turtles on display inside the temple symbolize the golden turtle said to have lived in the lake five centuries ago.

Hue has often been called the "city of pagodas," because of the many religious shrines that filled its streets and the surrounding plains. Each was protected by a temple guardian, in this case a military mandarin clothed in ceremonial dress.

In the nineteenth century, Emperor Gia Long built the Imperial City at Hue, a smaller copy of the Palace City in Peking. The Cua Ngo Mon or Central Gate, pictured here, was designed to receive the full light of the midday sun. The pond in the foreground was once a protective moat filled with spikes.

Although to the French, and later to the Americans, Hue was the "ancient" city of emperors, it was only at the beginning of the nineteenth century, after a bitter civil war, that the Emperor Gia Long made Hue the capital of a reunited Vietnam.

Located on a broad plain traversed by the Perfume River, Hue was geographically isolated halfway between the Red and Mekong deltas and further protected from the outside world by lagoons and by pine-covered mountains called the "Screen of Kings."

Within this secluded city Gia Long built a new imperial citadel. Three con-

Two major structures dominate the city of Hue, the Imperial City constructed in the early nineteenth century, and a citadel dating much earlier. In the 1970s South Vietnamese troops used the ruins of the older citadel as an ammunition dump and artillery training site.

centric walls enclosed the "Capital City," the "Royal City," and the "Forbidden Purple City," which was reserved for the exclusive use of the emperor, his family, and his concubines. Dotting the countryside to the south stood the elaborate tombs of the Nguyen dynasty.

Hue's eminence lasted less than a century. After seizing control of Vietnam, the French made Hanoi the center of their colonial administration. Hue became a ceremonial capital, where a succession of puppet emperors endured three generations of French rule.

Worse was to come. Hue was the scene of brutal fighting in both the French and American wars. During the Tet offensive of 1968, and the American bombing raids of 1972, many of the royal buildings and religious shrines which had been its special glory and a source of national pride for all Vietnamese, were destroyed.

Hue

South of the magnificent Pass of the Clouds, where the mountains run down to the sea, lies Da Nang, set between forested hills and one of the most beautiful bays in Southeast Asia.

For centuries Da Nang's deep, picturesque harbor has attracted traders and soldiers alike. It was from what they called Tourane Bay that the French launched their conquest of Vietnam. A century later, on March 8, 1965, American Marines landed in Vietnam on the beaches north of the city, the first time American combat troops—rather than advisers—had been committed to Vietnam.

During the colonial era the French looked primarily to Saigon and Hanoi for commercial investment, leaving Da Nang

relatively untouched. As late as 1963 its narrow streets of small houses and shops held a population of no more than eighty thousand people.

Then war came in earnest, bringing with it the gigantic U.S. air and naval base, and along the city's main street, Doc Lap Boulevard, a rash of bars. By 1973 Da Nang's population had swelled to nearly five hundred thousand, its crowded refugee settlements providing safe cover for Vietcong guerrillas who menaced the air base with sniper and rocket attacks.

The fall of Da Nang to the North Vietnamese in March 1975, signalled the beginning of the end for South Vietnam. The new regime returned many of the refugees to their homes in the countryside and returned Da Nang itself to its historic role as an accommodating port to international commerce.

Da Nang

The profusion of shops along a busy downtown street mirrors Da Nang's three centuries as a city of merchants and traders.

Twelve miles of white sand fringe the blue-green waters of Da Nang Bay. It was a playground for American airmen stationed here during the war, but for this young woman the beach is also a source of food: Her baskets are heavy with seaweed and small crabs.

Behind a Buddhist monastery near Da Nang, a series of dark passageways leads into a small mountain and then down a subterranean staircase to a vast cavern in the center of the hill. This is the Marble Mountain. Illuminated by light from an opening in the top of the hill, a Buddhist priest kneels to chant his sutra at the central altar.

Situated but four miles from the Vietcong-controlled mountains to the west, security was a constant concern at the giant U.S. air base at Da Nang. This small Buddhist temple, ringed with barbed wire, fell within the perimeter defenses designed to deter sabotage attempts.

The great bay which has long lured the ships of many nations to Da Nang also provides a place to live. In the shallows these fishermen have built a small "neighborhood" on stilts. Across the bay the city stretches out along the beach front.

Only weeks after the Communist victory in 1975, the normal hubbub of Da Nang's commercial district replaces the chaos of the South Vietnamese retreat and surrender.

In the aftermath of war the former U.S. air base at Da Nang was transformed into a huge refugee camp. Many of the families crowded into these Quonset huts, which once served as barracks for American airmen, returned to their villages in the countryside.

Resistance

When the young emperor, Ham Nghi, together with his court, fled Hue in July 1885 for the security of the mountains of central Vietnam, the Vietnamese resistance to French colonial rule began. The decision to resist the imposition of the French protectorate was sudden, but not unplanned. One of the regents responsible for the government of the thirteen-year-old Ham Nghi was Ton That Thuyet. He had long urged a more vigorous defense against French force and had prepared a mountain retreat, supplied with food, ammunition, and gold. But only a series of insults by French military commanders and an attempt to deprive the court at Hue of all power and influence finally convinced the royal family that its honor, at least, required an active military defense.

On his flight from Hue, Ham Nghi issued a royal declaration known as the "Loyalty to the King Edict." True to Confucian belief, the emperor accepted full blame for the calamities that had

befallen the country but insisted upon strict obedience to the new edict. Loyalty to the monarchy and hatred of the French were sufficiently strong to produce a twelve-year guerrilla resistance against the French. It drew its leaders from loyal mandarins and other local scholars and has been named the "Scholars' Revolt." Until the French captured Ham Nghi in 1888, the Scholars' Revolt centered around him.

With the French in hot pursuit of the fleeing court, the would-be rebels were unable to reach the mountain retreat they had selected in advance. The supplies stored there fell, instead, into French hands. The rebels moved farther into the mountains, quickly becoming dependent upon the support of small villages.

The guerrilla war begins

In the early years the rebels were highly effective. Selective Vietnamese ambushes prevented French troops from gaining a major foothold in the mountains. Ton That Thuyet reportedly had more volunteers than he could use. The classic pattern of guerrilla warfare emerged. By day the forces kept to the security of the mountains. At night they entered villages to resupply and to gain new recruits. Everywhere the French appeared to be in control of the villages, but nowhere were they safe.

With these early successes Ton left the young emperor in the care of his sons and traveled to China, hoping in vain to enlist the support of Peking. The French, too, began to seek support elsewhere. Their demand for more money and more troops from France was met in Paris by criticism from the Chamber of Deputies, which had previously been so enthusiastic about the protectorates.

The French then turned south to their colony of Cochin China, in hopes of enlisting support. Twenty years of colonial rule had had its effect there. A large number of Vietnamese already held stakes in the French rule. These tested collaborators proved willing to raise armies to fight their fellow Vietnamese in the North. One of the wealthiest of the Cochin Chinese, Tran Ba Loc, also proved to be one of the most ruthless of the antiguerrilla fighters. He literally wiped a score of villages off the map.

The French also sought other allies. After Ham Nghi's flight they had installed a new emperor, Dong

Khan. They called upon the mandarins to support this "rightful" ruler, making a highly enticing offer: Rebels who voluntarily surrendered would be pardoned; those caught would be summarily executed. However, many mandarins refused to recognize the new emperor and at best remained neutral. Much like the Americans nearly a century later, the French also exploited the guerrillas' reliance upon Vietnam's ethnic minorities in the mountains, especially the Muong. Small bribes were often enough to gain the cooperation and loyalty of the ethnic troops.

The French used this last connection to capture Ham Nghi and strike a fatal blow to the resistance. While in the care of Ton That Thuyet's sons, he was guarded by Muong tribesmen. The French approached the Muong chief, offering him opium and a military title in exchange for his betraying the emperor. Ham Nghi was captured in November 1888. True to the Confucian tradition of obedience to the father, one of Ton's young sons fell in defense of his monarch. The other, shamed by his inability to carry out his father's instructions, committed suicide. The

A French collaborator, Le Tong Doc of Hanoi, sits with his attendants. The French used Le and other mandarin officials to gain Vietnamese support against the Scholars' Revolt after 1888.

Preceding page. The execution of a bandit chief in Hanoi. Many Vietnamese saw bandits as heroic Robin Hoods, but to the French they were merely outlaws.

sixteen-year-old Ham Nghi behaved with dignity, refusing to communicate even his name to his French captors. He would not meet with relatives who had returned to the court at Hue and lived the rest of his life in exile in the French colony of Algeria.

The end of the Scholars' Revolt

The capture of Ham Nghi was a turning point in French pacification efforts. More and more mandarins saw the wisdom of accepting the French offer and returned to their duties, this time in the service of the French. Others followed the Confucian tradition of retirement to their home villages. It became increasingly easy for the French to consolidate their rule without aid from Paris. Mandarins were able to conscript native troops to battle the remaining insurgents, and taxes were heavily increased to pay for the military campaigns.

For a minority, however, the capture of Ham Nghi only intensified their efforts. Plans were laid for a long-term struggle. One guerrilla group captured

Conscripted Vietnamese peasants set up French artillery to rout guerrillas from a stronghold in the mountains. The French brought many Vietnamese to their side, ending early resistance to colonial rule.

and beheaded the Muong betrayer of Ham Nghi. Others developed increasingly sophisticated guerrilla tactics and began the manufacture of replicas of the most advanced French weapons. But the French developed a strategy that ultimately led to the end of guerrilla resistance. Focusing their entire attention on a particular area, they built a series of fortifications around the guerrillas' mountain base. Slowly moving in, they trapped the guerrillas in an ever-tightening noose. Ultimately the guerrillas' only hope was exactly what the French wanted: a frontal attack attempting to break through the French ring. These tactics destroyed the mass of the guerrilla movement. Those who were left fell victim to disease, starvation, and sometimes honor: many committed suicide.

By 1897 the last of the guerrilla forces in the mountains of Tonkin had been subdued. A decade of peace commenced, during which the French could begin the process of developing their new possessions. But the rebellion lived in the memory of the people, providing lessons both by what it had accomplished and what it had not.

The Scholars' Revolt failed largely because of the limitations of its guiding philosophy, Confucianism. The appeal to scholars provided Ham Nghi's court with its only link to the masses and gave the move-

ment its popular appeal. But it was also the major cause of its failure. The scholars commanded their own village peasants' loyalties, but unlike the guerrillas of the 1950s and 1960s, they had little support from other villages, much less a national leadership. This localism made it difficult for guerrillas, once forced from their native areas, to reestablish bases with close ties to neighboring villages—an essential element in the guerrilla strategy.

The Scholars' Revolt was also hampered by traditional Confucian loyalty to the family. The French tactic of arresting and threatening death to the parents of resistance leaders was cruel, but successful. Those Vietnamese who chose the good of the country over their filial responsibilities often went through extreme mental anguish. One creative mandarin tried to convince his peers that Vietnam was the parent of all its people and that fighting for one's country was the equivalent of ancestor worship. "Now I have one tomb," he argued, "a very large one that must be defended: the land of Vietnam. ... If I worry about my own tombs, who will worry about defending the tombs of the rest of the country?" But in 1890 he was a remarkable exception and convinced almost no one.

Finally, the Scholars' Revolt suffered from its conservative goals. Its aim was the restoration of the Nguyen court and its mandarin bureaucracy. Village loyalties were strong enough to enable local scholars to raise small guerrilla armies. Ultimately, however, peasant apathy and the promises of the French to bring the benefits of "civilization" to the Vietnamese robbed the Nguyen regime of its support.

Despite its failure, the Scholars' Revolt marked the beginning of the Vietnamese resistance movement. The heroic deaths, such as those of Ton's sons, inspired by Confucian honor, became a source of inspiration for the next generation of Vietnamese. Especially among mandarin families, the wish to avenge the death of a father, uncle, or older brother provided the psychological impetus for the rebirth of the resistance movement after 1900.

While peace dominated the years following the repression of the Scholars' Revolt, its glory was kept alive. Veterans told stories of the revolt, stirring schoolboys. Inevitably a new generation of scholars arose for whom the study of classical Chinese military tactics attained an importance equal to the study of classical Chinese philosophy. By 1903 these young men began plotting, with independence as their goal. The victory of the Japanese over the Russian empire in 1904 was proof that an Asian country could defeat

The resistance leader Phan Boi Chau, trained as a mandarin, originally envisioned a revolution against the French in the name of Confucian principles.

a western power and stimulated the second generation of Vietnamese resistance. The struggle of this new generation centered, above all, around two men: Phan Boi Chau and Phan Chu Trinh.

The birth of a revolutionary tradition

Phan Boi Chau was born in 1867 in the central province of Nghe An. His father had passed the mandarin examinations but declined government service. He chose instead the honorable but poor existence of a village teacher. When the Scholars' Revolt began in 1885, young Phan put his studies aside and organized his classmates into a candidates corps. As the French entered his home village, the corps dissolved in panic. Phan felt that he was unable to prevent the panic because he lacked the prestige of a mandarin's degree, and he returned to his studies. His fa-

Prince Cuong De, Phan Boi Chau's choice for a royal pretender to the throne. As part of his Confucian ideals, Phan Boi Chau believed the Vietnamese needed a monarch to lead them. Prince Cuong De later collaborated with the Japanese in the 1930s and 1940s.

ther's failing health made it all the more important that he establish himself. In 1900 he passed his examinations. Later that year his father died, and Phan was free to embark on his real career: organizing Vietnam's anticolonial movement.

True to his upbringing, Phan began his struggle with an entirely traditional outlook. He first sought the support of leading veterans of the earlier rebellion, receiving the blessing of the famous Hoang Hoa Tham, whose defeat in 1897 marked the end of the Scholars' Revolt. Tham encouraged Phan to find a royal pretender to the throne around whom the resistance could gather a loyal following. Ironically, Phan's choice was a direct descendant of Prince Canh, the son of Gia Long, whom Pigneau de Behaine had brought to France in 1784 to be educated as a pro-French ruler. In 1903 Prince Cuong De accepted the offer and began a lifetime as the center of royalist attempts to gain Vietnamese independence.

As Phan deepened his commitment to the past, he started reading the works of Chinese mandarin reformers breaking away from their own Confucian heritage. Some spoke only of a reformed Confucianism, while others supported the republican ideas of Sun Yat-sen. Many of them, unwelcome in China, had found refuge in Japan. When news of its victory over Russia in 1904 reached Vietnam, the allure of Japan grew. Phan and his small band of allies agreed that Vietnamese independence could only be won with foreign support. Japan became the most logical candidate.

In 1905 Phan sailed for Japan, having written ahead to the famous Chinese reformer, Liang Ch'i Ch'ao. Liang warned Phan against any reliance on Japanese aid. Japanese support, he argued, would inevitably result in Japanese domination of Vietnam. Still, Liang graciously introduced Phan to leading Japanese liberal politicians.

Japan's liberals disappointed Phan. They ruled out military aid and suggested instead that Phan raise money to send young Vietnamese to Japan for advanced study in both military arts and modern technology. Liang urged Phan to accept the Japanese offer as the best hope for the moment.

Returning to Vietnam, Phan Boi Chau organized the "Exodus to the East," as the program to encourage study in Japan was called. To raise funds and coordinate the program, the "Public Offering Society" was formed. By the summer of 1908 two hundred young Vietnamese were studying in Japan. Among the Vietnamese in Japan was Prince Cuong De, by now hunted by the French because of his claim to the Vietnamese throne.

To raise funds, Phan's fledgling movement depended upon more than direct solicitation from wealthy Vietnamese. Sympathizers to the cause began to develop commercial enterprises—hotels, restaurants, even newspapers—and turned the proceeds over to the movement. Given the traditional Confucian aversion to commercial ventures, this in itself was a major break with the past.

Phan also began to reconsider his reliance on traditional philosophy. While never disavowing his support for the monarchy and Prince Cuong De, he gradually began to sympathize with the belief of Chinese reformers in democracy. Phan became convinced that an independent Vietnam required the active participation of its citizens, rather than the restoration of the rigidly hierarchical mandarin system. The resulting synthesis gave birth to Vietnamese constitutional monarchism.

Vietnamese prisoners placed in stocks by the French after arrests made during the ''poison plot.'' These participants and many others involved in the plot ended up executed or behind French bars.

The poison plot

Gradually the pieces began to come together. By late 1907 Phan felt that the time was ripe for an attempt to force the French out of Vietnam. His group developed a plan by which the French officers of the Hanoi garrison would be poisoned by low-ranking native troops, who would then seize crucial points in the capital. Broader planning was limited to assurances of support by former leaders of the Scholars' Revolt in central and southern Vietnam.

The French officers were poisoned as planned, but the French apparently had some inkling of trouble. Their intimations were confirmed when one of the poisoners headed straight for the confessional after committing the deed. The Catholic priest immediately

violated his vow of confessional confidentiality and informed the French authorities. Phan's plot was thwarted, and his supporters throughout the country wisely canceled their planned attacks on the French.

In the aftermath, colonial authorities executed thirteen of Phan's followers. Scores more were sent to prison. Phan himself, already wanted by the French police, avoided arrest by remaining in Japan during the ''revolt.'' The French, however, soon discovered the connection between the aborted revolt and the ''Exodus to the East'' program and prevailed upon the Japanese government to deport the Vietnamese studying there.

By 1908 Japan was flexing its muscles as a new imperial power, more concerned with maintaining good relations with other great powers than with supporting the independence movements of its small neighbors. Japan's short-lived role as the benign liberator of Asia was over. Most of the Vietnamese students in Japan avoided deportation to Vietnam by finding refuge in China. Phan and a small group of followers made their new home in Siam, where they smuggled propaganda tracts back into Vietnam.

The misconceived alliance with Japan underscored a dilemma faced not only by Phan Boi Chau but by all of his successors in the independence movement. The small nation required substantial outside assistance to regain its independence, but that assistance called for dependence upon another country. Whether dealing with Japan, the United States, China, or the Soviet Union, no Vietnamese ruler was ever wholly able to walk this tightrope.

Phan played a major role in resistance politics for another two decades. But 1908 marked the climax of his leadership. While his belief in direct, violent action makes him, in many ways, the father of modern Vietnamese revolutionary philosophy, his political philosophy and tactics were largely from another era. He felt that the masses still required the traditional symbol of the monarchy. Although he recognized the need for mass support in any anticolonial movement, he was unable to develop a modern strategy. He still believed that the peasantry would follow the scholar class out of a traditional sense of loyalty. Phan's mirror image was found in his contemporary, Phan Chu Trinh, the other father of modern Vietnamese nationalism.

Phan Chu Trinh and the western alternative

Phan Chu Trinh was born into a wealthy scholar's family in central Vietnam. His father fought in the Scholars' Revolt but, suspected of being a traitor, was killed by other leaders of the movement in 1885. Orphaned at age thirteen, Phan relied on his elder brother for education in the Chinese classics. By 1901 he had received the highest mandarin degree, apparently on his way toward continuing the family tradition. But he soon became attracted to the Chinese reformers and met Phan Boi Chau in 1903. In 1905 he made the break, resigning his post in the mandarin bureaucracy.

Whereas Phan Boi Chau considered the French the major enemy, Phan Chu Trinh leveled his attacks against the traditional Vietnamese court and mandarin bureaucracy. He rejected the monarchy in its entirety and called for the establishment of a democratic republican Vietnam. In Phan Chu Trinh's opinion, French rule was preferable to a restored

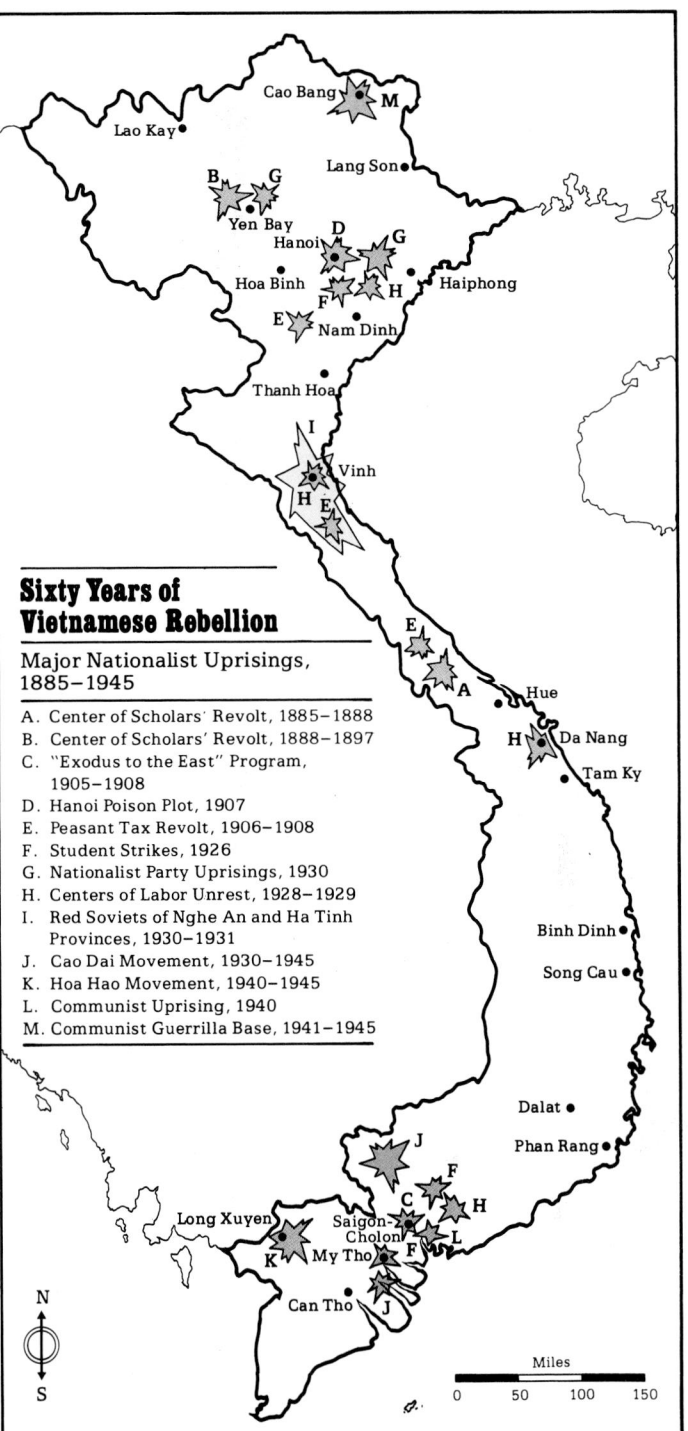

Sixty Years of Vietnamese Rebellion

Major Nationalist Uprisings, 1885–1945

A. Center of Scholars' Revolt, 1885–1888
B. Center of Scholars' Revolt, 1888–1897
C. "Exodus to the East" Program, 1905–1908
D. Hanoi Poison Plot, 1907
E. Peasant Tax Revolt, 1906–1908
F. Student Strikes, 1926
G. Nationalist Party Uprisings, 1930
H. Centers of Labor Unrest, 1928–1929
I. Red Soviets of Nghe An and Ha Tinh Provinces, 1930–1931
J. Cao Dai Movement, 1930–1945
K. Hoa Hao Movement, 1940–1945
L. Communist Uprising, 1940
M. Communist Guerrilla Base, 1941–1945

Nguyen regime. The two men respected each other, but their divergent views prevented them from working together.

Phan Chu Trinh's beliefs enabled him to maintain communication with the French. In 1906 he addressed a letter to Governor General Paul Beau requesting that the French live up to their civilizing mission. He called for the abolition of the vestiges of mandarin rule and the development of modern legal, educational, and economic institutions, including the industrialization of Vietnam. Phan also charged the French with responsibility for what had transpired in

Deadly Rivals

The rival leaders agreed that Vietnam should be independent, but Ho Chi Minh (left) and Ngo Dinh Diem (right) held radically opposing views of the way to attain that independence.

Out of the nationalist and revolutionary movements erupting in Vietnam during the first half of the twentieth century emerged two men who would one day symbolize to the world their country's bitter division: Ho Chi Minh and Ngo Dinh Diem. Both looked for guidance to earlier nationalist leaders; both were almost unknown outside of Vietnam before the end of World War II. But the path of each had been firmly established in the 1920s and 1930s.

Ho Chi Minh

Born in 1890 in Nghe An Province, the son of a wandering scholar, the man who would eventually be known to the world as Ho Chi Minh entered the National Academy at Hue in 1906, in preparation for a career in the colonial government. But after a year he left school and began a wandering life of his own, first as a

traveling scholar, then as one of the architects of modern communism. In 1912 he sailed from Saigon as a cook on a steamship line to fulfill his real ambition—to see the West. His travels took him to London and ultimately to Paris; he even visited the United States. In Paris he fell into the circle around Phan Chu Trinh and quickly emerged as a leader of Vietnamese nationalists living in France. It was in Paris that he adopted his first assumed name, Nguyen Ai Quoc.

His audacious presentation of a petition for Vietnamese independence before the Versailles Peace Conference in 1919 was typical of his later career. Simply by taking the initiative, he earned himself a lasting reputation as a man of action. Similarly, he eagerly accepted an invitation to represent Third World peasants at a meeting in Moscow, remaining to study at the Lenin School of Oriental Peoples. During the following two dec-

ades, Ho spent no time in Vietnam itself. But he was present at the major meetings of the Vietnamese Communist party: at its founding meeting in Hong Kong in 1930 and most importantly at its eighth plenum in 1941, where its postwar revolutionary strategy was developed. Like Phan Boi Chau, a committed revolutionary intent upon exploiting any opportunity afforded him, Ho recognized the enormous possibilities the war had brought the Vietminh: first to accelerate the weakening of both French and Japanese forces and then to leap into the power vacuum sure to emerge at the end of hostilities.

Ngo Dinh Diem

Ngo Dinh Diem was born in 1901 to a Catholic family in central Vietnam. His father, lacking a mandarin's education, had accumulated a large fortune serving in the government of the French puppet

emperors. When his master, Emperor Than Thai, was removed from office, he retired to his home village in traditional mandarin style. Young Diem received a Catholic education before entering Vietnam's highest institution of learning, the French College for Administration, in Hanoi. Upon graduation, he entered colonial government service in Annam. In 1933 he joined Emperor Bao Dai's cabinet as minister of interior, in hopes that the French would permit this reformed institution to take on more responsibility for governing Vietnam. When it quickly became apparent to him that the French would not take this native "shadow government" seriously, he resigned and, like his father, retired to his home village. Diem eschewed the violence of the increasingly radical Nationalists, but neither would he permit himself to become involved in schemes which would only brand him a collaborator.

When the Japanese gained virtual control of Vietnam at the outbreak of World War II, Diem saw another potential opportunity. He contacted Japanese officials, asking if their plans included an independent Vietnam. When the Japanese hemmed and hawed, he again retired to the sidelines. Diem, like Phan Chu Trinh, was essentially contemplative, reluctant to make enduring alliances, patient to wait for his moment to arrive. He was sufficiently opportunistic to entertain aid from any quarter but farsighted enough to maintain his own independence.

When the Japanese established an "independent" Vietnamese government in 1945, Emperor Bao Dai discussed with Diem the position of prime minister. However, the telegram formally offering the post to Diem was intercepted by the Japanese and never delivered. It was not until 1950, when Diem traveled to the United States for the first time, that he found an ally congenial to his temperament. He was an immediate hit with two American senators, Mike Mansfield and John F. Kennedy, intent upon finding a middle ground in Vietnam between the French and the Communists. Diem's wait was rapidly drawing to an end.

Like Phan Boi Chau and Phan Chu Trinh, Ho Chi Minh and Ngo Dinh Diem lived in widely divergent circumstances, following very different nationalist strategies. The complicated machinations of world power diplomacy kept them apart for two decades and then in 1954 brought them face to face, across the "demilitarized zone." But unlike their two predecessors, the differences between Ho and Diem could not be resolved by a respectful agreement to disagree. Rather, their differences were carried into a bloody twenty-year battle for the future of Vietnam.

Vietnam, particularly the exploitation of the countryside by Vietnamese collaborators. Phan's ideas soon won him a sympathetic audience among progressives in France itself.

These links also enabled Phan to organize and open the Hanoi Free School in 1907 with the permission of French authorities. The Free School's theory held that scholars must renounce their elitist traditions by learning from the masses and that peasants be given a modern education. The school's most successful enterprise was a series of free public lectures which frequently resulted in animated discussion by the audience. Hundreds in attendance were exposed to western ideas while debating various theories of modernization. To Phan, the major intent of these lectures was to overcome the Confucian philosophy that dominated Vietnamese political thought.

Within a year, however, the French closed the school. The Free School had scrupulously avoided any illegal activities, but the colonial authorities were convinced that it had ties to the more radical program of Phan Boi Chau. Peasant tax revolts had erupted in 1908, and the French were not willing to take any chances.

Phan Chu Trinh was arrested the following spring, charged with inciting the tax riots. He was condemned to death, but his progressive admirers in France intervened. The French resident superior commuted his sentence to life imprisonment. In 1911 the French pardoned him but placed him under house arrest. When Phan Chu Trinh then requested a return to prison rather than partial freedom, the French permitted him to travel to France.

In Paris Phan made contact with his French supporters who opened their journals to his attacks on French colonial rule. To support himself he found employment as a photo retoucher. He lived in Paris for more than a decade as a symbol, rather than a leader, of resistance. His home became an important meeting place of anti-French Vietnamese who made their way to France.

Phan Chu Trinh's more peaceful path to Vietnamese independence proved to be no more successful than Phan Boi Chau's. His political theory, never well developed, was unable to draw the fine line between reliance on the French to modernize Vietnam and full acceptance of the colonial regime. Not surprisingly, many of his associates eventually collaborated with the French rule. Like Phan Boi Chau, Phan Chu Trinh was unable to mobilize the peasants against the

French. He was more concerned with reforming the scholars than forming a mass political organization.

With the outbreak of World War I in 1914 another generation of Vietnamese resistance leaders had passed from the scene, the last group to enjoy leadership by virtue of its scholarly background. But this generation provided an essential link between traditional Vietnam and the modern political movements that followed in the 1920s. They began the process of sweeping away the ossified Confucian ideology. Phan Boi Chau developed the first violent revolutionary strategy; Phan Chu Trinh bequeathed his belief in a nonmandarin republican form of government. Their failures, too, were important. They taught the next generation the most important facet of modern politics: the need for mass organization.

"He who enlightens"

The initial blow for Vietnamese independence after World War I came from Paris. There, a twenty-nine-

Nguyen Ai Quoc (Ho Chi Minh) at the French Socialist Party Conference in Tours in 1920 after his bold appearance at the Versailles Peace Conference, where he petitioned for Vietnam's independence. At this meeting he became a charter member of the French Communist party.

year-old Vietnamese by the name of Nguyen Ai Quoc (Nguyen the Patriot) presented a petition for Vietnamese independence to the Versailles Peace Conference, then deciding the fate of postwar Europe. The petition caused the French government some embarrassment, but the peace conference quickly dismissed it. Not so easily dismissed was the young petitioner, Nguyen Ai Quoc. He had come to Paris as a ship's cook in order to learn about the West. There he met Phan Chu Trinh who taught him the trade of photo retouching and encouraged his patriotic spirit. For the rest of his life Nguyen Ai Quoc relentlessly pursued the goal of Vietnamese independence. A quarter of a century after appearing at Versailles, he changed his name to Ho Chi Minh, "he who enlightens."

But the 1920s were not a decade for the likes of

A facsimile of the document that Ho Chi Minh presented at the Versailles Peace Conference in 1919. It states the demands of the "Annamite people," the Vietnamese, but probably never reached Vietnam. Ho's demands included [point (1) on document] a general amnesty, (3) freedom of the press, (4) freedom to meet, and (5) freedom to travel. He also called for (6) reform of the educational system and (7) the replacement of the "regime of decree by a regime of laws" through (8) a Vietnamese parliament.

REVENDICATIONS

D U
Peuple Annamite

Depuis la victoire des Alliés, tous les peuples assujettis frémissent d'espoir devant la perspective de l'ère de droit et de justice qui doit s'ouvrir pour eux en vertu des engagements formels et solennels, pris devant le monde entier par les différentes puissances de l'Entente dans la lutte de la Civilisation contre la Barbarie.

En attendant que le principe des Nationalités passe du domaine de l'idéal dans celui de la réalité par la reconnaissance effective du droit sacré pour les peuples de disposer d'eux-mêmes, le Peuple de l'ancien Empire d'Annam, aujourd'hui Indo-Chine Française, présente aux Nobles Gouvernements de l'Entente en général et à l'honorable Gouvernement Français en particulier les humbles revendications suivantes:

    1° **Amnistie générale** en faveur de tous les condamnés politiques indigènes.

    2° **Réforme de la justice** indochinoise par l'octroi aux Indigènes des mêmes garanties judiciaires qu'aux Européens, et la suppression complète et définitive des Tribunaux d'exception qui sont des instruments de terrorisation et d'oppression contre la partie la plus honnête du peuple Annamite;

    3° **Liberté de Presse** et d'Opinion;

    4° **Liberté d'association** et de réunion;

    5° **Liberté d'émigration** et de voyage à l'étranger;

    6° **Liberté d'enseignement** et création dans toutes les provinces des écoles d'enseignements techniques et professionnels à l'usage des indigènes;

    7° **Remplacement du régime** des décrets par le régime des lois;

    8° **Délégation permanente** d'indigènes élus auprès du Parlement Français pour le tenir au courant des désiderata indigènes;

Le Peuple Annamite, en présentant les revendications ci-dessus formulées, compte sur la justice mondiale de toutes les Puissances et se recommande en particulier à la bienveillance du Noble Peuple Français qui tient son sort entre ses mains et qui, la France étant une République, est censée l'avoir pris sous sa protection. En se réclamant de la protection du Peuple Français, le Peuple Annamite, bien loin de s'humilier, s'honore au contraire: car il sait que le Peuple Français représente la liberté et la justice, et ne renoncera jamais à son sublime idéal de Fraternité universelle. En conséquence, en écoutant la voix des opprimés, le Peuple Français fera son devoir envers la France et envers l'Humanité.

Pour le Groupe des Patriotes Annamites:
NGUYÊN AI QUÂC

Nguyen the Patriot. Anticolonial politics were dominated instead by Vietnam's new elite—the increasingly wealthy urban middle class. As the worldwide prosperity of the post-World War I period reached Vietnam, a new generation emerged with closer cultural ties to the French. Many, perhaps the majority, relied upon that regime for their wealth, accepting the dependent status which French rule guaranteed. But others, in one way or another, joined the nationalist cause.

The most moderate among them avoided politics altogether but still made a valuable contribution to Vietnam's new sense of nationalism. Especially in Cochin China, they established newspapers, journals, and books, all published in *quoc ngu*. But these earliest ventures were largely initiated with French support, often with French capital, and limited to cultural and pedagogic themes. Still, they continued the work of Phan Chu Trinh by attacking Confucian philosophy and opening the minds of many Vietnamese to western ideas.

Other nationalists shared the beliefs of their apolitical countrymen but could not keep silent about their political grievances. Prior to World War I they coalesced around a French-language newspaper, the *Native Tribune*. In the 1920s they emerged as the Constitutionalist party, led by the *Tribune*'s publisher, Bui Quang Chieu. By the mid-1920s they had developed a platform for the political development of the Vietnamese nation. Ultimately they hoped to achieve a separate constitution for the country, with a relationship to France modeled after Canada's dominion status in the British Empire. For this the French colonialists branded them Bolsheviks.

The Constitutionalists' immediate demands included an expansion of educational opportunities for Vietnamese and the development of a university in Hanoi on equal footing with those in France. They also called for the creation of a representative council of Vietnamese elected through a wide suffrage. As an intermediate step they called for equal representation among French and Vietnamese within the Colonial Council.

The Colonial Council was, in fact, reformed in 1922, increasing Vietnamese representation to ten of the twenty-four seats. In the early 1920s the Constitutional party routinely won every Vietnamese seat on the council. This was indicative of their support but also resulted from the restricted suffrage laws. Only twenty-two thousand Vietnamese had the right to vote.

The failure of the moderates

Post–World War I agitation reached an early climax in the years 1925 and 1926. In November 1925 Alexandre Varenne arrived in Saigon as the new governor general of Indochina, appointed by the leftist coalition that had just won the French elections. The Constitutionalists presented him with a list of demands, insisting upon greater political rights for Vietnamese and development of their economic and cultural life.

Earlier in the year, Phan Chu Trinh had returned to Vietnam from Paris, by then a sick man. He died in March 1926. His funeral included a long procession from Saigon to Tan Son Nhut, where he was buried. Thousands upon thousands of Vietnamese lined the streets to pay tribute to the father of the Vietnamese independence movement. Bui Quang Chieu of the Constitutionalists made a speech but disappointed the crowd by calling for Franco–Vietnamese harmony. It was a fatal mistake, revealing that the Constitutionalist party had fallen behind the times.

In the aftermath of the funeral, student strikes erupted in Saigon, Hanoi, and My Tho, which housed three leading secondary schools of Vietnam. But there still existed no means of linking this new urban unrest to the village masses. By mid–1926 this small crisis had passed. Varenne's rule proved remarkably tranquil. A few badly needed reforms were initiated, but the political forces were dispersed. The Constitutionalists had lost their dynamism and posed no further threat to the French. One Vietnamese nationalist asked in anguish, "Have we all forgotten Phan Chu Trinh?"

The Vietnamese Nationalist party and the Chinese model

Not all had. On Christmas night, 1927, a small group of anticolonialists met in great secrecy near Hanoi to found the Vietnamese Nationalist party. The party was a conscious imitation of the Chinese Kuomintang, the Nationalist party of Chiang Kai-shek. Its major achievement was the development of the first revolutionary organization in Vietnam. Although it employed certain rituals traditional to Asian secret societies, it also adopted Lenin's modern organizational principles. An elected central committee issued orders down through the party structure, organized into small cells, to diminish the chances of detection

Middle–class in her dress and jewelry, this woman is one of the Vietnamese who benefited from the prosperity following World War I. In turn the prosperity gave these Vietnamese closer ties to the French colonists.

by the French police. In political theory the new party was less innovative. It simply adopted the platform of Chinese Nationalists.

According to the French secret police, the party grew to fifteen-hundred members in 120 cells by early 1929. It was the first party to draw its membership from outside the scholarly or wealthy elite. It encompassed students, small merchants, and a few landlords, but few peasants. Still almost none were scholars or came from mandarin families.

The party's promising beginnings, however, were soon destroyed. A group of Vietnamese workers approached the party asking that the French supervisor of labor recruitment in Indochina be assassinated. Labor recruitment, which was often forced, and the working conditions on plantations had long been scandalous. Peasants complained that those "recruited" never returned home. The Nationalist party shared the hatred of the workers for the recruitment practices but refused the assassination on strategic grounds: The recruiter's death would not weaken French rule and would lead to reprisals. Turned down by the party, the workers, who may have been party members, assassinated the French bureaucrat on their own.

The French reacted by arresting every party member they could find. Their lists were quite accurate. Eventually four hundred arrests were made, resulting in seventy-eight convictions. The leadership of the party was decimated. The party's founder, Nguyen Thai Hoc, escaped and regrouped his forces in a village near Haiphong. A heated discussion took place. Nguyen pointed to unrest among Vietnamese troops in French regiments and called for a major uprising. It appears, however, that he was aware that the uprising would not succeed. Instead, he was convinced that the French police would soon destroy the remnants of the party. He wished to see the Nationalist party end in action rather than through passive arrests.

The uprising was scheduled for February 9, 1930. At the last minute Nguyen Thai Hoc attempted to postpone the uprising for a week, but his messenger was captured by the French. Other forces, unaware of the postponement, began the rebellion as planned. In several garrisons native troops attacked French officers, but within nine hours the French had restored order. Almost all of the remaining party leaders were arrested. Nguyen Thai Hoc was beheaded. The few members who escaped arrest headed for sanctuary in southern China. There, riven with factionalism, they were unable to form any alliance with other resistance fighters in exile. They played only a small role in the 1930s but reemerged during World War II, when their strength came almost entirely from an external source—the Chinese Nationalists, after whom they had fashioned their party.

The Constitutionalists were in many ways the heirs of Phan Chu Trinh, although the party's attacks on French rule lacked the sharpness and radicalness of his ideas. The Nationalists were the heirs of Phan Boi Chau. Both parties advanced the development of the prewar resistance movement and introduced new elements of political thought and organization. But neither achieved a synthesis between the ideas of the two fathers of Vietnamese nationalism. More important, neither could reach the Vietnamese peasantry. By the late 1920s, however, new organizations emerged, perhaps less active politically than their forerunners but with roots deep in village Vietnam.

The Vietnamese alternative

In the 1920s a true counter-culture emerged in the villages of Vietnam. The spearhead of this alternative both to the French and the traditional Vietnamese bureaucracy was various religious movements, including a revitalized Catholic church. Later, in the 1930s, the Communist party emerged out of this counter-culture, offering not only a cultural and philosophical alternative to French rule but a political one as well.

The emerging counter-culture was not really anything new. Rather, it brought together elements long a part of traditional Vietnamese life. Alongside the official mandarin scholars with their court-approved interpretation of Confucius had stood the local village scholars. These scholars had been trained like the mandarins in the Chinese classics. But after failing their examinations or being dismissed from government service they had returned to their home villages. Some who were otherwise qualified had simply refused government service. Many had chosen the career of village teacher.

Their presence always represented an unofficial alternative to mandarin Confucianism. While a mandarin, for example, might emphasize the heavenly mandate of the ruler and the necessity of strict obedience, the local scholars would argue that the ruler's mandate really came from the people and insist upon the right of rebellion against an ineffective emperor. In Vietnam's times of crisis this divergence often led to civil war: the Tay Son found substantial support from among the local unofficial scholars.

Scholars who refused government service also found other occupations as chiefs of bandit gangs. Banditry played a substantially different role in Vietnamese society than the term implies. The French referred to most of the guerrillas who opposed the establishment of their rule as bandits, and they were not entirely wrong. Many bandits in Vietnam traditionally played a semipolitical role. Peasants forced to leave their villages, perhaps for unpaid debts during bad harvests, frequently had no alternative but to join a bandit gang.

One of the most famous of these gangs was led by Cao Ba Quat, considered the most brilliant scholar of all Vietnam. Cao Ba Quat, lacking the right contacts at the Nguyen court, was angered at being refused a government post. In 1854 he led an uprising against the Nguyen called the "Locust Revolt." Cao Ba Quat whipped up support for his rebellion among discontented peasants in the area of Son Tay, where locusts were ravaging the fields and inflicting severe hardship. The bandits roamed the countryside for several years before the Nguyen army could quell the revolt and finally pacify Son Tay.

The increased landlessness and indebtedness of

the peasantry under French rule resulted in the growth of such bands. Led by disaffected village scholars like Cao Ba Quat, they contained the seeds of political opposition to French rule. They were a constant headache to the French, but little more. They lacked the means of organizing into larger groups or of making their political opposition widely known. Still, the French could not ignore the political side of banditry when the gangs robbed, with substantial local peasant support, the warehouses of wealthy landlords.

The importance of banditry really lay in its leadership, made up largely of well-educated men. Like the local schoolteachers, the bandit leaders had sufficient knowledge of the ruling system of government to exploit it for the advantage of the peasants who followed them. That is, the bandit seemed to have many of the attributes of the middleman who did so much to exploit the peasantry. The two occupied roughly the same position in society, but with a crucial difference. The middleman operated for his own personal benefit, the local scholar and, often, the bandit leader for the benefit of the community. The key to the organization of an effective anticolonial movement proved to be the development of a new class of middleman that could understand and manipulate the French system

As the peasants' existence worsened, many took to banditry or political activity. The French made no distinction—they called them all bandits. Beheading was often their fate.

for the *welfare* of the peasants. The pioneers in this new form of organization were religious: the Cao Dai sect in Cochin China and reformed Catholicism in Annam and Tonkin.

Cao Daism

The Cao Dai sect has long fascinated western observers, who have usually concentrated on its apparently flamboyant theology. It offered itself as a synthesis of Vietnam's three great religions: Buddhism, Confucianist-Taoism, and Christianity. But the nature of its organization left the greatest mark on Vietnamese history.

Cao Dai was organized as a religion in 1926, but its roots are several years older. In 1902 a young Vietnamese serving in the French bureaucracy, Ngo Van Chieu, began experimenting in seances and spiritism. During the course of a seance in 1920 a spirit calling itself Cao Dai, or "High Tower," appeared before him. Ngo immediately recognized Cao Dai as the Supreme Being.

In 1924 Ngo's career returned him to Saigon where he gathered a group of disciples around him. One disciple, Le Van Trung, an official of the Colonial Council of Cochin China and member of the Indochinese Supreme Council, emerged as the leading member. During a seance on Christmas Eve, 1925, Cao Dai made his second appearance, this time before Le Van Trung. Cao Dai announced that he was

The "all-seeing eye" (above) is the symbol of the Cao Dai religion and adorns most of the movement's temples.

Le Van Trung (left) was one of the founders of the Cao Dai sect. The spirit Cao Dai appeared before Le in 1925. He then set about converting others to the religion, which worshipped a diverse group of spirits, ranging from Buddha and Jesus Christ to Charlie Chaplin and Joan of Arc.

As the Cao Dai sect grew, so did its political influence. This cathedral in Tay Ninh was the center of many activities which eventually included an army to protect church members. The banner (center) reads "May the Cao Dai Pope live ten thousand years."

the spirit who had been revealed through Jesus Christ. With this revelation Le Van Trung became convinced that the purpose of Cao Daism was to unite the world's religions.

A split developed, however, between the founder Ngo and his disciple Le Van Trung. Ngo opposed Le's desire to attract converts to Cao Daism. Rather, he believed that the "elect"—those who had been moved by Cao Dai—should retire to a quiet existence and prepare themselves for the afterlife. Le proceeded without Ngo, requesting government permission in 1926 to carry on missionary activities. Although official governmental recognition was not granted until 1938, neither did the French issue a ban. The new religion proceeded to grow.

In November 1926 the religion was officially inaugurated in its "home village" in Tay Ninh Province. By 1930 it had one-half million adherents in Cochin China (whose total population was only 3.5 million). Alarmed at the religion's popularity, the French prohibited its exportation to Tonkin, Annam, and Cambodia.

Although the Cao Dai sects became a major political force in Cochin China in the 1930s, they never became a threat as a political party. The religion was anti-French, but it lacked any political program. On the contrary, its activities were largely directed toward increasing the number of faithful rather than organizing them toward any political goal. Still, as the energy of resistance politics of the 1920s diminished, many frustrated nationalists and students found a home in the Cao Dai movement. The religion also attracted many native officials in the French bureaucracy, a tradition begun by Cao Dai's founders. But any movement of one-half million people in Cochin China drew heavily from the peasantry. The religion thus became the first organization with substantial roots in the countryside.

Cao Daism attracted so many peasants because it offered a new way of dealing with the colonial administration. The members of the religion within the French bureaucracy maintained informal ties. French officials charged that they were forming an alternative bureaucracy. Peasant members of the religion were able to call upon their coreligionists for aid in dealing with French law. No longer were they forced to rely upon the culture brokers. In the depression, the Cao Dai sects established social work branches, forming an informal welfare network to aid needy members. In 1938 a private army was founded to protect the property of its members.

In short, the Cao Dai movement took on all the attributes of a counter-culture. Leading members were educated and held positions of importance in the French bureaucracy. They were thus able to use their skills to mediate between their less fortunate coreligionists and the French rulers and to provide services to the peasantry which the colonial regime neglected.

The bonds that united the members of Cao Daism proved to be among the strongest created as a response to French rule. Almost alone among Vietnamese organizations, the Cao Daists were able to avoid inroads into their movement by the Communists. Indeed, they proved to be one of the stablest, if most independent, allies of the French fighting the Communist Vietminh after 1945. Even Ngo Dinh Diem, upon assuming the presidency of South Vietnam, had trouble controlling the semiautonomous Cao Dai army. Only direct military pressure could "convince" its leaders to accept positions within the regular South Vietnamese Army.

The Catholic revival

The story of the Catholic revival in Vietnam in the 1920s and 1930s is less dramatic but runs parallel to the development of the Cao Dai. Like the Cao Dai movement, the Catholic church was able to provide poor peasants with trustworthy access to political and economic power. Local priests were almost universally Vietnamese, and the church offered western education and western know-how, thus appealing to Vietnam's new elite. They were able to call upon their coreligionists within the French bureaucracy to aid fellow Catholics.

Also like the Cao Dai, the church formed its own counter-culture. Peasants were able to rely upon village priests to decide disputes among Catholics. Corrupt middlemen were thus avoided. Local priests were also able to serve as welfare officials, using charity raised by the church in support of needy peasants.

With ties extending from the highest reaches of Vietnamese colonial society to the humblest peasant, Catholicism attracted an impressive number of converts. By 1945, 20 percent of the peasants of Tonkin and Annam had joined the church, mostly from the poorest areas. The church was even less inclined than the Cao Dai to wage a frontal assault on the French presence, but the dissatisfaction with that rule was always implicit in its success.

The development of mass organizations reaching

deep into the villages provided the last ingredient for the formation of an effective resistance movement. With the waning of the Constitutionalists and the decimation of the Nationalists, the path was clear for a new party capable of synthesizing the three elements: the revolutionary thrust of Phan Boi Chau, a modern political ideology such as Phan Chu Trinh's, and the ability to develop roots in village organization. It was left to Nguyen the Patriot to put all of the pieces together. But his victory was hardly inevitable: He would have to wait for World War II to bring the onset of Vietnamese independence.

Nguyen Ai Quoc led a busy life after gaining notoriety at the Versailles Peace Conference. At that time he was not a Marxist, but sometime early in the 1920s he became attracted to Lenin's "Theses on the National and Colonial Question," the first major Communist work to address itself specifically to the freedom of colonized peoples. Nguyen associated himself with the more radical French socialists and joined them when they split with the moderates to form the French Communist party in 1920. He was soon called to Moscow to serve as a delegate to the Peasants' International and remained to study at the Lenin School of Oriental Peoples. Late in 1924 he returned to Asia, with instructions to organize a Communist association in Vietnam.

Communism takes hold

Arriving in Canton, China, Nguyen met with Phan Boi Chau and talked with the remnants of his followers and other exiles there. Through his contacts with the old revolutionaries, he founded in June 1925 the Revolutionary Youth League of Vietnam, the country's first Communist organization. Most of the members of this new organization were high school students or veterans of urban revolutionary groups sought by the French police. Their social status was significant: Nguyen Ai Quoc was attracting Vietnamese with the ability to understand the French regime. Since the Communists and Nationalists maintained an uneasy alliance in China until 1927, the Revolutionary Youth League was also able to offer its recruits educational opportunities in China as well as military training. Its members, once trained, found their ways to factories, plantations, and other places where they could agitate among the masses.

The league attempted to forge alliances with other revolutionary groups, but for the first of many times was undercut by changing political directions from Moscow. When in 1928 Moscow ordered all Marxist parties to refrain from alliances with bourgeois elements, the movement soon found itself in disarray. More adventurous members from Hanoi formed their own group, the Communist party of Indochina and competed against the youth league. The remnants of the league formed a second party. Negotiations to merge the two failed.

Nguyen Ai Quoc had been traveling in Europe and Asia during this split. Moscow, displeased with the disunity in Vietnam, ordered Nguyen back to southern China to hold an emergency unity conference. There, in February 1930, the Vietnamese Communist party was formed. Nguyen Ai Quoc solidified his unchallenged leadership of Vietnamese Communists by getting the competing factions to cooperate. Six months later, again under instructions from Moscow, the party changed its name to the Indochinese Communist party (ICP). Comintern leaders in Moscow wanted the party to include Cambodians and Laotians, ignoring the traditional rivalry among Indochinese peoples. But party members came largely from Vietnam, providing that country with an early leadership of all Indochinese Communists, a leadership that Hanoi continues to assert today.

The Red Soviets of Vietnam

The Communist flag waved for the first time in Vietnam not in an urban center but in the villages, during the revolt of the so-called Red Soviets in Nghe An and Ha Tinh provinces in 1930 and 1931.

When the world depression reached Vietnam in

The French temporarily lost control of Nghe An Province outside of its capital, Vinh, during the revolt of the Red Soviets in 1930. Here, the Vietnamese governor receives the submission of the people, flanked by his protectors—the French administration and the commander of the foreign legion—after the brutal suppression of the revolt.

1930 its effect was immediate: The market price of rice in Saigon fell by 50 percent and continued downward. Tax revolts broke out in central Annam in early 1930. The French were able to control the situation in the cities, but in the countryside peasant bands began to form, waving red flags. The peasants in Nghe An Province formed an alliance with striking factory workers. Soon French rule in the countryside disappeared. Mandarins and French bureaucrats headed for the provincial capital of Vinh. Local Communist leaders attempted to contact the party central committee for instructions but in the meantime were forced to develop their own tactics. The Communists, young and inexperienced, had not organized the revolt and were barely able to keep up with events. But the appearance of the red flag meant that their propaganda had penetrated the countryside.

Forced to develop their tactics as they went, the local Communist leadership presented a sophisticated five-point program that called for: (1) the development of peasant associations, (2) the organization of a village militia for defense, (3) the annulment of all taxes and lowering of rents, (4) the redistribution of former communal lands taken by notables, and (5) the distribution of excess rice to the needy.

On September 12, 1930, the first Red Soviet was formed in Nghe An. Soon soviets spread throughout the province and in Ha Tinh. The soviets, or peoples councils, included all residents of the village who chose to participate. They selected executive committees and formed associations for youth, women, and workers. By common consent, they simplified traditional Vietnamese religious ceremonies, such as marriage and funerals, and thereby reduced costs. There seemed to be a collective sigh of relief as the soviets relieved the peasants of the tremendous financial burden of these traditional observances.

French air attacks

The French responded with the first use of air power in Vietnam. Almost two hundred Vietnamese died in air attacks. On the ground, the French foreign legion moved in to subjugate the soviets. But the Vietnamese resorted to guerrilla tactics. Although the legionnaires earned a reputation for brutality, the going was slow. Finally, a famine came to the aid of the French. The soviets were simply unable to feed their people, and the French required an identification card to establish eligibility for famine relief. The guerrillas were forced to reappear or starve.

By May the leadership of the ICP had been destroyed by arrests. Even Nguyen Ai Quoc was arrested at France's request by the British in Hong Kong and served eighteen months in jail. In August 1931 the last soviet fell. In all, the French arrested one thousand accused Communists. Eighty were executed and four hundred deported. The revolt had been a remarkable display of Communist strength, but the party required three years to nurse its wounds.

Unlike the fate of the Vietnamese Nationalist party, the decimation of the Communist party did not mean its demise. The party was brought back to health in part by Comintern officials in Moscow and in part by political developments in France. The party sent new recruits to Moscow for training, supplying the ICP with an ever-increasing leadership cadre. Paris aided the cause by granting amnesties to those arrested for Communist activities.

By 1933 the renewed ICP allied with a Trotskyist group in Saigon, even though Stalin was in the midst of his violent anti-Trotskyist crusade in the Soviet Union. A combined slate of Communists and Trotskyists won a majority of the seats on the Saigon municipal council in the mid-1930s, ending the domination of the Constitutionalist party. The municipal council, a reform the French had instituted to "teach" the Vietnamese about democracy, was a good indication of public opinion. It was elected by much wider suffrage than the Colonial Council. The ICP's major handicap during these years came from officials in Moscow, who directed the party to recruit solely among workers. The promising initiatives of the party in the villages were sacrificed to adherence to the Moscow line.

But the ever-changing winds from Moscow came to the aid of the party in 1935. With his eye on the growing power of Nazi Germany, Stalin called for cooperation between national Communist parties and progressive bourgeois parties. The most dramatic effect was the building of the Popular Front government in France, a government supported by the French Communist party. The Communists were given increased freedom for peaceful political agitation, both in France and in colonies like Vietnam. In addition, the Vietnamese Communists were encouraged to pursue alliances with middle-class anticolonial organizations in Vietnam itself. Under Nguyen Ai Quoc's leadership, the party developed a new, more moderate platform. The party now sought to gain reform of the greatest abuses of French rule in

Vietnam but avoided embarrassing the Popular Front government. If Stalin had his eye on Nazi Germany, Nguyen had his on the aggressive Japanese.

The fall of the Popular Front government in France in 1938, followed by the Nazi-Soviet pact in August 1939, had predictable consequences in Vietnam. The former led to a mild increase in the suppression of political activities. Party newspapers were closed, a few radicals arrested, and political demonstrations limited. The Nazi-Soviet pact, coming just weeks before the outbreak of World War II, made the Soviet Union—and the ICP—a potential enemy of the French Republic. In Vietnam the French outlawed the Communist party and drove its leadership underground or into exile. Like the French and Soviet Communist parties, Vietnamese Communists opposed the French war effort after hostilities began in September 1939. The Vietnamese, however, were more concerned with the Japanese and continued to call for united resistance to any Japanese attack, as well as opposition to French colonial rule.

The fall of France

When France fell to the Nazi armies in May 1940, the remaining leadership of the Communist party, centered in Saigon, thought their moment was at hand. In November 1940 they staged an uprising in Cochin China. But the local leadership had been totally cut off from the national ICP leadership hiding in southern China. They planned the insurrection on their own initiative, without any national coordination. The French secret police were well aware of the plot. Within fifteen days the uprising was crushed; over six thousand arrests followed. The insurrection yielded only one positive contribution to the resistance movement. For the first time Communists struggled under their own flag, now familiar—a gold star against a red background.

When word of the insurrection reached the party leadership in southern China the actions of the Cochin China leaders were condemned. The party would again have to reorganize from the ground up. But there were several promising notes. Nguyen Ai Quoc returned from his world travels to take over personal supervision of the reconstruction. Moreover, two young leaders of exceptional ability had been sent to join him: Vo Nguyen Giap, the mastermind of the Communist guerrilla strategy, and Pham Van Dong, later to be premier of North Vietnam. Finally, as the Soviet Union itself entered the war, the Viet-

French and Japanese officials arrested thousands of members of the Indochina Communist party in Cochin China in November 1940 after a short revolt. The Communists felt that the time was ripe for rebellion after the fall of France in June 1940 in World War II. Ho Chi Minh condemned the revolt.

namese Communists were free to develop their own strategy, independent of Moscow. The Vietnamese Communists were at last able to benefit from contact with their Chinese counterparts, now rapidly organizing peasants.

As Vietnam entered World War II, the Indochinese Communist party had displayed its ability to organize and lead periodic large-scale protests against colonialism, but it had yet to build an organization that could truly threaten the French regime. In the French secret police they more than met their match. Most of the party's leaders had experienced the harshness of French prisons, sometimes called "schools of Bolshevism." But World War II gave them the opportunity to develop their potential, to concentrate on peasant organization, and to enlist other groups against the French regime. If on the eve of World War II the Communists could not yet directly challenge French rule, they had already established themselves as the unrivaled leaders of the Vietnamese independence movement.

Bao Dai

Bao Dai, thirteenth Nguyen emperor of Vietnam, was a man born not so much to rule as to serve. Like his father and grandfather before him, he would spend most of his life as a convenient figurehead for French domination of his native land.

The last emperor of Vietnam, he was the first sent to Europe for his education. He left the royal household for Paris at the age of nine and, save for one brief return to Hue on the death of his father, remained in the French capital for the next ten years. There, he was placed in the care of a former high colonial official. His training had one purpose: to prepare him to rule his country under the guidance of the French colonial administration. Although he was reasonably diligent, his schoolmates remembered him most vividly as a "husky, amiable boy who liked to ride and play tennis." He also became a popular figure at Paris nightclubs and a frequent guest at weekend hunting parties.

French by education, by training, by inclination, Vietnamese by birth alone, Bao Dai ascended the emperor's throne in 1932 with words of gratitude for his benefactors. Knowing he could count on the French for their "affectionate support and clear counsel," he pledged in return, "the most complete and loyal cooperation." He would rule, he declared to his people, "in the spirit of close and confident collaboration with the protectorate government."

In truth, Bao Dai proved a gratifying instrument for the colonialists. As emperor, he observed all the ancient traditions of his station, while at the same time displaying a mild penchant for reform. He abolished the royal harem, required that prospective Vietnamese officials study political science, and did away with the ancient mandarin custom of touching the forehead to the ground when addressing the emperor. Yet, when the French discouraged his attempts to revitalize the political role of the emperor, he accepted their decision with equanimity. Careful in public always to wear traditional Vietnamese garb, in private he lived the life of a wealthy Frenchman, spending his time playing tennis and bridge, driving racing cars, and enjoying big-game hunting. The young woman he took to be his empress was the daughter of an aristocratic Vietnamese family. She was also a classmate of Bao Dai's in Paris and a Roman Catholic.

If he found favor among the French, however, he was judged harshly by Vietnamese intellectuals. "The emperor suffers from being looked upon as a puppet of the French by the nationalists," wrote a contemporary observer, "too useless and expensive." Another critic was even more graphic, describing the emperor as "a drop of water. Like water, he will rot everything he touches."

An amiable man, a reasonable man, a man "who resisted nobody," Bao Dai was able to "adjust" to the Japanese occupation in 1940. He became head of state of the Japanese-directed government in March 1945, only to abdicate in August at the behest of Ho Chi Minh and his victorious Vietminh. Having served first the French, then the Japanese, he saw no reason not to serve the Democratic Republic. And as plain Mr. Nguyen Vinh Thuy, he accepted the meaningless position of "supreme political adviser" to the new government.

In the years to come there would be exile and, during the postwar French attempt to regain control of their colony, a temporary return to the emperor's throne. But for the moment, as he declared in his message of abdication, "We shall be happy to be a free citizen in an independent country. Long live the independence of Vietnam! Long live our Democratic Republic!"

Educated from his youth in Paris, Bao Dai would remain wedded to the adornments of French culture.

As emperor, Bao Dai was always careful to observe the traditions of his station. On his arrival in Da Nang in 1932, he shed his western dress in favor of traditional Vietnamese ceremonial garb and, flanked by the French resident superior of Annam and the Vietnamese prime minister, began the last stage of his journey to the imperial residence at Hue.

Embarking on one of his many return trips from France to Vietnam, Bao Dai says good-bye to well-wishers at a Paris train station.

World War II—Occupation and Liberation

One of the first acts of the new French government that succeeded the fallen Popular Front coalition in August 1938 was to appoint General Georges Catroux governor general of Indochina. The appointment of Catroux, the first military governor general since civilian rule began in 1879, reflected the single greatest concern of the new government: defense of the homeland, defense of the empire. While the home government worried about the Nazi menace, Catroux's anxieties centered on the Japanese, who had invaded China in July 1937 and were still fighting there. The capture of Canton in 1938 and the island of Hainan early the next year had brought Japan to Vietnam's doorstep, but no closer to gaining a Chinese surrender. The Japanese were convinced that their difficulties in subduing the Chinese were caused by the supplies transported to the Chinese government over the railroads and highways of Tonkin.

When France entered World War II against Japan's ally, Nazi Germany, in September 1939, the Japanese began a propaganda and diplomatic campaign against this French life line to the Chinese government. But as long as the French government stood, the Japanese were unwilling to risk in a war in Indochina what they might quickly gain if France were defeated by Germany. They bided their time.

In the spring of 1940 Nazi tanks rolled virtually unchallenged through western Europe, culminating in the capitulation of the French in June. The Nazis chose to occupy only the northern part of France and turned over the rest of the country to a puppet regime known as the Vichy government. Nominally the Vichy government remained in control of France's colonial possessions; the Germans were unwilling to devote resources to the direct administration of territory vastly larger than France itself. To Britain, France's former ally, and to a watchful America, this arrangement was the best that could be hoped for. At least France's possessions had not fallen into enemy hands.

Japan turns the screw

The developments in Europe provided the Japanese an opportunity in Southeast Asia. Scarcely had the ink dried on the Franco-German armistice in June 1940 than the Japanese vigorously renewed their demand that France cease supplying the Chinese via Tonkin. While this ultimatum was being delivered to French officials in Hanoi, a Japanese diplomatic mission went to Berlin to gain German support for their move. The Germans stalled, the Vichy government stalled, but Catroux, in Hanoi, had to decide. Notified that he would receive no military aid from England or the United States, he capitulated, promising to cut the supply lines between Vietnam and China. The Japanese had won the first round.

In Vichy, Catroux's decision was attacked. Vichy military leaders realized that he had no alternative but to give in. But they were angered that he had first approached the British, a move that subverted Vichy France's cultivation of ties with Germany in Europe. Catroux was dismissed and replaced with the commander-in-chief of the French naval forces in Asia, Admiral Jean Decoux.

A test of nerves for supply drivers, the route between Vietnam and China snakes through the mountains of southern China.

But the Japanese had only begun. In August they sent a second ultimatum demanding permission both to transport their own troops across Tonkin to China and to occupy French airfields. Admiral Decoux seemed to accept the new demands, but the Japanese quickly complained that he was not cooperating. Japan renewed its ultimatum in September. Vichy France looked in vain to Germany to restrain its ally. The Nazis were concerned that a "yellow race" might gain control of Indochina but were unwilling to endanger their alliance with Japan. Just as Decoux again capitulated, the Japanese struck, their troops pouring south across the Chinese border into Tonkin. Within three days French resistance was crushed. The French had learned their lesson—they could not defeat the Japanese in Indochina. Japan exacted permission to establish three air bases in Tonkin and to garrison Japanese troops on Vietnamese soil.

In the winter of 1940 the Japanese tried a different tack. They encouraged Thailand to invade French Indochina's western flank, Cambodia. The Thai government sought to recover territory that it had lost to France in Cambodia and Laos in the early twentieth century. France could ill afford an extended war with Thailand and in March 1941 agreed to a Thai proposal that the Japanese arbitrate the dispute. Thailand received most of the contested territory but was forced to protect the rights of French citizens in the area. For itself, Japan secured a guarantee that it would receive 80 percent of Indochina's rice exports. The real winner, of course, was Japan. It could boast of being not only a "peacemaker" in Asia but also a

Preceding page. Japanese occupation troops bicycle into Saigon in 1941. Japan used Vietnam as a staging area for its advance into Southeast Asia.

A U.S. naval truck transports supplies from Tonkin to China to help the Chinese in their battle against Japan.

protector of Asian nations fighting European domination.

Japan solidified control of Vietnam in July 1941. A month earlier Germany had invaded the Soviet Union. Berlin, urgently in need of Japan's aid in this enormous undertaking, hoped that its ally would attack Russia's Asian coast. To encourage the Japanese to declare war against the Soviet Union, the Nazis forced the puppet Vichy government to sign an accord for the "common defense" of Indochina.

The Japanese now had a free hand in Indochina. They could station troops wherever they wanted. They could use army and naval bases for their own military purposes. The Japanese could now even install their own police force. Vichy signed separate economic agreements that guaranteed to Japan virtually all of Vietnam's rice, rubber, and mineral exports. In payment the French received restricted Japanese yen, which could be spent only in Japan itself. The agreements did confirm France's sovereignty in Indochina. But the French would share their sovereignty with the Japanese. Although French Indochina was not technically occupied by Japan, the two countries settled down to an uneasy joint control.

For Vietnamese Nationalists this joint control was an economic nightmare. The country's wealth, long exploited by the French, was now bled dry by the Japanese in order to finance their all-out imperial military effort. But politically it provided an opportunity undreamed of five years earlier. The French and Japanese began to compete for the affection of the Vietnamese.

The "policy of regard"

The French, left in control of most of the administration of the country, instituted a new program, known as the "policy of regard." Itself a biting critique of earlier French practices, the new policy had as its centerpiece a prohibition of brutality against native Vietnamese. But the French went much further. Through propaganda they reminded the Vietnamese of their own history, especially their long struggle against domination by Asian neighbors. French officials also increased the pay and prestige of native members of the bureaucracy, especially those residing in villages.

Most important, they began a wholesale, European-style organization of the masses, in particular, the Vietnamese Youth Movement. It soon boasted more than 1 million members and represented a major break with the Vietnamese tradition that respected old age, not youth. Through the movement an entire generation of Vietnamese gained a distinct sense of themselves. Nationalists, led by Communist agitation, soon dominated the youth movement. Most important of all, the youth members received an extensive paramilitary education, including training in the use of modern firearms. Unwittingly, the French were training a revolutionary army.

Still, eighty years of misrule proved to be too much to overcome. Despite their efforts, the French won few adherents to a continuation of their rule. Perhaps their most serious mistake was the importation of the Vichy legal system, a system that the new French government had itself borrowed from Nazi Germany.

Japan's Vietnamese friends

Japan's limited presence in Vietnam inhibited its ability to compete with the French. The major arm of Japanese efforts was the *Kampeitai*, the Japanese secret police. Ostensibly brought to Vietnam to seek out agents of the Chinese, their real purpose was to support potential pro-Japanese nationalists and protect them from the French.

In 1941 the Japanese possessed no clear view of a future Indochina. Expecting to win the war, they certainly had no intention of permitting the French to remain after a Japanese victory. Nor was a truly independent Vietnam a part of their postwar planning. Vietnamese Nationalists who had hoped for an early independence under Japanese protection were, like their counterparts elsewhere in Southeast Asia, bitterly disappointed. The Japanese were content to let France continue the financial burden of administering the colony.

But some Nationalists were willing to wait and place their future in Japanese hands. Prince Cuong De had lived for most of the 1930s in Japanese exile, hailing that country's military advances. Many of his supporters from the Phan Boi Chau era worked with the Japanese in the hopes that the royal pretender would ultimately win the throne. More important, the Vietnamese religious sects, Cao Dai and the newer Hoa Hao, proved to be willing collaborators.

The Hoa Hao sect had been founded by Huynh Phu So, whom the French called the "mad monk." He was born in 1919 to a leading family in the village of Hoa Hao. A sickly youth, he had resisted all medical treatment until entering a monastery in 1939. There he received a "miraculous cure" and proceeded to found a new Buddhist sect. His oratorical skills, spiced with violent anti-French diatribes, soon won him a following of peasants numbering tens of thousands. In 1940 the French arrested him and placed him in a psychiatric hospital. When instead of responding to treatment he converted his doctor, his fame and reputation spread.

The French then decided to exile him to remote northern Laos, but the Japanese secret police stepped in. Calling him a spy for China, they placed him under "house arrest" in Saigon, where he was able to receive his followers and direct the Hoa Hao move-ment. French protests to end the sham arrest were ignored. His followers grew to more than forty thousand, forming an army of potential use to the Japanese empire.

Japanese policy was to encourage groups like the Cao Dai and Hoa Hao that adhered to their "Asia for Asians" line, a propaganda policy calling for the elimination of western ideas and influence in Asia. The problem with this strategy was that the Japanese did not know what to do with their allies. They were unwilling to champion a popular uprising, since they did not want to see a total breakdown of French rule. Instead they merely collected potential allies. Naturally, their support gradually dwindled.

In 1943 and 1944 the Japanese government itself became alarmed at the extent of *Kampeitai* support for Vietnamese independence groups. *Kampeitai* activity was sharply curtailed, leaving the French free to crack down on the pro-Japanese groups. But it was already too late. Increasingly anti-French, the Cao Dai and Hoa Hao were now too strong to be eliminated by the colonial regime. With their strong roots in the peasantry, they emerged as the only groups capable of vying with the Communists for control of postwar Vietnam.

Imperial turnabout. French Admiral Jean Decoux (left) leads the commander of Japan's Indochina forces past a line of French troops after an early Franco-Japanese conference. In the review of Japanese troops on the right, Japanese envoy Matsumiya (right) marches ahead of two French officers.

Vietnam and China–the circle dance continues

While anti-French forces committed to traditional Asian philosophies were protected by Japan, pro-French forces in Vietnam prospered under the reformed colonial system. But Communists and other radically anti-French nationalist groups suffered under the repressive Vichy legal code. After 1940 they relied even more on their traditional sanctuary—southern China. The Vietnamese Nationalists had already found a home in China after their devastating defeat in 1930. Now, with Chinese Nationalists—the Kuomintang—and Communists agreeing to a truce in their civil war in order to fight the Japanese invasion, even Vietnamese Communists could operate freely in southern China.

With Japan established in Vietnam after the "agreements" of 1941, the Chinese government sought to create a unified front among the Vietnamese anticolonialists in China. It hoped to convert this political force into an espionage network capable of providing accurate intelligence on Japanese troop movements. A truly effective Vietnamese national front, thought the Chinese leaders, might even be able to engage in guerrilla-style harassment of Japanese forces and supply lines in Vietnam.

The first step of the Chinese was to unite the Vietnamese Nationalists. In their China exile the Nationalists had split into two groups, one based in Canton, the other in Yunnan Province. The Chinese established the Vietnam Liberation League in 1940, as a united front group and, indeed, it included members of the Communist party. Its leadership, however, was firmly in Nationalist hands. The Chinese Nationalists, never completely comfortable with their own alliance with Chinese Communists, were anxious to support their ideological kin in Vietnam. Supported with Kuomintang funds, the league secured military training for over five hundred of its members.

The Nationalist-led Vietnam Liberation League, however, greatly disappointed its Chinese sponsors. Since 1930 the Nationalists had been little more than a minor émigré party with no real roots in Vietnam itself. It lacked the contacts necessary to build a viable espionage network. Chinese military leaders in southern China became convinced by 1943 that they were simply throwing their money away. Almost in desperation they turned to the Communists.

By then, the Communist party had recovered from its defeats of 1940. After the remnants of the Communist party had regrouped in southern China in 1940, Nguyen Ai Quoc made two fateful decisions concerning the future of the party. First, he realized that workers and peasants were not the only ones interested in ending French rule. The weakness of France in protecting Vietnam against the Japanese had persuaded many from the middle class, including some landlords, to support the independence movement. Second, unlike the Nationalist leaders, Nguyen Ai Quoc refused to convert his party into an

émigré group based in China. Rather, he was convinced of the necessity of finding a secure base on Vietnamese soil itself. In late 1940 and early 1941 members of the party infiltrated Cao Bang Province along the Chinese border. Establishing ties with the mountain peoples of the area, the party made the village of Pac Bo their base of activities in Vietnam.

The birth of the Vietminh

On May 10, 1941, the Vietnamese Communists daringly assembled on Vietnamese soil in the village of Pac Bo for their eighth party conference. For the first time since the founding of the party in February 1930, the plenum was chaired by Nguyen Ai Quoc. This meeting approved and implemented the new strategy developed by Nguyen, constructing a new party platform that eliminated the emphasis on workers' organizations. Instead, the party's goal would now be to organize all Vietnamese "whether workers, peasants, rich peasants, landlords, or native bourgeoisie, to work for the seizure of independence." Accordingly, the party dropped its plans to redistribute the lands of all landlords and instead promised that only the lands of the French and their collaborators would be confiscated.

To organize all anticolonial forces a new organization was formed: the Vietnam Doc Lap Dong Minh (Vietnam Independence League). The league would become known to the world as the Vietminh. Within the Vietminh, various subgroups called National Salvation Associations were formed. The new associations included such traditional groups as students, peasants, workers, and women, and for the first time, a National Salvation Association of landlords and an association of intellectuals. Each association was to be developed at the village level, headed by democratically elected committees.

At the top of a pyramid including village, district, and provincial committees stood the central executive committee. The Vietminh and its National Salvation Associations were, of course, led by Communists, but adherence to party doctrine was not necessary for membership or participation. Ultimately the Vietminh attracted a substantial number of Vietnamese unwilling to declare themselves Communists but wishing to participate in what rapidly became the most effective anticolonial movement.

The second part of Nguyen's strategy called for the development of guerrilla bases on Vietnamese soil. Copying the example of Mao Tse Tung, Nguyen

hoped to establish a base in a remote area of the country from which the Communists could spread their influence and which would also serve as a sample of "liberated" Vietnam. The province of Cao Bang had already been selected as a primary site. The party's goal was to control the villages in Cao Bang, replacing the colonial rule with their own. Paying close attention to the needs of the minorities, the Vietminh were enormously successful. By the end of 1941 they had organized one-third of the villages in Cao Bang. A training base for guerrillas was established, furnishing the party forty prepared fighters every ten days.

The emergence of Ho Chi Minh

In accordance with this new party platform, in 1941 the Vietminh eagerly joined the Vietnam Liberation League organized by Chinese Nationalists. However, the views and strategies of the league's varied members soon diverged. Nationalist leaders complained that the Communists were attempting to dominate the league and pointed to the "Moscow-training" of Nguyen Ai Quoc. In early 1942 Chinese military leaders, heeding the pleas of Vietnamese Nationalists, drove the Vietminh underground and arrested Nguyen Ai Quoc. It was the last the world was to hear from Nguyen the Patriot. His foresight, however, saved the bulk of his party from arrest; they were able to find refuge in the new Vietminh base in Cao Bang Province.

Nguyen Ai Quoc could view the situation only from his Chinese jail. But within a year he became aware of the ineffectiveness of the Vietnamese Nationalists' espionage efforts and the increasing Chinese displeasure with the Vietnam Liberation League. Arranging a meeting with the Chinese general, Chang Fa-K'uei, Nguyen Ai Quoc offered the services of his party to organize a new intelligence and guerrilla network against the Japanese. Chang Fa-K'uei accepted and arranged for his release from prison. Upon learning of Nguyen's Communist background, he became fearful lest his superiors criticize his decision. He suggested that Nguyen Ai Quoc change his name. In early 1943 a new man emerged to lead Vietnamese forces in China: Ho Chi Minh.

When the Chinese selected the Vietminh to lead the Vietnamese against Japan in 1943, the league automatically received the support of the U.S. mission in China, which bankrolled virtually the entire Chinese war effort. U.S. policy makers, already con-

cerned about postwar plans for Indochina, found themselves tied to Ho Chi Minh's Vietminh.

Peasants carry ammunition to the Vietminh's army in remote mountain hideaways. Such efforts helped keep alive Vietnam's World War II resistance against the Japanese.

America becomes involved

After the fall of France in 1940 American diplomats faced an extremely thorny problem. They had no fondness for the pro-Nazi Vichy government in France but did not want to do anything that would weaken France's hold on its colonies and pave the way for a German occupation. The U.S. thus recognized Vichy diplomatically and encouraged the government in its attempts to resist Japanese demands. U.S. officials were angered at the "joint defense" of Indochina agreement signed by Vichy and Japan in July 1941.

In many ways this agreement marked the point of no return in relations between Japan and the United States. On the eve of World War II the United States depended upon Indochina for 50 percent of its raw rubber. Japanese control of the area thus deprived the U.S. of its major source of this strategic resource. The U.S., acting in concert with Britain and Holland, retaliated by cutting off Japan's oil supplies. In negotiations that took place in the fall of 1941 with Japan, the United States made several demands, including the evacuation of Vietnam by Japanese forces. The Japanese response to the American proposals was the attack on Pearl Harbor.

The entry of the U.S. into the war did not solve any of these problems; on the contrary, they became more complicated. In addition to the diplomatic dilemma, American policy makers now had to face questions of military strategy. The Japanese intended to use Vietnam as a staging ground for an assault on Dutch Indonesia. As Japanese carriers steamed away from the wreckage at Pearl Harbor, Japanese planes bombed the Dutch colony. Southeast Asia quickly became a prime source of raw materials for the Japanese war machine: rubber from Malaya, rice and rubber from Vietnam, oil from Indonesia. Increasingly, the Japanese made use of Vietnamese ports, especially Saigon, Haiphong, and Cam Ranh Bay, as depots for these supplies on their long trek back to the Japanese islands.

Cutting the supply lines from Southeast Asia to Japan and preventing Japan from using Vietnam as a base for its continued operations in China became one of the major objectives of General Claire L. Chennault's American Volunteer Group (AVG), better known as the Flying Tigers. The Flying Tigers, a collection of volunteers operating under the command of the Chinese Nationalist Army, were reorganized in July 1942 into the China Air Task Force, a part of the U.S. Army Air Force. One of the stated objectives of the task force was to "damage seriously

Japanese establishments and concentrations in Indochina, Formosa, Thailand, Burma, North China."

In January 1942 Chennault's Flying Tigers flew their first mission over Vietnam, attacking Japanese positions in Hanoi. The mission had an unusual international flavor: Chinese pilots flew old Russian-made bombers and were escorted by the American Flying Tigers in their P-40s. On May 12, 1942, Chennault's group suffered the first American death in Vietnam. A former Navy pilot, John T. Donovan, was shot down by Japanese antiaircraft fire. Donovan had been piloting his old P-40, used as a fighter-bomber, in a strafing and bombing mission over Hanoi.

The bombing of targets in Vietnam was a minor part of Chennault's strategy. Above all he was ham-

A Chinese sentry watches over the famous P-40s of U.S. Brigadier General Claire L. Chennault's Flying Tigers. From bases in China the Flying Tigers, all of them volunteers, flew bombing missions against Japanese bases in Vietnam and China before the U.S. entered World War II.

pered by the absence of airfields within easy striking distance of Vietnam. His planes could reach only as far as Haiphong. In 1943 Chinese forces, with American assistance, managed to retake some airfields from the Japanese in southeastern China. But a year later, in Japan's last successful offensive in China, the bases were lost. Not until 1945, after America recaptured the Philippines, were the Allies able to undertake effective bombing missions against the Japanese supply lines and ports in Indochina.

Roosevelt insists on Vietnamese independence

In Washington these military considerations mixed with, and sometimes intensified, the diplomatic problems. American diplomats still wanted to support Vichy France's claims of sovereignty over the French colonies in order to forestall any move by the Germans to occupy them. In addition, America now had

to face the headstrong leader of the Free French, General Charles de Gaulle, their new ally.

President Franklin D. Roosevelt and other administration figures assumed contradictory postures on the Indochina question. On the one hand, the U.S. announced its firm opposition to a restoration of European empires in Asia, thus drawing the wrath of Britain's prime minister, Winston Churchill. Roosevelt and Churchill worked out a tacit agreement that the U.S. would not force England to relinquish its empire, especially India. But FDR was more direct when he spoke about Indochina. In January 1944 he wrote to Secretary of State Hull that "France has had the country . . . for nearly one hundred years, and the people are worse off than they were at the beginning. . . . France has milked it for one hundred years. The people of Indochina are entitled to something better than that."

In public, however, Roosevelt was forced to pacify the French. He did not want to give Vichy France a major propaganda opportunity: to argue that only Vichy could maintain France's glory and that an Allied victory would result in the dismemberment of the French empire. De Gaulle was well aware of the tensions in U.S. policy but had no means of gaining the sort of commitment from Washington that Churchill had received. Neither of the eastern Allies, Russia or China, would side with de Gaulle since their leaders, Stalin and Chiang Kai-shek, shared Roosevelt's views. De Gaulle turned to his fellow imperialist, Winston Churchill, for aid. The result was one of the most serious disputes in the Grand Alliance.

The war on the Asian mainland had been divided into two theaters. The Southeast Asia Command (SEAC) was formed in 1943 under British control. The China theater had been established in 1942, under

The Invasion that Didn't Happen

The Franco-Japanese joint defense treaty for Indochina, signed in 1940, caused many headaches for American military planners. One of these headaches emerged fully only two years later, when the Japanese captured Burma. The joint defense treaty closed one of the major supply routes to Allied forces fighting the Japanese in southern China. Only the famed Burma Road remained to tie the Chinese with their American and British allies. After taking Burma in March 1942, the Japanese closed this supply line, forcing the U.S. to deliver all supplies to southern China by airlift. Initially only ten thousand tons of food, clothing, and military equipment could be delivered to the beleaguered Chinese forces each month.

It was natural under these circumstances that American military planners would consider an offensive into northern Vietnam in an attempt to reopen to Allied supplies the railroad from Haiphong to Yunnan Province. General Hugh Drum made the first proposal to Secretary of War Henry L. Stimson, suggesting that the thrust come from Thailand across to Hanoi and Haiphong. Stimson thought highly of the plan but was unwilling to divert the necessary resources from other theaters of war, especially from Europe.

General Joseph W. Stilwell, Chiang Kai-shek's chief of staff, made a similar suggestion to the Generalissimo, calling for an invasion of Vietnam by Chinese forces along their common border. But Chiang, like Stimson, was unwilling to divert the manpower. Presumably he reasoned that Chinese troops sent to Indochina would be unavailable for what he saw as their most important mission: keeping close watch over his Chinese Communist allies.

In the end, no invasion of Vietnam was attempted. But it is interesting to speculate what a successful invasion might have meant. Allied control of Vietnam and the surrounding water would have seriously impaired Japan's war effort. Maintaining the railroads in Vietnam and the supply lanes of the South China Sea was essential for Japan in supplying its armies in China and the Japanese mainland itself. An Allied invasion of Vietnam might have been a turning point in the war in the Pacific.

It is even more tempting, but more difficult, to speculate on the effect that such an invasion might have had on Vietnamese history. The liberation of the country from Japanese domination would have been accomplished under very different circumstances. American and Chinese forces would have predominated, perhaps even fighting the Vichy French forces still collaborating with the Japanese. With President Roosevelt's firm insistence that the French not be permitted to return to Vietnam, it is possible that much of Vietnam's bloodshed after 1945 would have been avoided.

Provinces of Colonial Vietnam

1. Lai Chau
2. Phong Tho and Lao Kay
3. Ha Giang
4. Cao Bang
5. Yen Bay
6. Tuyen Quang
7. Bac Kan
8. Lang Son
9. Son La
10. Phu Tho
11. Vinh-Phuc Yen
12. Thai Nguyen
13. Phu Lang Thuong
14. Hai Ninh
15. Ha Tay
16. Bac Ninh and Gia Lam
17. Kien An
18. Quang Yen
19. Hoa Binh
20. Hung Yen
21. Hai Duong
22. Ha Nam
23. Thai Binh
24. Thanh Hoa
25. Ninh Binh
26. Nam Dinh and Bui Chu

27. Nghe An
28. Ha Tinh
29. Quang Binh
30. Quang Tri
31. Thua Thien
32. Quang Nam
33. Quang Ngai
34. Kontum
35. Binh Dinh
36. Phu Yen
37. Darlac
38. Khanh Hoa
39. Phan Rang
40. Haut Don Nai
41. Thuan
42. Thu Dau Mot
43. Tay Ninh
44. Bien Hoa
45. Ba Ria
46. Gia Dinh
47. Cholon
48. Go Cong
49. Tan An
50. My Tho
51. Sadec
52. Long Xuyen

53. Chau Doc
54. Ha Tien
55. Rach Gia
56. Bac Lieu
57. Soctrang
58. Tra Vinh
59. Can Tho
60. Vinh Long
61. Ben Tre

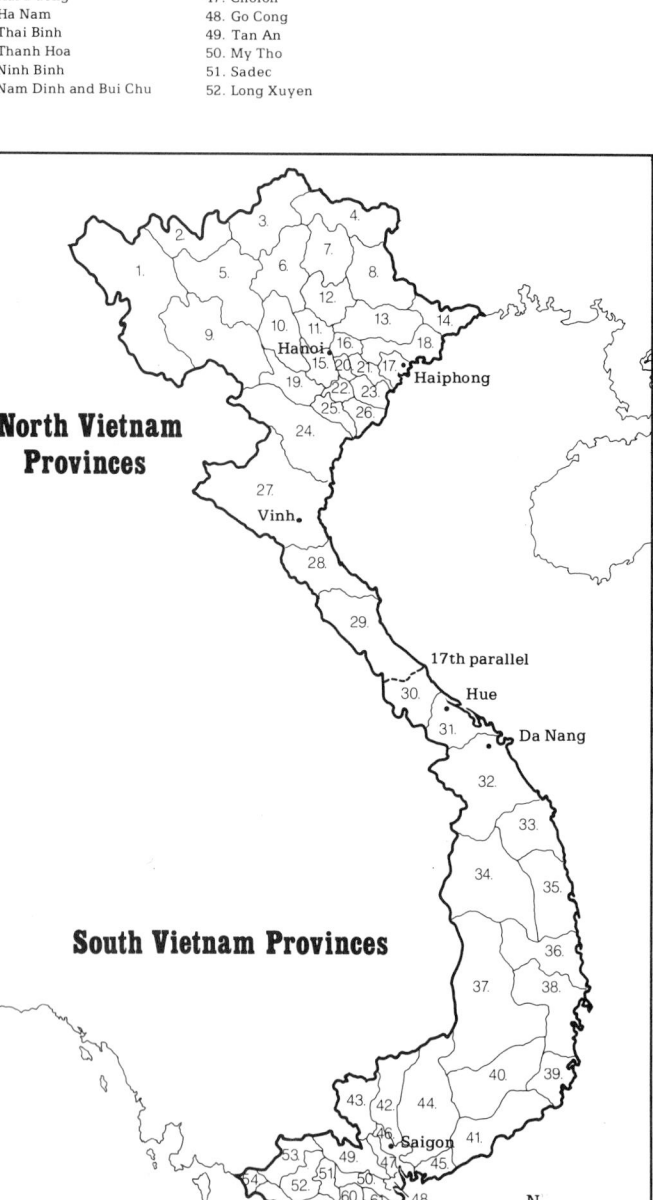

Chinese command, acting in consultation with the U.S. China mission headed after 1944 by General Albert C. Wedemeyer. Indochina had been placed in the China theater in 1942, but when the British established SEAC, they argued that Indochina should be shifted to its jurisdiction. U.S. intelligence reported that the British planned to refuse cooperation with any native organizations in Vietnam and to aid only the French. It was clear that Britain wanted wartime control of Indochina in order to restore the colony to France at the conclusion of hostilities.

Roosevelt was not deceived. He ordered that under no circumstances should any aid be accorded French forces in Indochina, nor should France be consulted about the area's postwar future. The dispute between the U.S. and Britain over command jurisdiction in Indochina was not fully resolved until the Potsdam Conference in 1945, but an interim agreement was worked out whereby the British could take action in Indochina after first clearing its plans with the China command. At Potsdam, Britain's claims were partially conceded. To supervise the approaching Japanese surrender, Indochina was to be divided at the sixteenth parallel, British forces stationed south of the line and the Chinese occupying the northern portion.

While Roosevelt was doing his best to prevent a return of the French to Vietnam, he was also developing alternative plans for Indochina. One of his first proposals was to place Vietnam under Chinese control. Chiang Kai-shek had not been known for his restraint during the course of wartime diplomacy, but in this instance he struck a rare note of realism. When asked if he wanted to govern Indochina, he replied, "Under no circumstances!" He then added, "They are not Chinese. They would not assimilate into the Chinese people." Two thousand years of Vietnamese history had taught him a lesson that the French were soon to learn at a heavy cost.

Following Chiang's refusal, Roosevelt toyed with the idea of an international trusteeship to administer Vietnam until the Allies deemed it ready for self-government. This trusteeship, which Roosevelt later included in his proposals for the United Nations, would include both Vietnamese and French, but also Chinese, Russians, and Americans. At the Teheran Conference of the Allied leaders in November 1943 Roosevelt, Chiang, and Stalin affirmed the plan. Only Churchill opposed the idea, fearing that a chain reaction of independence movements might reach India.

U.S. supports Ho Chi Minh

While the U.S. was using international summit diplomacy to try to insure postwar independence for Vietnam, Ho Chi Minh and the Vietminh were happy to receive the support of the U.S. mission in China, especially from the forerunner of the CIA, the Office of Strategic Services (OSS). When U.S. policy makers finally decided after World War II that Ho Chi Minh was an enemy, the extent of OSS assistance became a matter of controversy. OSS officials, perhaps fearful of accusations that they had aided Communists, insisted that only a few side arms had been given. They also disputed how much help the Vietminh had given in fighting the Japanese. The Chinese, however, appeared to be satisfied with the performance of their new allies, the Vietminh. Chinese complaints concerning the lack of intelligence information from Vietnam ended in 1944.

The Vietminh made skillful propaganda use of their new connection. Tales of Vietminh guerrillas meeting with American OSS officials circulated throughout northern Vietnam. The Vietminh portrayed themselves as the chosen resistance group favored by the popular Americans. They were not entirely wrong. The U.S. clearly favored their efforts over those of the pro-Japanese and pro-French groups.

Use of their new American "friends" was only one aspect of the Vietminh effort to secure undisputed leadership of the Vietnamese independence movement as the war neared its conclusion. In December

1943, speaking from Algeria, de Gaulle announced his plans for postwar Indochina. He acknowledged the necessity for thorough reform and an entirely new relationship between France and Vietnam but specifically ruled out an independent Vietnam. The Vietminh strongly attacked de Gaulle. Although they were willing to compromise their Marxist ideology for the sake of independence, they would make no compromise on independence itself. Exactly one year later, in the mountains of northern Vietnam, they officially formed the military wing of the Vietminh, the Vietnam Liberation Army.

America strikes in Asia

As Asia headed into its last year of World War II, it became evident that the Japanese empire was doomed. By late 1944 American victories in Malaya, Indonesia, and especially the Philippines had forced the Japanese into a steady withdrawal. In November, the headquarters of the Japanese Southern Army moved from Manila to Saigon. In January 1945 retreating troops were used to reinforce Japanese strength in Vietnam. Field Marshall Terauchi was given strict orders to hold Vietnam at all costs. With the Americans again entrenched in the Philippines, Japan feared an imminent invasion of Indochina.

The United States did all it could to encourage Ja-

Officials of the Allied forces greet the new commander of the China theater, U.S. Major General Albert C. Wedemeyer, in 1944. From left to right: General Carton De Wyart, Chungking representative of Prime Minister Churchill; Chinese Minister of Foreign Affairs T. V. Soong; Major General Patrick J. Hurley, personal representative of President Roosevelt; Major General Thomas G. Hearn, Chief of Staff; Wedemeyer; and General Ho Yong Chin, Chinese Minister of War.

Roosevelt and Churchill, meeting at the Yalta Conference, constantly disagreed on the future of European colonies in Asia. FDR did not want the French returned to control of Indochina after the war.

pan's fears. Vietnam was now within easy reach of American fighter-bombers flying from Vice Admiral William F. "Bull" Halsey's Third Fleet and later B–24s and B–25s taking off from Clark Field in the Philippines. On January 12 Halsey struck at Saigon as thousands of French and Vietnamese watched, hundreds from the city's roof tops. Five hundred American fighter-bombers sank four cargo ships and two oil tankers in Saigon harbor. Oil storage tanks along the river front exploded. Towering columns of black smoke reached a mile into the sky. In all, fourteen enemy warships and thirty-three merchant ships were destroyed, the largest number sunk by the U.S. Navy in any one day in the entire war.

The real purpose of these and other raids was to destroy Japanese shipping lanes. But the Americans knew that the sustained bombing would also encourage Japanese fears of invasion. On March 10, B–25s sank a tanker in Da Nang Harbor; on April 26, B–24s claimed four large merchant vessels in the Saigon River. By April few enemy convoys could expect any protective air cover. With the sea lanes closed, Japan began to rely upon Vietnamese railroads, transporting their supplies into southern China and then over water to Japan. On May 7 and 8, this last link was broken. Fourteen B–25s and forty-eight Liberators knocked out a string of bridges from Saigon to Binh Dinh Province and damaged several rail yards.

The end of French rule

The importance of these developments was not lost on the French population remaining in Indochina. Many of them had openly supported the Vichy government in collaborating with the Japanese. But the attractiveness of cooperation with the Axis powers decreased as they recognized the opportunity to fight for the liberation of Indochina under the French flag. The Japanese, too, were aware of this change in atti-

The USS Essex *cruises off Vietnam to launch the Avengers' bombing raid (top). The* Essex *returned to Vietnam in 1954 carrying a nuclear weapon when President Eisenhower considered aiding the French at Dien Bien Phu. Still in operation during the Vietnam War, the* Essex *served as a training carrier in the Caribbean in the 1960s.*

TBF Avengers from the carrier USS Essex *fly over the southern Vietnamese coast on their way to attack Japanese airfields and shipping in the Saigon area, January 12, 1945 (middle).*

Japanese ships burn along the Saigon river front, destroyed by the Avengers' bombing mission.

A Question of Intelligence

United States intelligence units made contact with Ho Chi Minh during the latter stages of World War II. Thereafter our intelligence agencies maintained America's most extensive and consistent network of contact with Vietnam—North and South. Yet two generations of American policy makers regularly overlooked the assessments emerging from intelligence activities—both when those activities supported Ho during World War II and afterward when American intelligence directed large-scale covert operations against the Communists.

OSS officers cooperated with the anti-Japanese efforts of Ho's Vietminh during 1944 and 1945. Americans who worked with Ho during those years characterized him as a "brilliant and capable man ... who speaks for his people" and as a moderate "ready to remain pro-West." Yet, postwar American aid went instead to the French in their vain attempt to regain control of Indochina, a decision that helped deplete the enormous prestige America enjoyed as a liberator at war's end.

After World War II, American intelligence—first the OSS and then the CIA—undertook a program of escalating covert operations and intelligence gathering within Vietnam. Before the 1954 French withdrawal, Colonel Edward Lansdale headed a sabotage team operating in Vietnam. During one of Lansdale's missions the team dumped sugar in the gas tanks of Vietminh trucks in Hanoi.

In 1955 small-scale effort gave way to a native South Vietnamese paramilitary unit deployed in the North but operating under Lansdale's authority. From 1955 to 1959 the CIA secretly trained South Vietnamese police forces under the auspices of a Michigan State University research team, and in 1958 it began financing an anti-Communist army in Laos. By 1961 the CIA role in Vietnam had become so extensive that the agency blocked a plan to use lie detectors to ferret out Vietcong agents in the Saigon government because it feared exposing the rapidly increasing number of CIA-paid government officials.

As CIA activity and contact increased, however, its optimism diminished, and more and more of its reports conflicted with those of the military. The CIA focused its assessments on the political, rather than on the purely military, context. Well before 1965 it doubted the capacity of the South Vietnamese government to successfully carry out the war and retain the support of its people. Later it questioned the effectiveness of the massive bombing of the North.

But just as the earlier optimistic reports of the OSS had been disregarded, so now the CIA's pessimistic assessments were ignored. When Desmond FitzGerald, the number four man at the CIA and an expert on Asia, presented one of his weekly briefings to Secretary of Defense Robert S. McNamara in 1964, he questioned McNamara's insistence on putting everything into numbers. He told McNamara that many of the military's statistics were misleading and that they regularly conflicted with good intelligence reporting which was, FitzGerald believed, too often overlooked. McNamara nodded curtly and never asked FitzGerald to brief him again.

Ho Chi Minh, now established as head of the Vietminh guerrilla movement, and Vo Nguyen Giap (in the white suit) meet with Americans from the Office of Strategic Services (OSS) in the summer of 1945 to discuss operations against the Japanese.

tude. With its troop strength reinforced in January, Japan decided to tighten its belt in preparation for a final defense.

On March 9, 1945, Japan ended nearly one hundred years of French rule in Indochina: Shortly before midnight on March 9 Japanese soldiers entered the governor general's palace and arrested Admiral Decoux. Simultaneous attacks secured all the major administrative buildings, public utilities, and radio stations for the Japanese. French troops throughout the country were caught off guard. Whole regiments surrendered without a shot, though many others fought bravely even when encircled and outnumbered. Thousands of French were taken prisoner. A few hundred escaped to the mountains. There they were surprised to find a well-coordinated network of guerrillas, experienced in helping Allied soldiers, especially downed pilots, escape from the Japanese. The French had met the Vietminh. True to their promise to aid any Frenchman willing to fight Japanese aggression, the Vietminh cared for many Frenchmen, helping them escape into China.

Meanwhile, playing the role of liberators, the Japanese attempted to secure their hold in Vietnam with the establishment of an "independent" government. On March 9 Emperor Bao Dai had been in Quang Tri Province, entertaining French officials at a hunting party. Upon his return to Hue, he was informed by a Japanese commander that his country was free and asked to assume his full responsibilities as emperor. Bao Dai convened his cabinet and on March 11 accepted the Japanese offer to head a new government. Despite his long-standing friendship with the Japanese, Prince Cuong De waited in vain for his call to the throne. The Japanese were more interested in maintaining continuity in the Vietnamese government than in rewarding a loyal ally.

Members of Bao Dai's cabinet soon had second thoughts about the new arrangement. Two ministers, including a royal prince who later joined the Vietminh, persuaded their colleagues to resign in favor of a more broadly based government. Bao Dai was forced to form a new cabinet. His choice for prime minister was Ngo Dinh Diem, but the Japanese vetoed that appointment. A new government of middle-class intellectuals was formed. They quickly realized that Japan's defeat was imminent and that they, in the process, would be discredited. This chilling reality paralyzed the government, and it accomplished almost nothing of substance. Japan exercised real control over the country.

The Vietminh prepare to strike

With the French defeated, the Vietminh moved to consolidate their position. The Vietminh forces in the North had already been augmented in 1944, when the British Royal Air Force parachuted into guerrilla-held territory many Vietnamese Communists who had been interned on the French island of Madagascar. In April 1945 the Vietminh began to plan for a national liberation, placing the Vietnam Liberation Army under the command of Vo Nguyen Giap. By this time the Vietminh had expanded their "liberated zone" beyond Cao Bang Province to include seven provinces in the North.

In the aftermath of the Japanese coup, Vietminh contact with American intelligence officials also intensified. The Americans had relied on pro-Allied French officials for information concerning Japanese movements in the country, but with the French defeated they turned to the Vietminh as the best source of intelligence. Meanwhile, the British, with French support, had established their own commando operations in Vietnam's northern mountains. After March 9 these commandos were joined by many French soldiers fleeing the Japanese coup.

Relations between the two groups of guerrillas were not smooth. The Vietminh believed that the French were more interested in reestablishing their rule in Vietnam than in defeating the Japanese. The Americans believed the Vietminh. American commandos routinely joined with the Vietminh, not the Anglo-French guerrilla forces. By the end of the war not only were OSS teams cooperating with the Vietminh, they were joined as well by Air-Ground-Air-Service teams (AGAS) aiding downed pilots, by units of the Joint Army-Navy Intelligence Service (JANIS), and by a team of officers under Colonel Steven L. Nordlinger, charged with the repatriation of American prisoners of war.

The Deer Mission

One of the most unusual American commando missions was the so-called Deer Mission, led by Major Allison K. Thomas. On July 16, 1945, Thomas along with two other Americans, a French officer, and a

Giap and Ho in 1945. Giap would become commander of the Vietminh Vietnam People's Army after a brief tenure as minister of the interior in Ho's independent Vietnamese government.

Vietnamese, were parachuted into Vietminh-held territory. They were met by a Vietminh official who escorted them to a nearby village. Posted on the village bamboo gateway was a simple sign: "Welcome to our American Friends." The commandos were soon joined by Ho Chi Minh and treated to a banquet, including fatted calf and Hanoi beer. But Ho insisted that the French officer be sent back to China. He would not cooperate with the French. Ho said that, while he liked some Frenchmen, he hated what they had done to Vietnam, and his countrymen would never accept French support.

Thomas was instructed to establish a guerrilla training center and to build a commando unit to cut Japanese land transportation. He quickly became convinced that the Vietminh's own training center was ideal for the purpose and began drilling one hundred guerrilla fighters. Thomas' only disappointment was the Japanese capitulation. Instead of fighting, he was forced to stand on the sidelines and watch as the Vietminh accepted the surrender of Japanese troops.

By the summer of 1945 the Vietminh had moved far beyond the confines of the mountainous North. Aided by former political prisoners of the French released by the Japanese, they began to infiltrate more heavily populated areas. The Vietnam Liberation Army was soon joined by most of the French-organized youth movement. Japanese attempts to root out the Vietminh were totally ineffectual. With their unrelenting call for independence, the Vietminh had become, in effect, the Vietnamese people.

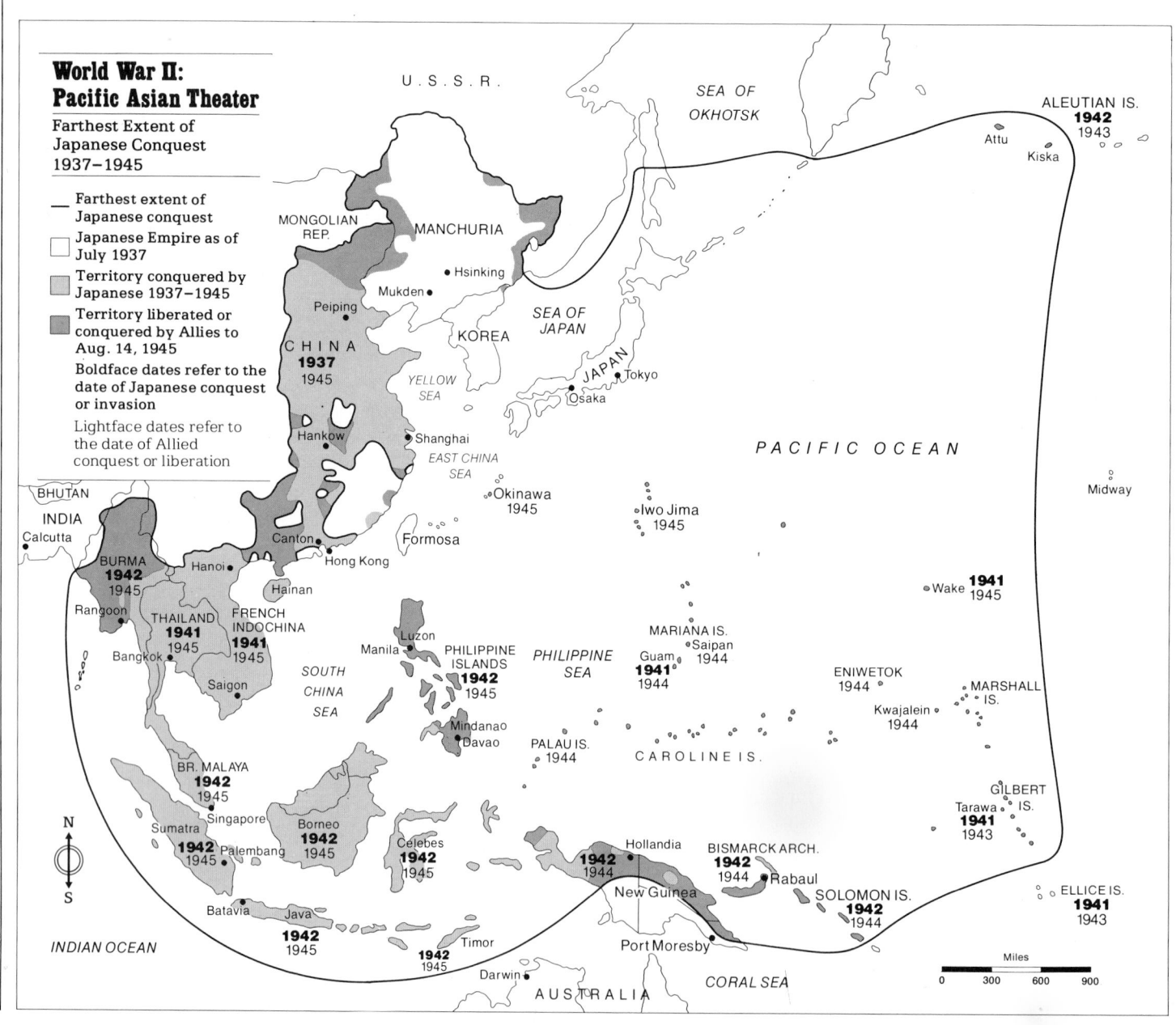

World War II: Pacific Asian Theater

Farthest Extent of Japanese Conquest 1937–1945

— Farthest extent of Japanese conquest

☐ Japanese Empire as of July 1937

Territory conquered by Japanese 1937–1945

Territory liberated or conquered by Allies to Aug. 14, 1945

Boldface dates refer to the date of Japanese conquest or invasion

Lightface dates refer to the date of Allied conquest or liberation

As President of the Provisional Government of the Democratic Republic of Vietnam, Ho Chi Minh (behind microphone) delivers his declaration of independence, based largely on the American Declaration of Independence, to a crowd in Hanoi on September 2, 1945.

Independence for Vietnam

The final capitulation of the Japanese empire in August 1945 eliminated the last force between the Vietminh and independence. Japanese troops still occupied Indochina. But in what was perhaps a final attempt in defeat to keep "Asia for Asians" they surrendered to the Vietminh, rather than to Allied forces. No doubt a vast quantity of weapons fell into Vietminh hands as a result of the Japanese method of surrender. Later the French argued that the Vietminh had thereby received overt Japanese assistance. The charge was groundless; the Vietminh had consistently fought Japanese aggression and fought it more effectively than the French themselves.

The revolution engulfed the entire country. There was little opposition. In the villages, councils of notables were overturned in favor of "peoples committees." The ranks of the Vietminh National Salvation Associations swelled. Hanoi, Hue, and Saigon were soon governed by Vietminh committees. The French were gone, the Japanese had surrendered, but in Vietnam, a country deemed "incapable of self-government," order prevailed, not anarchy. There was no secret to the Vietminh success. It had simply done what generations of Vietnamese had wanted to do: proclaim Vietnam's independence.

The author of Vietnam's Declaration of Independence was none other than Ho Chi Minh. As early as May 1945 Ho had sought out a young American lieutenant who had parachuted into the northern Vietnamese mountains with the OSS. "He kept asking me if I could remember the language of our declaration," the lieutenant later recalled. "I was a normal American, I couldn't." Eventually he realized that Ho knew more about the American proclamation of freedom than he did himself. On September 2, 1945, Ho Chi Minh addressed a crowd assembled in Hanoi, and indeed, the entire world, with these words:

We hold truths that all men are created equal, that they are endowed by their Creator with certain unalienable Rights, among these are Life, Liberty and the pursuit of Happiness.

This immortal statement is extracted from the Declaration of Independence of the United States of America in 1776. Understood in the broader sense, this means: All peoples on the earth are born equal; every person has the right to live to be happy and free.

These are undeniable truths.

* * *

We, the members of the Provisional Government representing the entire people of Vietnam, declare that we shall from now on have no connections with imperialist France; we consider null and void all the treaties France has signed concerning Vietnam, and we hereby cancel all the privileges that the French arrogated to themselves on our territory.

After eighty years of French rule, Vietnam was again independent and again united. That unity, more than just political, expressed the deepest wishes of the Vietnamese people. The Vietminh had taken control of the country virtually without opposition; a Vietminh army of only two thousand men had been sufficient to secure the city of Hanoi for the new government. Within days, Emperor Bao Dai abdicated, promising to support the new government as a private citizen.

This peace in Vietnam was to be short-lived. Already the French were regrouping, waiting to reenter the country on the heels of the British occupation force in southern Vietnam. There would be a year of negotiations with Vietnam, an attempt to create a new relationship between Vietnam and France. But the die was already cast. France, now under the political leadership of Charles de Gaulle, was simply unwilling to give away the "jewel" of its empire. The revolution of August 1945 was to usher in not a new era of peace for the Vietnamese but the bloodiest and most destructive thirty years in its history.

Following page. A prophetic banner hangs above a street in Hanoi.

Bibliography

Bain, Chester. *A History of Vietnam from the French Penetration to 1939.* University Microfilm, 1957.
Baskir, Lawrence M., and Straus, William A. *The Draft, the War, and the Vietnam Generation: Chance and Circumstance.* Alfred A. Knopf, 1978.
Berger, Carl, ed. *The United States Air Force in Southeast Asia, 1961–1973.* Office of Air Force History, 1977.
Bodard, Lucien. *The Quicksand War: Prelude to Vietnam.* Trans. Patrick O'Brian. Atlantic–Little Brown, 1967.
Borri, Christoforo. *Cochinchina.* n.p., 1633.
Brocheux, Pierre. "Grands propriétaires et fermiers dans l'ouest de le Cochinchine pendant la période coloniale." *Revue Historique,* 499 (1971), pp. 59–76.
Buchanan, Albert R. *The Navy's Air War: A Mission Completed.* Harper and Brothers, 1946.
Buttinger, Joseph. *The Smaller Dragon.* Praegar, 1958.

Cady, John F.:
  "The French Colonial Regime in Vietnam." *Current History,* 50 (1966), pp. 72–78, 115.
  The Roots of French Imperialism in Eastern Asia. Cornell University Press, 1954.
Cairns, James Ford. *The Eagle and the Lotus: Western Intervention in Vietnam, 1847–1968.* Lansdowne Press, 1969.
Chaliand, Gérard. *The Peasants of North Vietnam.* Trans. Peter Wiles. Penguin, 1969.
Chen, King. *Vietnam and China, 1938–1954.* Princeton University Press, 1969.
Chesneaux, Jean:
  "Stages in the Development of the Vietnamese National Movement, 1862–1940." *Past and Present,* 37 (1955), pp. 63–75.
  "The Historical Background of Vietnamese Communism." *Government and Opposition,* 4 (1969), pp. 119–35.
  The Vietnamese Nation: Contribution to a History. Current Book Distribution, 1966.
Chuyen, Uong D. "FDR and Indochina." *Giao dan,* 1 (1969), pp. 11–24.
Coedès, G. *The Making of South East Asia.* Trans. H. M. Wright. University of California Press, 1964.
Cohen, Joan Lebold. *Angkor: Monuments of the God-Kings.* Harry N. Abrams, 1975.
Conti, Flavio. *Tribute to Religion.* Trans. Patrick Creagh. HBJ Press, 1979.
Cotter, Michael. "Towards a Social History of the Vietnamese Southward Movement." *Journal of Southeast Asian History,* 9 (1968), pp. 12–24.
Craven, Wesley F., and Cate, James L., eds. *The Army Air Forces in World War II.* Vols. 4, 5. University of Chicago Press, 1950, 1953.
Crawford, Ann. *Customs and Culture of Vietnam.* C. E. Tuttle Co., 1966.

Dawson, Alan. *55 Days: The Fall of South Vietnam.* Prentice-Hall, 1977.
Decoux, Jean. *À la Barre de l'Indochine: Histoire de mon gouvernement Général, 1940–45.* Plon, 1952.
De Rhodes, Alexandre. *Rhodes of VietNam: The Travels and Missions of Father Alexandre de Rhodes in China and Other Kingdoms of the Orient.* Trans. Hertz Solange. The Newman Press, 1966.
Drachman, Edward R. *United States Policy Toward Vietnam, 1940–45.* Farleigh Dickinson University Press, 1970.
Duiker, William J.:
  "The Red Soviets of Nghe-Tinh: An Early Communist Rebellion in Vietnam." *Journal of Southeast Asian Studies,* 4 (1973), pp. 185–98.
  The Rise of Nationalism in Vietnam 1900–1941. Cornell University Press, 1975.
Durand, Maurice. *Imagerie Populaire Vietnamienne.* Vol. 47. L'École Française d'Extrême-Orient, 1960.
Dutt, Sukumar. *Buddhism in East Asia.* Indian Council for Cultural Relations, 1966.

Emerson, Gloria. *Winners and Losers.* Harcourt Brace Jovanovich, 1976.
Encyclopaedia Britannica. s.v., "World Wars."
Ennis, Thomas E. *French Policy and Developments in Indochina.* University of Chicago Press, 1936.

Faivre, Jean Paul. *L'Expansion Française dans Pacifique de 1800 à 1842.* Nouvelles Editions Latines, 1953.
Fall, Bernard B.:
  Hell in a Very Small Place: The Siege of Dien Bien Phu. Vintage, 1966.
  "The Political Religious Sects of Vietnam." *Pacific Affairs,* 28 (1955), pp. 235–53.
  The Two Vietnams. Praeger, 1963.
FitzGerald, Frances. *Fire in the Lake: The Vietnamese and the Americans in Vietnam.* Atlantic–Little Brown, 1972.

Garner, Reuben. "Watchdogs of the Empire: The French Colonial Inspection Service in Action: 1815–1913." Ph.D. dissertation, University of Rochester, 1970.
Ghosh, Manomohan:
  "French Colonization of Vietnam: The First Phase (1861–1885)." *Calcutta Review,* 172 (1964), pp. 119–29.
  "French Conquest of Vietnam." *Calcutta Review,* 170 (1964), pp. 273–310.
Giap, Vo Nguyen, and Chinh, Truong. "The Peasant Question (1937–1938)." Trans. Christine Pelzer White. Southeast Asian Program Data Paper no. 94. Cornell University Press, 1974.

Glimpses of Vietnamese Classical Tradition. Foreign Languages Publishing House, 1972.
Gopal, Sarvepalli. *British Policy in India, 1858–1905.* Cambridge University Press, 1965.
Gourou, Pierre. *The Peasants of the Tonkin Delta.* Vols. 1, 2. Humane Relations Area Files, 1955.
Gran, Guy. "Vietnam and the Capitalist Route to Modernity: Village Cochinchina 1880–1940." Ph.D. dissertation, University of Wisconsin, 1973.
Groslier, Bernard. *The Art of Indochina.* Crown Publishers, 1962.
Grosser Historischer Weltatlas. III Teil. Bayerischen Schulbuch-Verlag, 1967.

Halberstam, David. *The Best and the Brightest.* Random House, 1969.
Hall, Daniel:
  Atlas of Southeast Asia. Macmillan, 1964.
  A History of Southeast Asia. St. Martin's Press, 1955.
Hammer, Ellen Jay:
  The Struggle for Indochina, 1940–1955. Stanford University Press, 1966.
  Vietnam, Yesterday and Today. Holt, Rinehart & Winston, 1966.
Hejzlar, J. *The Art of Vietnam.* Trans. Till Gottheiner. Hamlyn Publishing Group, 1973.
Hickey, Gerald C. *Village In Vietnam.* Yale University Press, 1964.
Ho Chi Minh. *Le Procès de la Colonization Française.* Éditions en Langues Étrangères, 1962.
Hosmer, Stephen, et al. *The Fall of South Vietnam.* Rand Corporation R-2208-OSD (Hist.), Report prepared for Office of the Secretary of Defense, 1978.
Hotz, Robert B. *With General Chennault: The Story of the Flying Tigers.* Coward-McCann, 1943.

Kahin, George McTurnan, and Lewis, John W. *The United States in Vietnam.* Dial Press, 1967.
Kiem, Thai Van. "Les Premières Relations entre le Viêtnam et les Étas Unis d'Amérique." *Bulletin de la Société des Études Indochinoises,* 37 (1962), pp. 286–310.
Kirby, V. S. Woodburn. *The War Against Japan.* Vols 4, 5. H.M. Stationery Office, 1965, 1969.

Lamb, Alastair. *The Mandarin Road to Old Hue: Narratives of Anglo-Vietnamese Diplomacy from the 17th Century to the Eve of the French Conquest.* Chatto And Windus, 1970.
Lamb, Helen. *Vietnam's Will to Live.* Monthly Review Press, 1972.
Lancaster, Donald. *The Emancipation of French Indochina.* Octagon Books, 1974.
Lavalle, A. J. C., ed. *Last Flight from Saigon.* U.S.A.F. Southeast Asia Monograph Series, n.d.
Lewy, Guenter. *America in Vietnam.* Oxford University Press, 1978.

McAleavy, Henry. *Black Flags in Vietnam: The Story of the Chinese Intervention.* Allen & Unwin, 1968.
Manguin, Pierre Yves. *Les Portugais sur les Côtes du Viêt-Nam et du Champa.* L'École Française d'Extrême-Orient, 1972.
Marr, David G. *Vietnamese Anticolonialism, 1885–1925.* University of California Press, 1971.
Mole, Robert L. *The Montagnards of South Vietnam: A Study of Nine Tribes.* C. E. Tuttle, 1970.
Mordant, Eugene. *Au Service de la France en Indochine, 1941–45.* IFOM, 1950.

New York Times:
  February 18, 1979.
  February 20, 1979.
Nguyen-din-Hoa. *The Vietnamese Language.* Department of National Education, 1960.
Nguyen Khac Vien. "Confucianisme et marxisme au Viet-Nam." *Pensée,* (1962), pp. 3–26.
  ed. "Traditional Vietnam: Some Historical Studies." *Vietnamese Studies,* no. 21 (1969).
Nguyen Ngoc Bich. *A Thousand Years of Vietnamese Poetry.* Alfred A. Knopf, 1975.
Nguyen-van-Thai. *A Short History of Vietnam.* Times Publishing Co., 1958.

Oliver, Victor L. *Cao Dai Spiritualism: A Study of Religion in Vietnamese Society.* E. J. Brill, 1976.
Osborne, Milton E.:
  River Road to China, The Mekong River Expedition, 1866–1873. Liveright, 1975.
  The French Presence in Cochinchina and Cambodia: Rule and Response (1859–1905). Cornell University Press, 1969.

Pilger, John. *The Last Day.* Mirror Group Book, 1975.
Popkin, Samuel L. *The Rational Peasant: The Political Economy of Rural Society in Vietnam.* University of California Press, 1979.

Robequain, Charles. *L'Indochine Française.* Colin, 1935.
Romanus, Charles F., and Sunderland, Riley:
  Stilwell: Mission to China. Office of the Chief of Military History. Department of the Army, 1953.
  Time Runs Out in CBI, 1959.

Schultz, George F. *Vietnamese Legends.* C. E. Tuttle Co., 1965.

Shawcross, William. *Sideshow: Kissinger, Nixon and the Destruction of Cambodia.* Simon & Schuster, 1979.

Shaplen, Robert. *The Lost Revolution.* Harper & Row, 1966.

Sherrod, Robert. *History of Marine Corps Aviation in World War II.* Combat Forces Press, 1952.

Shore, Captain Moyers. *The Battle for Khe Sanh.* U.S. Marine Corps, History and Museums Division, 1969.

Smith, Ralph B.:
  "The Cycle of Confucianization in Vietnam." *Aspects of Vietnamese History,* Hawaii University Press, 1973.
  "The Development of Opposition to French Rule in Southern Vietnam 1880-1940." *Past and Present,* 54 (1972), pp. 94-129.
  "An Introduction to Cao Daism: I. Origins and Early History." *London University Bulletin of School of Oriental and African Studies,* 33 (1970), pp. 335-49.
  "An Introduction to Cao Daism: II. Beliefs and Organization." *London University Bulletin of School of Oriental and African Studies,* 33 (1970), pp. 573-589.

Smithsonian Institution, *Art and Archaeology of Vietnam,* 1961.

Taylor, Keith. "The Rise of Dai Viet and the Establishment of Thang-Long." *Michigan Papers Asia,* 11 (1976).

The Great Retreat. *Newsweek.* March 31, 1975, p. 16.

Thich Nhat Hanh. *Vietnam: Lotus in a Sea of Fire.* Hill & Wang, 1967.

Thompson, R. Stanley. "The Diplomacy of Imperialism: France and Spain in Cochinchina, 1858-1863." *Journal of Modern History,* 12 (1940), pp. 334-56.

Thompson, Virginia. *French Indochina.* Allen & Unwin, 1937.

Tolson, Lt. Gen. John J. *Airmobility: 1961-1971.* Department of the Army, 1973.

Truong, Buu Lam. *Patterns of Vietnamese Response to Foreign Intervention, 1858-1900.* Southeast Asian Studies Monograph no. 11. Yale University Press, 1967.

U.S. Congress Senate Foreign Relations Committee Report. *Causes, Origins, and Lessons of the Vietnam War.* U.S. Government Printing Office, 1973.

Welty, Paul. *The Asians: Their Heritage and their Destiny.* J. B. Lippincott Co., 1963.

Westmoreland, William. *A Soldier Reports.* Doubleday & Co., 1976.

White, John. *History of a Voyage to the China Sea.* Wells & Lilly, 1823.

Whitmore, John. "The Vietnamese Confucian Scholar's View of His Country's Early History." *Michigan Papers Asia,* 11 (1976).

Wickberg, Edgar. *Historical Interaction of China and Vietnam.* Paragon Book Gallery, 1969.

Woodruff, Lloyd W. *The Study of a Vietnamese Rural Community.* 2 vols. Michigan State University, 1960.

Woodside, Alexander:
  Community and Revolution in Modern Vietnam. Houghton Mifflin Co., 1976.
  "Early Ming Expansionism, 1406-1427: China's Abortive Conquest of Vietnam." *Papers on China,* 17 (1963).
  "The Development of Social Organizations in Vietnamese Cities in the Late Colonial Period." *Pacific Affairs,* 64 (1921), pp. 39-63.
  Vietnam and the Chinese Model. Harvard University Press, 1971.

Poem on page 46, "A Farmer's Calendar," from *A Thousand Years of Vietnamese Poetry,* edited by Nguyen Ngoc Bich, translated by Nguyen Ngoc Bich with Burton Raffel & W. S. Merwin. Copyright © 1974 by Asia Society, Inc. Reprinted by permission of Alfred A. Knopf, Inc.

Photography Credits

Cover Photos
Clockwise from top right:
UPI; E. Boubat—Photo Researchers; UPI; Gilles Caron—Gamma/Liaison.

Chapter I
p. 11, 13, UPI. pp. 14-15, Jean-Claude Francolon—Gamma/Liaison. p. 16, Wide World. p. 18, top, Sygma; bottom, Wide World. p. 20, Wide World. p. 21, U.S. Navy. p. 22, Gamma/Liaison. p. 23, Michel Laurent—Gamma/Liaison. p. 24, J. A. Pavlovsky—Sygma. p. 25, U.S. Navy. p. 26, left, UPI; right, Buffon-Darquenne—Sygma. p. 27, left, UPI; right, Tiziano Terzani. p. 28, UPI. p. 29, top, Wide World; bottom, Tiziano Terzani.

Chapter II
p. 35, Milton M. Baroody—Cyr Agency. p. 36, Robert J. George. p. 38, George Cohen—Picture Group. p. 39, Wide World. p. 40, George Cohen—Picture Group. p. 41, Nicolas Tikhomiroff—Magnum. p. 42, top, Milton B. Baroody—Cyr Agency; bottom, Wade Nofziger—Cyr Agency. p. 43, U.S. Air Force. p. 44, Jean-Claude Labbé—Gamma/Liaison. p. 45, Tibor Hirsch—Photo Researchers. p. 46, top, Jean-Claude Labbé—Gamma/Liaison; right, René Burri—Magnum. p. 47, top, Bruno Barbey—Magnum; bottom, E. Boubat—Photo Researchers. p. 49, Archives Nationales—Service Outre-Mer. pp. 50-51, Courtesy of the Fogg Art Museum, Harvard University. p. 52, E. Boubat—Photo Researchers. p. 54, Werner Forman Archive. p. 55, Maurice Durand Collection of Vietnamese Art—Yale University Library. pp. 56-57, Werner Forman Archive. p. 59, Durand Collection—L'École Française d'Extrême Orient.

Chapter III
p. 61, © Werner Forman Archive, reproduced courtesy of Hamlyn Publishing Group. p. 62, Maurice Durand Collection of Vietnamese Art—Yale University Library. p. 63, Wan-go Weng—Gemini Smith. p. 64, Asian Art Museum of San Francisco—The Avery Brundage Collection. p. 65, Courtesy of Chatto And Windus. p. 67, Wide World. p. 68, Durand Collection—L'École Française d'Extrême Orient. p. 69, Agence France-Presse. p. 71, Howard Sochurek—LIFE Magazine, © 1962, Time Inc. pp. 72-73, *Churchill's Voyages*—Courtesy of the Trustees of the Boston Public Library. p. 74, Courtesy of Chatto And Windus. p. 75, *Galerie Illustrée*—Courtesy of the Trustees of the Boston Public Library. p. 76, Courtesy of Chatto And Windus. p. 77, Wide World. p. 79, Courtesy of the Library of Congress. pp. 80-83, Marc Riboud—Magnum.

Chapter IV
p. 85, *L'Illustration.* p. 87, Courtesy of Chatto And Windus. p. 88, *Tour du Monde,* Courtesy of the Trustees of the Boston Public Library. p. 89, Giraudon. p. 92, *Tour du Monde,* Courtesy of the Trustees of the Boston Public Library. p. 94, Peabody Museum of Salem. p. 95, U.S.S. Constitution Museum. p. 97, *London Illustrated Times*—Courtesy of the Trustees of the Boston Public Library. p. 99, top, Collection Viollet; bottom, Courtesy of The British Library. p. 101, top left, Collection Viollet; top right, *Voyage d'Exploration,* F. Garnier—Courtesy of the Trustees of the Boston Public Library; bottom, John Launois—LIFE Magazine, © 1962, Time Inc.

Chapter V
pp. 103-105, Collection Viollet. p. 109, Bibliothèque Nationale. pp. 110-112, Collection of D. Seylan. p. 113, top, Collection of D. Seylan; Maurice Durand Collection of Vietnamese Art—Yale University Library. p. 115, Tallandier. p. 117, Jack Birns—LIFE Magazine, © 1949, Time Inc. pp. 118-119, Claude Johner—Gamma/Liaison. pp. 121-122, Collection of D. Seylan. pp. 125, 127, Collection Viollet. p. 129, Collection of D. Seylan. p. 130, George Holton—Photo Researchers. p. 131, Jean-Claude Labbé—Gamma/Liaison. p. 132, Aubrey K. Belknap—Cyr Agency. p. 133, top, D. Turner Givens—Woodfin Camp; bottom, Van Bucher—Photo Researchers. p. 134, George Cohen—Picture Group. p. 135, Dirck Halstead—Gamma/Liaison. pp. 136-137, George Cohen—Picture Group. p. 138, Ngo Vinh Long. p. 139, George Cohen—Picture Group. p. 140, top, Aubrey K. Belknap—Cyr Agency; bottom, Ngo Vinh Long. p. 141, Bruno Barbey—Magnum. p. 142, Tom Friedmann—Photo Researchers. p. 143, left, D. Turner Givens—Woodfin Camp; top, Marilyn Silverstone—Magnum. p. 144, top, Jerry Howard—Photo Researchers; bottom, Robert F. Holly—Cyr Agency. p. 145, Gamma/Liaison.

Chapter VI
pp. 147-148, *L'Illustration.* p. 149, *Une Campagne au Tonkin,* Hoquard. pp. 150-151, Georges Boudarel. p. 152, Gamma/Liaison. p. 154, UPI. p. 155, Keystone. p. 156, Agence France-Presse. p. 158, Collection of D. Seylan. p. 160, Collection Viollet. p. 161, top left, Keystone; top right, Archives Nationales—Service Outre-Mer; bottom, UPI. p. 163, Historical Pictures Service, Inc., Chicago. p. 165, UPI. p. 166, The Bettman Archive. p. 167, top, Historical Pictures Service, Inc., Chicago; bottom, Photoworld.

Chapter VII
p. 169, Wide World. pp. 170-171, photographs by Rey Scott, Courtesy LIFE Magazine. p. 172, Wide World. p. 173, Keystone. p. 175, Eastfoto. p. 176, UPI. p. 179, left, UPI; right, Wide World. p. 180, National Archives. p. 181, Allan Squires. p. 183, Wide World. p. 185, Eastfoto. pp. 186-187, Tallandier.

Map Credits

p. 17—Map by Diane McCaffery. Reproduced by permission from *Newsweek,* Inc.
pp. 32-33—Maps by Mary Reilly.
p. 48—Map by Carol Keller. Reproduced by permission from D.G.E. Hall, *Atlas of Southeast Asia* (Macmillan, London & Basingstoke, 1964).
pp. 90-91—Map by Dick Sanderson. Source: *Grosser Historischer Weltatlas,* III. Teil, Neuzeit, Bayerischer Schulbuch-Verlag, München 1967³, Seite 199.
p. 107—Map by Mary Reilly. Reproduced by permission from André Masson, *l'Histoire de l'Indochine* (Paris: Presses Universitaires de France, 1949), a volume in the series *Que sais-je?*
p. 108—Map by Dick Sanderson. Reproduced by permission from D.G.E. Hall, *Atlas of Southeast Asia* (Macmillan, London & Basingstoke, 1964).
p. 153—Map by Dianne McCaffery.
p. 178—Map by Mary Reilly. Reproduced from Gérard Chaliand, *The Peasants of North Vietnam,* (Pelican Books, 1979) p. 247. Copyright © Librairie Francois Maspero, 1968. Translation copyright © Penguin Books Ltd., 1969. Reprinted by permission of Penguin Books, Ltd.
p. 184—Map by Dick Sanderson. Copyright, Hammond Incorporated, Maplewood, N.J. 07040. Reproduced by permission.

Acknowledgments

Boston Publishing Company wishes to acknowledge the kind assistance of the following people: Charles R. Bryant, Southeast Asia Collection, Yale University Library; Vincent Demma, Army Department Center for Military History; Edward Doctoroff, Widener Library, Harvard University; George Esper, Associated Press, Boston; Glenn MacDonald, *The Daily Journal,* Elizabeth, New Jersey; Clarence F. Shangraw, Southeast Asia Collection, Asian Art Museum of San Francisco; Rita Spurdle, Chatto And Windus Publishers Limited, London.

Index

Angkor, 80, *81, 82, 83, 100*
Annam, 37, 38, 40, 41, 64, 73, 86, 120, 123, 155, 160, 162, 164, *167*
Army of the Republic of Vietnam (ARVN), see South Vietnamese military
A Shau Valley, 43
Au Lac, 44, 48, 59

Bach Dang, battle of, 59, *59*, 60
Bach Dang River, 70
Bac Ninh Province, 125
Banditry, 159-60, *160*
Bank of Indochina, 116, 127
Bao Dai, Emperor, 86, *104*, 155, 166, *166, 167*, 182, 185
Bassac River, 115
Bien Hoa Province, 97
Binh Dinh Province, 39, 180
Black River, 37
Bonzes, see Buddhism, monks
Brévié, Jules, 114
Buddha, *56, 57*, 58
Buddhism, *56, 57*, 58, 59, 62, *62*, 65, 66, 67, 75, 78, *133, 143, 144*, 160, 172; followers of, 58, 65, 66, 67, 76, 77; monks (bonzes), 58, 59, 67, *67*, 77
British East India Company, 90, 94
British Empire, see England
Burma, 34, 88, 90, 118, 176, 177

Cambodia, 34, *36*, 40, 41, 64, 73, *80, 81*, 87, 89, 93, 97, 100, 106, 162, 170; people of, 37, 163
Cam Ranh Bay, 20, 21, 175
Cao Bang Province, 174, 182
Cao Dai, *133*, 160, *161*, 162, 172
Catholic Missionaries, see Missionaries, Roman Catholic
Catholics, Catholicism, see Roman Catholic Church
Central highlands, 12, 13, *13*, 17, 22, 39, 120
Central Intelligence Agency (CIA), 23-4, 39, 119, 179, 181
Champa, 64, 65, 75; people of, 64, *64*, 87
Charner, Admiral, 97
Chau Doc Province, 97
Chennault, General Claire L., 176, *176*
China, 34, 38, 86, 88, 89, 96, 98, 99, 100, 148, 163, 165, 168, 170, 171, *171*, 173, 174, 176, *176*, 177, 178, 179, 182, 184; commerce of, 34, 51, 74, *74*, 75, 79, 90, 95, 96, 98, 100, *100*, 120; cultural influence of on Vietnam, 34, 44, 45, *46*, 49, 50, 51, 53, *53*, 56-7, *57*, 58-9, 62, 65, 75, 78, 84, 86, 87, 118, *121, 139*, 150, 151, 153, 158; occupation of Vietnam by, 48, 49, 50, 51, 53, *53*, 54, *54*, 55, 56-8, 59, *59*, 60, 62, *63*, 64, 68, 70-1, *71*, 78, *79*, 178; people of, 88, 95, 171; support of for Vietnamese independence movements, 37, 63, 151, 153, 158-9, 163, 165, 173, 174, 175, 179 (see also Manchu dynasty, Ming dynasty, T'ang dynasty, Yunnan Province)
Churchill, Winston S., 177, 178, *179*
Clear River, 37
Cochin China, 37, 41, 42, 79, 97, 98, 104, 106, 107, 108, 109, 114, 115, 117, 120, 123, 124, 125, 129, 148, 157, 160, 162, 165, *165*
Communism, 72, 78, 163, 164-5, 171, 177, 181
Communist party, Chinese, 165, 173
Communist party, French, *156*, 163, 164
Communist party, Indochinese (ICP), 159, 163, 164-5, *165*, 173, 174
Communists, 12, 60, 71, 155, 162, 163, 164-5, *165*, 173, 174, 182
Confucianism, 50-1, 58, 59, 62, 65-6, *65*, 68, 72, 75, 78, 84, 86, 87, *87*, 89, 104, 107, *121*, 122, 127, 128, *139*, 146, 148, 149, 150, *150*, 151, *151*, 156, 157, 159, 160
Confucius, 50, 56, 65, 159

Congress, United States, see United States Congress
Cuong De, Prince, 151, 172, 182

Dai Co Viet, 64
Da Nang (Tourane), 16, *16*, 17, *18*, 19, 20, 21, 22, *22*, *36, 43*, 48, *49*, 74, *74*, 93, 95, *95*, 96, 97, *97*, 143, *144*, *145, 167*; bay of, 40, *143*
de Behaine, Pigneau, 77, 79, 87, 151
de Courcy, General, 99
de Gaulle, Charles, 177, 179, 185
de Genouilly, Admiral Rigault, 96, *97*
de la Grandière, Admiral, 97, 100, 108
De Minh, 45
Depuis, Jean, 98
de Rhodes, Alexandre, 75-6, *75*
de Vilers, Le Myre, 98, 108-9, 123
Diem, Ngo Dinh, 58, 66, 67, *67*, 77, *77*, 128, 154-5, *154*, 162, 182
Dien Bien Phu, 28, 40, 43, 114, *180*
Dinh Bo Linh, 62, *62*, 64
Dinh Tuong Province, 97
Dong Nai River, 41
Dong, Pham Van, 165
Doumer, Paul, 114
Dung, General Van Tien, 22, 31
Dupré, Admiral, 98
Dutch, see Netherlands, the

England, 75, 79, 86, 90-1, 93, 94, 95, 96, 104, 114, 118, 157, 164, 170, 175, 177, 178, 185

Faifo, 74, *74*, 75
Flying Tigers, the, 175, 176, *176*
Ford, Gerald R., 19, 26, 29, *29*
French East India Company, 79, 90

Garnier, Francis, 98, *99*, 100, *100*
Geneva accords (1954), 39, 73, 77, 106, 128
Germany, Nazi, 164, 165, 168, 170, 175, 176
Gia Dinh Province, 97
Gia Long, Emperor (Nguyen Anh), 77, 79, 86-7, 89, 119, *140*, 151
Giap, General Vo Nguyen, 22, 39, 69, *69*, 165, *181*, 182, *182*

Haiphong, 37, *59, 110*, 159, 175, 176, 177
Ham Nghi, 99, 146, 148, 149
Han dynasty, 49, 50, 51, *51*
Hanoi, 12, 37, 38, *38*, 39, 41, *47, 56, 57*, 73, 78, 86, 98, 99, *111*, 114, *122*, 126, *135, 136, 139, 148*, 152, 155, 156, 158, 170, 176, 181, 184, 185, *185*
Ha Tien Province, 97
Ha Tinh Province, 163, 164
Hoa Hao, 172
Ho Chi Minh (Nguyen Ai Quoc), 39, 58, 63, 69, *69*, 71, *135*, 154, *154*, 155, 156-7, *156, 157*, 163, 164, 165, *165*, 166, 173, 174-5, 179, 181, *181, 182*, 184, 185, *185*
Ho Chi Minh Trail, 40
Hong Bang dynasty, 45
Ho Qui Ly, 70
Ho Xuan Huong, 78
Hue, 16, *16*, 21, *22*, 54, 64, 73, 76, 79, 86, *86*, 96, 97, *97*, 98, 99, 104, 124, *140, 141*, 146, 149, 154, 166, *167*, 182, 185

India, 34, 36, 51, 58, 64, *64*, 68, 74, 75, 79, 90, 104, 114, 116, 128, 177, 178

Indochina Peninsula, 34, 37, 64, 106
Indochinese Communist party (ICP), see Communist party, Indochinese
Indonesia, 74, 128, 175,
Irrigation systems, 38, *38*, 42, 53, 60, 68, 80, 86, 115

Japan, 63, 74, 89, 95, 128, 150, 151, *151*, 153, 154, 155, 165, *165*, 166, *170*, 171-2, *171*, *172*, 173, 174, 175, *175*, 176, *176*, 179, 180, *180*, *181*, 182, 184
Jesuits, 75, *75*

Kennedy, John F., 77, 155
Khe Sanh, battle of, 12, 40, 43
Khmers, 73, *81*, *82*, *83*, 87
Kuomintang, see Nationalists, Chinese
Ky, Nguyen Cao, 21, *21*, 23, 39

Lac Long Quan, 45
Laos, 34, 38, 40, 57, 64, 70, 87, 88, 90, 100, *100*, 106, 118, 120, 163, 170, 172, 181
Le Duan, 12
Le dynasty, 72, *72*, *73*, *79*, 97
Le Loi, 71, *71*, 72
Linh River, 73
Loc Duc, 45
London, 154
Ly Bon, 57, 58, 59
Ly dynasty, *62*, 65

Mac Dang Dung, 72
Malaya, 90, 120, 128, 175, 179
Malaysia, 34
Manchu dynasty (China), 78, *79*
Mandarins, 65-6, *65*, 68, 75, 76, 78, 87-9, 93, *93*, 94, 96, 97, *121*, 123, 127, *127*, *148*, 149, 150, *150*, 151, 153, 154, 158, 159, 164, 166
Martin, Graham A., 17, 21, 22, 24, 26, *27*, 28
Mekong Delta, *36*, 41, 42, *42*, 73, 74, 76, 96, 97, 117
Mekong River, *36*, 37, 41, *41*, 42, 87, 98, 100, *100*
Ming dynasty (China), 70, 71
Minh, Duong Van "Big," 22, *28*, 29
Minh Mang, 87-9, *87*, 93, 94
Missionaries, Roman Catholic, 75-6, *75*, 77, 78, 79, *87*, 89, 91, 93, 96, 107, 122 (see also Jesuits)
Mongols, 68, *68*, 70
Montagnards (mountain people), 38, 39, *39*,
Moscow, 154, 163, 174

Nam Viet, 48, 49, 51, 53
Napoleon III, 93, 96, 97, 98
Nationalism, 157
Nationalists, Chinese (Kuomintang), 158, 159, 173, 175
Nationalists, Vietnamese, 60, 155, 158, 159, 163, 164, 166, 171, 172, 173, 174
Netherlands, the, 74, 90, 175
Nghe An Province, 150, 154, 163, *163*, 164
Ngo Quyen, 59, *59*, 70
Nguyen Ai Quoc, see Ho Chi Minh
Nguyen Anh, see Gia Long, Emperor
Nguyen dynasty, 73, 74, 76, *76*, 86, 87, 88, 93, 150, 153, 159
Nguyen Hoang, 73
Nguyen Kim, 72
Ngu, Madame, Ngo Dinh, 58
Nixon, Richard M., 37
North Vietnamese Army (NVA), 10, 12, *27*

Office of Strategic Services (OSS), 179, 181, 182, 185

Page, Admiral, 96, 97
Paris Agreements of 1973, 10, 19
Phan Boi Chau, 150, *150*, 151-3, *151*, *152*, 154, 155, 156, 159, 163, 172
Phan Chu Trinh, 150, 153, 154, 155, 156, 157, 158, 159, 163
Philastre, M., 98
Phnom Penh, 97, 100, 106
Phuoc Long Province, 12
Pleiku, 12, 13, 16, 39, 40, *49*
Portugal, 74, *74*, 75, 90
Poulo Condore, 97

Quang Tri Province, 16, 182

Red River, 37, *38*, 41, 42, 53, 98, 100, 126
Red River Delta, 37, 38, *38*, 41, 48, 64, 71, 86, 117
Rice cultivation, 37-8, 41, *46*, *47*, 48-9, *53*, 60, 115, 117, 126, 170
Rivière, Captain Henri, 98, *99*
Roman Catholic Church, 21, *21*, 22, 23, 27, 39, 66, 75, *75*, 76, 77, *77*, 87, 89, *89*, 98, 107, 154, 155, 159, 160, 162, 166
Roosevelt, Franklin D., 177-8, *179*
Russia, see U.S.S.R.

Saigon, 12, 13, 17, *18*, 19, 21, *27*, 41, *67*, 72, 76, 78, 79, 86, 94, 96, 97, 98, 100, *113*, 114, 117, 118, 122, 124, 125, 128, *131*, *133*, *134*, 154, 158, 160, 164, 165, *170*, 172, 175, 180, *180*, 181, 185; fall of, 10, 12, *15*, 17, 21, *21*, 22-9, *27*, *29*
Scholars' Revolt, the, 148, *148*, 149, 150, 151, 152, 153
Siam, see Thailand
Smith, Major General Homer, 26
Song Be, 12
South Vietnamese military, *14*, *18*, 40, 41, 44, 48, 68, 71; Air Force, 12, 13, 25, *25*; Army, 12, 20, 21, 68, 162; Marines, *18*, 20
Spain, 90, 96, 97
Spellman, Francis Cardinal, 77, *77*

Talon Vise, Operation, 23, 24, 26, 27
Tanan Province, 107
T'ang dynasty (China), 59
Tan Son Nhut, *18*, 23, 24, *24*, 25, 26, 27
Tay Ninh Province, *161*, 162
Tay Son, *76*, 78, 79, *79*, 84, 86, 89, 159
Tet festival, *44*, *45*
Tet offensive, 41
Thai Binh River, 37
Thailand (Siam), 34, 64, 87, 88, *88*, 89, 93, 96, *100*, 106, 118, 153, 170, 176; Gulf of, 37, 79
Thieu, Nguyen Van, 12, 17, 19, *20*, 21, 22, 23, 66, 77, 119, 128
Thieu Tri, Emperor, 93
Tonkin, 37, 38, 41, *73*, 97, 98, 99, 100, 120, 121, 123, 125, 149, 160, 162, 168, 170, *171*; Gulf of, 37
Tourane, see Da Nang
Tran dynasty, 65, 68, 70
Tran Hung Dao, 68, 69, *69*, 70, 71
Transbassac, 115
Trieu Au, 55
Trinh dynasty, 73, *73*, 74, 75, 76, *76*, 78
Trinh Kiem, 72, 73
Trung sisters, 54, 55, 56, 58
Truong, General, 16
Tu Duc, 93, *93*, 95, 97, 98, 99

United States, 10, 17, 19, 20, *29*, 40, 41, 44, 48, 69, 71, 94, *94*, 95, 153, 155, 170, 174, 175-82, *176*, 184; aid to South Vietnam, 19, *29*, 128, 181; Air Force, 21, 43, *43*; Congress, 17, 19; Defense Attache Office (DAO), 24, 25, 26, 27; Department of Defense, 17, 24, 118; Marines, 26, *26*, 27, 28, *36*, 43; military in Vietnam, *36*, 37, 43, 118-9, *119*, 143, *144*, 184; military leadership, 39, 43, 119, 177; Navy, 20, 23, 26, 94, 95, *171*, 182; Special Forces operations, 39, 40
U.S.S.R. (Russia), *22*, 37, 63, *134*, 153, 164, 165, 171, 178

Van Lang, 44, 45, 48, 59
Varenne, Alexandre, 114, 158
Vietcong, 53, *144*
Vietminh (Vietnam Doc Lap Dong Minh, Vietnam Independence League), 39, 43, 63, 69, 154, 162, 166, 174, 175, 179, 181, *181*, 182, *182*, 184, 185
Vietnam Liberation Army, 179, 182, 184
Vietnamese language, 48, 57, 59, 73, 75, 78, 107, 122, 123, 157
Viets, 39, 48, 53
Vinh Long Province, 97

Westmoreland, General William C., 39

Xuan Loc, 21

Yunnan Province (China), 37, 98, 114, 177